JAMES WALLACE OF MACALESTER

Portrait of James Wallace, by Ozni Brown of New York, Presented to Macalester College by The New York Mac Clan.

JAMES WALLACE
OF MACALESTER

by

Edwin Kagin

With a foreword by his son,

DeWitt Wallace

Editor of *Readers' Digest*

1957
Doubleday & Company, Inc.
GARDEN CITY, NEW YORK

The quotation on page 248 is from *Green Pastures*, copyright 1929 by Marc Connelly, copyright renewed 1957, reprinted by permission of Rinehart, Inc.

To
M. F. J. K. and J. E. K.

At Wallace' name, what Scottish blood
But boils up in a spring-tide flood!

ROBERT BURNS

Acknowledgments

AT a banquet on the occasion of my retirement from active teaching at Macalester College, St. Paul, Minnesota, in 1951, President Charles J. Turck asked me, "How would you like to head a faculty committee to write the life of Dr. James Wallace?" This seemed a pleasant task, especially since I was a colleague of Dr. Wallace in the department of religion, and a close friend during his later years. The necessity of further teaching in an emergency, however, delayed the work.

Robert and Nina Wallace were the custodians of intimate family letters dating back to the courtship days of Dr. Wallace. They also had a large collection of letters, newspaper clippings, reports, sermons, and speeches dealing with his manifold activities. This gold mine of biographical material they placed at my disposal.

After the research got under way it seemed wise that I should do all of the work and write the story. It was believed that this procedure would result in a more unified biography.

I am indebted to Dr. Turck for the inception of the idea, for providing a delightful workshop by placing the Neill Room of the college library at my disposal, and for making it possible to have student secretaries for transcribing the many excerpts from the source material and for typing my manuscript.

To Robert Wallace and his wife Nina I owe a debt of gratitude for the material furnished, for sustained interest in the project, for reading the first draft of the manuscript, for friendly criticism and helpful suggestions.

A number of the alumni of the college responded to an appeal to share with me some of their recollections of Dr. Wallace. I am indebted to the following persons for anecdotes or other interesting material connected with the life of James Wallace: H. S. Alexander, H. D. Baker, Harold H. Baldwin, Herbert E. Dierenfield, Margaret M. Doty, Asa J. Ferry, Charles Gerlinger, John L. Harvey, Esther Jerabek, Ernest W. Johnson, Mary Frances Johnstone Kagin, William P. Kirkwood, B. H. Kroeze, William Marvin, Gladys Reutiman, L. H. Schock, George Scotton, Ann Elizabeth Taylor, Robert S. and Nina Wallace, Grace B. Whitridge, and others.

I am also indebted to the college librarian and his staff for many courtesies while working in their midst.

For background material I am greatly indebted to the voluminous writings of Edward Duffield Neill, the founder of Macalester College; to Dr. H. D. Funk's *History of Macalester College;* to Dr. Maurice D. Edwards' *History of the Synod of Minnesota of the Presbyterian Church U.S.A.;* and to Dr. Huntley Dupre's *Edward Duffield Neill.*

Special credit is due Miss Lucy Lillian Notestein, a niece of Dr. Wallace, for condensing my manuscript and for helpful additions from her own store of knowledge of the life of her uncle.

I am greatly indebted to my wife for her painstaking work of proofreading the finished manuscript.

Foreword

A S one of the younger members of the James Wallace family,
I lived through much of the period here recorded and was conscious of my father's and my mother's struggles. Yet as I read
this manuscript I was profoundly shocked, for this is a saga essentially of suffering, acute and prolonged. The reader cannot help
but ask, as I have done: Why did my father do this? Why did
he continue through these almost hopeless years? Why didn't
he go elsewhere? Why did he subject himself, his wife, and his
family to such hardship? I do not know in full.

Yet I knew my father and in him I can read, I think, at least
some of the answers. Minnesota, when he went to it, was still a
young and rather raw country. Now we call it Middle West.
Then it was the Northwest, a frontier. The little train through
the stump fields, the puffing engine with its broad flaring smoke-
stack, was but a symbol. Minnesota was a pioneer country, and
my father was a pioneer at heart. He breathed air with the tang
of the woods still in it; there were hard work and broad horizons;
there the world in a sense lay before him, and his every nerve
tingled to these promptings. Education there was still a rather
rare and precious thing; only the most eager and forward-looking,
those who were willing to make sacrifices for their own futures
and the future of the great Northwest, would be coming to college. There he would be shaping leaders.

But that was not all. Behind and beyond this was his unbounded
faith in God, who was to him an ever-present help. When things
grew hard, when Presbyterians showed no real inclination to support their college, when the great depression of that day struck
and lasted, why did he not give up? Deep in my father was a
streak of Scottish stubbornness. He was still master of his fate;

11

he would not be overcome; he, too, was fighting a battle of Bannockburn. Against him were massed overwhelming forces, but within him was the heart not just of a Wallace but of a Bruce. He would not yield. In the end he won—but at what a cost!

One asks again, not why, but how? How could he keep on enduring? What kept him from breaking? I offer two explanations. My father found delight in the small things of life. He could sit down on a stump in an orchard somewhere with his penknife and cut and eat peach after peach or apple after apple, praising his Maker meanwhile for creating such fruit. He could go to the theater, as he often did in his later years when he visited us in the East, and rejoice in every nuance or clever phrase. He did not miss a trick. I well remember how when he saw *Green Pastures*, there were moments when he laughed delightedly at the portrayal of God—but that implied no irreverence at all. It couldn't for him.

Many a man might have become bitter from his experience. Not my father. Subject to the "blues," he nevertheless had great resilience of spirit. He was always ready to enjoy or tell a joke. His sense of humor was one thing that kept him going. The struggles of his spirit were never altogether unrelieved, for he could laugh, even at himself. Devotion to a cause alone—and that, of course, he had—sometimes proves a mighty burden. With it one must be endowed with lightness of heart. That my father had also.

If the readers of this story feel as I, and I hope and believe they will, they will not allow such suffering to have been in vain. Macalester College must and will continue to grow in importance and in strength, fulfilling its destiny of Christian leadership of which my father dreamed.

DeWitt Wallace

"High Winds,"
Mount Kisco, N.Y.

Contents

	Acknowledgments	9
	Foreword	11
	Introduction	17
I	Scottish Origins	19
II	Jimmy Wallace Grows Up	29
III	Beginning with Aesop	37
IV	The Year in Greece	47
V	Separation	57
VI	Father, Professor, Crusader	67
VII	A Pioneer Goes North	77
VIII	Again Alone	91
IX	Postmarked Wooster	105
X	Settling In	115
XI	Dean	129
XII	President and Tramp	145
XIII	On the Campus	165
XIV	With His Family	177
XV	The End of a Chapter	187
XVI	On Leave	195
XVII	War Years	211
XVIII	Retirement	223
XIX	Looking to the Future	233
	Postscript	249

Illustrations

Portrait of James Wallace, by Ozni Brown of
New York, presented to Macalester College
by The New York Mac Clan   *Frontispiece*

In Greece in 1877: James Wallace, DeForrest,
Davidson, Carr, Leonidas   *Facing page* 52

Janet Morris Davis (1877) married James Wallace September 2, 1878   *Facing page* 64

The country home of Benjamin Wallace and
Janet Bruce Wallace, three miles southwest of
Wooster, Ohio. Here the two youngest children were born and here all grew to manhood
or womanhood   *Facing page* 70

Mrs. James Wallace and her three oldest children, Benjamin, Helen, and Robert (the
youngest in the group)   *Facing page* 72

Macalester College Co-eds pinning a home-
coming button on Dr. James Wallace in his
89th year   *Facing page* 242

Introduction

JAMES WALLACE, the hero of this story, came of that virile stock that had grown sturdy in the mist-covered hills of Scotland and the bogs of northern Ireland. Religion, industry, and frugality were the accepted bases of the homes of his immigrant grandparents, the basis also of the farm home in Ohio in which he grew up. From his father and mother he inherited a love for learning, and a habit of serious thinking. They had determined that their children should have the education denied themselves. With their aid and his own hard work and intense application he put himself through college, went on to further study and a graduate degree. He became a teacher in Wooster, Ohio's Presbyterian college. With a missionary spirit, he allowed himself to be persuaded to join the educational pioneers in a new college founded for and by the Presbyterians of Minnesota. There, as professor, later as president, he risked his health and his economic security, all but forfeited his chance to pursue his scholarly interests, to try to keep this floundering young college above the surface. It seemed often a hopeless task, and over and over again he was tempted to give up, yet always he felt the prickings of his Calvinistic conscience; God would not hold him guiltless if he failed to do his utmost to save this college and so help provide a Christian leadership for the rapidly developing Northwest. He fought on and on, and at length he won his battle.

Out of the travail of his soul James Wallace grew strong, efficient, influential. He helped to mold the political, social, and religious thought of the state. He fired many of his students with a passion for righteousness, knowledge, and service to country and church. They still remember "Dr. Jimmy" with honor, admiration, and deep affection.

The life of James Wallace is a tribute to this land which opened to him a fair field, a tribute also to an educational system which makes it possible for eager and imaginative youth to acquire the knowledge and skills they need. It is a challenge to gifted youth to go and do likewise: to develop their God-given talents to the enrichment of a many-faceted America.

I

Scottish Origins

O Caledonia! stern and wild,
Meet nurse for a poetic child!
Land of brown heath and shaggy wood,
Land of the mountain and the flood,
Land of my sires! what mortal hand
Can e'er untie the filial band,
That knits me to thy rugged strand!
SIR WALTER SCOTT

THIS was Jimmy Wallace's big day. His mother had dressed him in a new gingham outfit of pants and blouse. His face washed and hair combed, he took the hand of his older brother Will and started to school. School meant the old log schoolhouse, five miles west of Wooster, Ohio, near Plain Church. It was on the edge of some woods, and a good mile and a half or more from the farm. Around the walls where segments of logs had been cut out, long windows had been inserted. On the inside, facing these, sat the older pupils. The smaller children occupied the benches and desks just in front of the teacher. Here Jimmy Wallace was shown his place. All morning long he sat watching the other children as they studied and recited, envying the older ones who could, through the windows, watch the birds and the squirrels in the woods outside. At the noon recess he and Will ate their lunches and played games with the others. Then school resumed.

About two o'clock the teacher looked at him and said: "Will Jimmy Wallace come up and say his ABCs?" Jimmy advanced slowly and timidly. Mr. Downing held before him a primer and, pointing to a letter with his penknife, asked kindly: "What letter is this?" Jimmy stiffened. "Papa doesn't want me to say my ABCs," he replied. "Oh yes, he does," the teacher said; "that is what little boys come to school for." "Mother does not want me to say my ABCs," Jimmy retorted. But under the patient and persistent persuasion of the teacher, Jimmy finally identified A, B, and C, and nearly all the letters of the alphabet. He had already learned them at his mother's knee. He saw the smiles of approval on the faces of the other pupils and took his seat with a feeling of triumph. Jimmy was now about six years of age. He had been born on March 12, 1849.

So began the school career of James Wallace, Greek scholar, educator, student of international affairs, outstanding churchman, president of Macalester College, and the leader in a heroic struggle by devoted faculty members and trustees to save this college founded in poverty, nurtured in penury, and nearly starved to death by a severe economic depression.

For several years Jimmy, with his brother, trudged to this same school. Joseph H. Downing, the teacher, was reading law in the hope of being admitted to the Bar. He was kind and also just, and he succeeded in impressing his pupils with his sense of justice. He believed in the old adage that sparing the rod spoils the child. On occasion he was known to keep after school hours boys who had failed to do their studying or had been guilty of misconduct. If the process of disciplining reached to the evening-meal hour, he would tie a rope around the waist of the culprit, fasten the other end of the rope to the leg of the big stove that heated the building, and go off to his boarding place nearby. After supper he would return to complete the discipline.

One day Will Wallace fell afoul of the teacher's rules and was ordered to remain. A brief play period always preceded the final assembly. Before these closing exercises Will took Jimmy by the hand and stood near the cap hooks. At the moment of dismissal he grabbed his cap and Jimmy's, ran out the door and down the road, dragging his little brother as fast as Jimmy's shorter legs would allow. When Mr. Downing looked around he saw the two running figures far down the road on the way to the Wallace farm. The next day he sternly inquired of Will why he had not remained. Will stood and pleaded that they lived far away, that it was late, and that they would have had to walk through dark woods to get home. The teacher apparently thought the lad had justice on his side and accepted the defense. He was later to become Judge Downing of the Wayne County court.

Jimmy had been named for his grandfather, born in 1771, of Scottish ancestry, near Cookstown, County Tyrone, North Ireland. There his grandfather had lived the first thirty-nine years of his life. At twenty-three he had married a sturdy Scottish lass, Mary Barefoot, from the next county. She had been visiting an aunt nearby and had been walking on the road one day when he had caught up with her and entered into conversation. They were the same age and were immediately taken with each other, so much so that on getting home each made inquiries, to find the other highly recommended. "Go for him with all your might," her aunt advised. In the fifteen years they were still to live in North Ireland she bore him five sons and two daughters. This James Wallace was a "fair giant of a man," more than six feet tall, erect, well built, clean-shaven. She was smaller but comely. Both were Presbyterians, grounded on the Shorter Cathechism and the Scriptures.

Of course, he belonged to the peasantry, leasing his forty-acre farm from Lord Castle Stewart, and paying him for it, in two installments a year, the equivalent of eight hundred dollars. Their life was very simple, their home a long, low, thatched cottage of two rooms with fireplaces for heat. In these they burned peat from a neighboring bog. Cottagers were not allowed to cut trees, though James Wallace did cut one once and defended his action by explaining that he had planted two. Their food was largely oatmeal. Flax, of course, they grew and scutched and wove into linen.

This grandfather had been a man of great physical strength, with an equal reputation for integrity. On one occasion, it is related, he left a web of linen in town with a tradesman to be sold. The money, however, was to be paid directly to him, and not to any middleman. The merchant nevertheless pocketed the shillings. James Wallace heard of the sale and when he met the merchant on the road demanded what was his. The trades- man denied having received any money; whereupon James Wal- lace threw him to the ground, tore open his coat, seized his wallet, and extracted the price of the linen. The stricken man cried, "Robber! Murder!" and went to the court to have Wallace arrested. The magistrate knew Wallace's reputation, and, mak- ing his own deductions, asked the merchant to bring Wallace to him so that he could hear both sides. There the matter dropped. James Wallace was not a man to be put upon.

In 1810 this doughty peasant made up his mind to take his fam- ily to America, whither his wife's sister and brother-in-law had already gone. Lord Castle Stewart asked his reasons. "I can do nothing here," Wallace replied, "but pay rent." In the summer, therefore, he and his family sailed from Londonderry aboard the American brig *Louisiana*. They paid eleven guineas each, at least for the adults, for passage. The voyage was rough and took eleven weeks. Fortunately they had taken supplementary food with them, meat and bread and a few staples. At length, in the fall, they came to Hampton Roads and there went ashore on a small island and saw their first growing cotton and their first Negro slaves, and then finally they came to Baltimore, where they landed and drove overland to Franklin County, Pennsyl- vania. Here at the home of Henry Taylor and Mary's sister, Jane Barefoot Taylor, they stayed until March of 1811. In the meantime this father of the family had not been idle. In Juniata County he had found a two-hundred-acre farm and with his meager savings he had bought it. There, in the spring of the year, they moved and there their eighth child, Margaret Jane, arrived, the only one of the flock to be born in America. Hard work, good health—in his eighty-four years, it is said, James Wallace had a doctor but once—and frugality enabled the fam- ily to prosper in their new home.

Cheerful, optimistic, with a strong sense of humor, James Wallace readily made friends and fitted himself into the com- munity life. Deeply religious and a student of the Bible, he came to be an elder in the Presbyterian church. He was outspoken, also, almost to the point of bluntness. On one occasion he took his minister to task for what he considered unorthodox preaching. When criticized for his temerity, he took the matter to the presbytery and was sustained. One day on the road he met an acquaintance, an uneducated Methodist minister. He inquired on what subject he would be preaching on the Sabbath day. The minister replied that he would preach whatever the Lord put into his mouth. James Wallace made note of this and went to hear him at the chapel the following Sabbath morning. He listened closely. When the speaker gave utterance to what James Wallace thought unscriptural teaching, he rose from his seat and called out, "Jamie, Jamie, the Lord didna' put that in your mouth to say!"

Jimmy Wallace's father, Benjamin, was the third child of James Wallace. He, too, was born in North Ireland, February 21, 1800, and was a boy of ten when the family arrived in Pennsylvania. On the farm he became inured to hard labor. He cleared land, split rails, built fences, helped with buildings, tended livestock. In short, he did a man's work. They were accustomed on this farm to doing even their own shoemaking. Under the influence of the simple piety of his mother and the vigorous faith of his father, he developed into a young man of deep religious convictions with a great love for the church. In his early twenties he married Ann Black, daughter of a neighboring farmer. Hearing that fertile land could be bought cheaply in Ohio, they determined to seek their fortunes there. They loaded their meager furniture and household goods on a wagon and turned their faces with hope toward the setting sun. Bidding her son farewell, Mary Barefoot Wallace, it is said, remarked with typical Scottish understatement, "You never gave your mother a sore heart." In Pittsburgh where they stopped, Benjamin Wallace went to a bookstore and invested twenty dollars of his two hundred dollars (which represented both patrimony and savings) in a three-volume, leather-bound set of Scott's *Commentary on the Bible*, a leather-bound copy of Brown's *Bible Dictionary*, and several smaller books on religious subjects.

Wayne County, Ohio, where they were bound, was a mildly

rolling country, full of woodland and little creeks draining into
the Killbuck. The soil was rich. Wayne was early ranked, agri-
culturally, among the first half dozen counties in the United
States; and it had drawn and was drawing a fine class of farmers.
Two strains had met there, the Scotch-Irish and the Germans.
Both were industrious and meticulous in their habits and the
care of their land. Arriving, Benjamin and Ann Wallace spent
their first winter in a puncheon-floored cabin north of Wooster.
He found work of various kinds to provide the necessities of
life. For one thing, he could split rails, and did, three hundred
for one dollar. The next year he rented a small farm and bought
a horse. When it died he used his own back for carrying the
harvest from the fields to the barn. Later when he had two
horses and one was killed by a falling tree, he teamed a cow
with his remaining horse and carried on farm operations as usual.
Shrewd, hard-working, and thrifty, he prospered and soon
bought his own farm of 160 acres, southwest of the village of
Jefferson in Plain Township. Ann Black bore him a daughter,
but by 1844 both daughter and wife had died, leaving Benjamin
a childless widower. He was not utterly alone, however, for he
and his wife had generously taken in the four orphaned daughters of Ann's sister, and these were to remain as members of the
household until they married and moved away.

Benjamin Wallace brought his certificate of church membership to the Associate Reformed Presbyterian Church of Wooster.
This later became a part of the United Presbyterian Church.
Before long he was chosen an elder by the congregation, and
for more than fifty-five years thereafter continued so to serve
his church. He always occupied a pew near the pulpit on the
left side of the aisle. On the other side, one row back, sat James
Bruce and his family. They were recent immigrants from Airth,
Stirlingshire, Scotland, near Bannockburn. Janet Bruce, born
in Scotland on November 9, 1823, a tall, energetic, and bonny
lass, caught the fancy of the lonely widower. She reciprocated
his affection and they were married in 1845. He was almost twice
her age. She bore him five sons, William, James, Robert Bruce,
John Taggart, and Benjamin Boyd—and two daughters, Margaret Janet and Mary Elizabeth.

By the time the children came along, Benjamin Wallace had
got past the age when he liked to be bothered much with them,
at least in their romping, battling stage. Besides, he had become
prematurely white-haired and prematurely deaf; the children
were not unaware of their advantage. Of an evening in the house,
he was absorbed in reading and only when the uproar broke
through the solid curtain of his concentration would he turn
and say, "Janet, Janet, can't you make the bairns be quiet!" She
it was who used the rod when all else failed. They knew that
what she did was reasonable and just and motivated by her love.

Father Wallace was rather the high priest of the household.
Every morning and evening his voice was lifted in a prayer of
thanksgiving to the Almighty for His goodness and mercy, and
in fervent petitions for his family and fellow men. Those prayers
and his running comments on the Scriptures as he read them
aloud were a cherished memory of his sons and daughters in
long after years. They seemed, even to boys and girls, no common prayers but meditation and communion with the God he
loved and reverenced.

In the Wallace household the Sabbath was a day of rest, and
worship, and spiritual nurture. Chores were cut down to a mini-
mum. In the morning all the family went to the United Presbyterian services and sang the Psalms and worshiped and listened
to the discourse. There was no instrumental music. In summer
they usually went packed in the high spring wagon; in winter
in the bobsled, with straw and blankets around them. At noon,
when the weather permitted, they sat under the locust trees
around the "kirk," eating their lunches and discussing the sermon with the other Scottish parishioners, many of them kinfolk—
Wallaces, Bruces, Douglasses, Frazers, Liddells, McKees, and Alexanders. They usually stayed for the afternoon service. Then
they returned home for the chores and an evening spent in
reading or discussion. The children were required to memorize
the 107 questions and answers of the Westminster Shorter Catechism, and on Sundays they recited these to their parents. Sometimes from weariness they compromised on 54 questions one
Sabbath, 53 the next. His mother singled out James for special
attention. Throughout one winter she awakened him long be-

fore breakfast and had him memorize psalm after psalm till he knew the first fifty by heart. In later years he looked back with deep gratitude to her for holding him to this task.

Benjamin Wallace was a good farmer, continued to prosper and to add to his acreage. He understood better than many of his period the wisdom of rotating his crops, his corn and wheat, rye and barley, or clover. He raised fat hogs and cattle for market, sheep as well. For them he erected large and sturdy barns, and for his family after some years, on the lower farm, a large brick home, which his son James fondly called Belvidere. In the farm work his sons helped when they were not in school, as did the daughters with the work about the house and with the cream in the springhouse, the butter and the eggs. There were usually also some hired helpers about the place. Benjamin Wallace rose early, throwing a bucket of water over himself at the pump before he dressed, and he retired early. Occasionally in the evening he would help his children with their problems, for he was good at figures, could work out fractions, compute interest, and solve square root.

Yet often of an evening he would read until he would fall asleep in his chair. Beside the Bible and the Commentaries, books in the house were few: Bunyan's *Pilgrim's Progress*, Boston's *Fourfold State*, Fox's *Book of Martyrs*, Edwards on *Redemption*, and later a history of slavery. He subscribed for the local newspaper, for Horace Greeley's weekly New York *Tribune*, the *American Agriculturist*, the *United Presbyterian*, and a religious monthly. Benjamin Wallace never read much because he had not much to read, but he pondered deeply what he had read. When he spoke, his words represented the distillation of long thought.

He was a civic-minded, solid citizen and took a real interest in local, state, and national politics. He contributed liberally toward the bringing of the Fort Wayne Railway (now Pennsylvania) through Wooster, could be counted on during the war period for contributions for the Union soldiers whenever they were sought, was a stockholder in the Wayne County Bank. He often entertained visiting ministers and local politicians. On these occasions there usually developed warm discussions on theology, slavery, tariff, prohibition, taxes, and the merits of local, state, or national candidates. Sometimes of an evening the community gathered in the schoolhouse for discussion and debate. Ben Wallace often entered into these debates, especially in the cause of emancipation. He was an ardent abolitionist, supporting his stand from the Scriptures, and practicing it in his daily life. For a time he had as a helper on the farm a colored man, known locally as "Ben Wallaces's nigger." This man sat regularly at the table with the family, knelt with them at family prayers. Because of this stand he drew to himself much criticism in the county from those who sympathized with the system in the southern cotton fields. Once he secretly transported a runaway slave to Oberlin, on the "underground railway" to Canada. Wayne County was not itself sufficiently hospitable to this underground to allow Benjamin Wallace himself to offer shelter. Slaves were directed farther west.

One of Ben Wallace's friends near Mansfield, who sometimes visited in the Wallace home, did carry on a way station of the undergound, and what he did Ben Wallace might well have done had he had the opportunity. One night Mr. Finney had secreted several Canada-bound slaves in his large haymow. Before breakfast in the morning officers arrived looking for Negroes and proposing to search the place. Mr. Finney invited them in, saying that they were just about to sit down for breakfast and would be glad to have the officers join them. They all sat down. Breakfast was hearty, and the men were urged to have more, then to join them in the usual family prayers. The head of the house chose for his reading the 119th Psalm, the longest of all, and he commented at length on passages as he went along. Then they all knelt. Mr. Finney had chosen his place so that on his knees he could look out at the barn. He prayed at length. After he had been given a sign that the colored boys had taken off and a sufficient time had elapsed, he said "Amen," rose, and offered to assist the men with their search. This was a story which James Wallace loved to tell. He remembered Mr. Finney from his boyhood.

In his earlier days Benjamin Wallace, as his father before him, had enjoyed and had served an occasional glass of toddy. But after the prohibition movement gained strength in the churches, he stopped doing so and became a supporter of the movement to outlaw alcoholic beverages.

Such was Jimmy Wallace's heritage and the atmosphere in which he grew up.

II

Jimmy Wallace Grows Up

There studious let me sit,
And hold high converse with the MIGHTY DEAD.
JAMES THOMSON

AS a boy Jimmy Wallace liked school and books. He enjoyed also the fun and fellowship of school. He liked to tell jokes and to hear them, to tease his fellows, write little ditties and pass them around to make the girls giggle, and to play pranks. He even carried a spit gun and, at least on one occasion, took a surreptitious shot at a teacher for whom the pupils did not care. He was not above putting "stickum" on a teacher's seat, or adjusting a stovepipe so that it would tumble at the slightest jar. Once when he saw punishment in the offing, he slyly made away with the teacher's rod, cut it nearly through, and replaced it. It broke on the first application. He played baseball, ran races, competed for the broad jump. At home he played croquet and pitched horseshoes, and often wrestled in the haymow. In all, he was a normal boy.

From the log school at Plain, he moved to the academy at Canaan. Here his cousin, William Wilson Wallace, ten years his senior, was principal. When after two years this cousin went on to the academy at Iberia, Ohio, James followed, sharing his cousin's room at the boardinghouse. In both academies he entered into both study and student life with zest. In programs open to the public, boys learned to declaim, read original essays, deliver orations, and debate. Through these exercises James Wallace was learning to stand before an audience, think quickly and clearly, and express himself in correct English.

When the Civil War broke out James was but a lad of twelve years. As Lincoln issued call after call for volunteers, James's brother Will and his cousin enlisted in the army and were stationed near Washington to help guard the capital. When word got about of the terrible sufferings and hunger of the Union prisoners at Andersonville, Georgia, people in the North were bitter and inclined to hold Jefferson Davis personally responsible. He was painted as an archfiend, gloating over his enemies. Schoolboys, of course, took up the cry against him. As Jimmy rode home from Wooster one day in the farm wagon with his father, he opened the latest Wooster *Republican* and with glee read aloud some verses calling for retribution on the head of the Confederacy:

> "Oh may that cuss, Jeff Davis, float
> In open sea, in open boat,
> In Iceland cold without a coat:
> Glory, Halleluia!
>
> "Oh may that cuss, Jeff Davis, dwell
> In darkest pits of deepest hell
> And there forever groan and yell:
> Glory, Halleluia!"

"Hush up!" his father said impatiently. Benjamin Wallace was too rational to hold one man accountable for sufferings inherent in war, and too earnest a Christian to consign even an enemy to so dire a fate. Not so his son, who was never inclined to let guilt go unpunished.

The war was followed in the Wallace household with profound concern. When news came first of the proclamation of emancipation, then of Gettysburg, and finally of the surrender of Lee at Appomattox there was great relief and satisfaction in the hearts of all. The Union was saved, the Negro was free, and Will and the other young men in the army could now come home. Then came the startling news of President Lincoln's assassination. Jimmy Wallace, growing up rapidly now, was moved to profound sorrow. There was much in common between the boy Abraham Lincoln had been and the young James Wallace. Both could swing a scythe, wield an ax, drive a team, and plow a deep furrow. Both were tall and rugged. Both had a passion for books and knowledge, especially of the Bible. Both were simple in their tastes, with contempt for sham and pretense. They were devoted to the cause of the common man, to justice, freedom for all, and to the preservation of the Union. From this time on James Wallace cherished the memory of Lincoln as the ideal statesman and the supreme example of American manhood. In later years when he came to Wooster he would ask to be driven out to the old farm, and always beside a certain field he would point out the spot where he had been standing when he first heard the news of Lincoln's assassination.

Some years went by. He had finished nearly four years at the academies, was twenty-one and doing a full man's work on the farm. But he was reading, too, at every opportunity. He longed for further education. One spring morning—and every single act that morning was indelibly recorded in his memory—he went out to plow. In the barn he laid his history book on the wagon seat, harnessed a team, hitched it to a wagon, and drove off down the rough lane, the big plow jolting about in the wagon bed. At last year's cornfield he stopped, pushed the plow to the ground, got down himself, unhitched the horses from the wagon, backed them to the plow, and hooked the traces to the single-trees. Skidding the plow along on its side, he drove his team onto the field and began. He would fix his eye on a tree or stump or rock ahead, depress the plow point, and drive forward to cut as deep and straight a furrow as he could, and so back and forth and back and forth till the sun marked halfway till noon and the horses' flanks were wet with sweat. He stopped them then at the edge of the field, took the bit out of their mouths, and let them graze. Then he took down his book, sat down with his back against a tree, and was soon absorbed in events of centuries ago. At the end of the chapter he put the book back and stood looking across the fields and past the woods to a hill four miles away. There he could see the walls of the first building of Wooster University taking shape. Could he—could he join the entering class in September? He hoped.

It was the spring of 1870. If he was going to college he should not wait too long. He loved the fields, the growing grain, the woods, the fruit trees, the fresh air, and the freedom of farm life, but his heart was also in his books. He dreamed of being a scholar, a teacher, an author of books, possibly even an eloquent minister—if he could overcome his shyness in public speaking. He was prepared in Greek and Latin and mathematics for college. Would his father consent? His father approved of college education, for he had donated one hundred dollars toward the fund to bring the college to Wooster, had later added another two hundred. Could his father spare him from the farm? He was getting along in years, now over seventy. Will had married and was living at the upper farm. Rob was seventeen and John was fourteen. With their father's oversight, he believed that they could run the place. He would speak to his father and mother about going to college; they might consent, might even help him financially. And he would make the matter a subject of prayer. He drove back to the house. For dinner that noon his mother had one of his favorite dishes, boiled dumplings. Somehow it seemed to him a good omen.

The summer passed quickly. By September the tall brick building on the far hill was completed and furnished. On the opening day of the new college the leading members of the Presbyterian Synod of Ohio were on hand. They were dedicating the building to the service of the Lord and inaugurating the first president of their college, the aged and distinguished Reverend Willis Lord. The university consisted of a preparatory department, college department, postgraduate department, all in Wooster, and a medical department in Cleveland. The college proper at Wooster opened that day with an enrollment of thirty-four students. When the roll of freshmen was called, a tall, sun-tanned, muscular young farmer, James Wallace, answered present. To his embarrassment he found himself seated on the young women's side of the chapel. His mind and heart were glowing at the privilege of attending college. The dream of years was being fulfilled. He was older than most of the boys in his class, and less sophisticated than some. Naturally shy, he had to fight a slight feeling of inferiority. But inwardly he was resolved: he would give no one ground to regard him as a dumb farmer.

Another farm boy from near Old Hickory, ten miles north of Wooster, had entered Wooster University that same fall. He had had his freshman year at Hudson (now Western Reserve University). The two had been chums at Canaan Academy, and in the summer, they had arranged this year to room together. Indeed Jonas Notestein was reported to have said that he was going to graduate at Wooster and marry Jim Wallace's sister Margaret (which he did). James Wallace found great comfort in his companionship, and the close association so begun continued throughout their lives.

They had much in common. Both had to earn, in part, their way in college. From his weekends at home James brought back food his mother had prepared, and during the week members of the family brought him in supplies. Both loved books and the intellectual life; both loved the church and all it stood for, though one was a Presbyterian, the other a United Presbyterian. They shared their attitude toward smoking, drinking, and what they called "loose morals," even shared many of their political opinions. Pretense of all sorts they hated, and had no patience with the wasting of time and money on "frivolity." Fraternities had been granted charters at Wooster, and to these and their ways they were bitterly opposed. The way some of these fraternity men lolled around, smoked pipes, neglected their studies, and wasted their parents' money roused James Wallace's indignation. It provoked him to see them in a highhanded manner writing the slates for class elections, pushing their mates forward into positions of honor and influence without regard to merit. Some of them, he knew, regarded him as a bookworm and a pious kill-joy from the psalm-singing United Presbyterian Church. He would show these fellows that he could forge to the front by Christian integrity and hard study without recourse to fraternity friendships.

The college year at Wooster was divided into fall, winter, and spring terms. The course of study was built on a solid liberal-arts foundation. Freshmen and spohomores had their studies prescribed. These were a groundwork for a later field of concentration. At the beginning of the junior year, students were required to elect the area in which they would continue their studies—the classical, philosophical, or scientific. James Wallace chose the classical course. He studied Greek for all four years, learning something of Xenophon, Herodotus, Demosthenes, Homer, Aeschylus, Thucydides, Euripides, and Plato. He studied Latin for three years—Cicero, Horace, Terence. In mathematics the course carried through analytical geometry. In science he was introduced to mechanics, optics, astronomy, chemistry, geology. He studied psychology, moral philosophy, logic, evidences of Christianity, English Bible, French, history, and English literature. He would have preferred to major in history, but since the curriculum did not allow for this, he chose his second-best love for concentration, Greek language and literature.

June 24, 1874, commencement day at Wooster University, found the small town astir early, seeing to the last details for the big event of the year. The young women put on their best and gayest dresses; prancing horses carried guests back and forth; the friends and families of the graduating class headed up the college hill. A platform had been erected under the oaks. Rows of chairs had been arranged before it, on either side a long aisle. These were fast filling up. Among those seated there in eager anticipation were Benjamin and Janet Wallace with some of their children. Dr. A. A. E. Taylor, who had succeeded President Lord, and the faculty were lined up, waiting. At length to the strains of a stirring march they filed down the aisle and up to the palm-decorated rostrum. The seniors in caps and gowns, led by their president and valedictorian, James Wallace, followed.

James Wallace had shown himself and his classmates that he could climb to the top on the basis of merit. He had achieved a general average for the four years of 97 plus, and this despite the fact that he had had to drop out of college for a term and then to take an extra load in catching up. He was now twenty-five, a mature young man. He had read many books, taken part in many discussions, and he had prepared a thought-provoking oration.

The program proceeded: an invocation, a hymn, a prayer, and then the student speakers in turn, at length the valedictorian. James Wallace, tall and angular, arose, bowed, and advanced to the pulpit to announce his enigmatic subject, *Where and When*. Benjamin and Janet sat tense in the audience, hoping he would not forget. Then James began, in a clear yet deferential tone: "What constitutes the progress of our age is the rapidity, clearness and fulness with which truth in all its diversified forms is revealed, and the divine plan unfolded." He believed that devout students of history can discern the when and where of the progressive fulfillment of this plan. The progress of truth in the present era had been marked by brilliant triumphs, he pointed out. "Superstitions and errors that have lasted for centuries are vanishing. False creeds and dogmas are dissolving. . . . The portals of the nations are opening to commerce and to Christianity. . . . Truth's progress is further manifested in that the human mind is wrought up to intense activity in every field of science; every system of religion and morality is being tested: and human rights defined, and the limits of freedom extended." He held that in the midst of this struggle between error and truth in the world, it behooves us all "to lay a foundation in thorough self-discipline and sound morality as this is the only law for the highest and noblest life."

As he continued, Benjamin Wallace sat as one entranced and tears of joy trickled down his wrinkled cheeks. All the years of toil and sacrifice to educate this boy were forgotten in the satisfaction of this moment. The learning and culture which had been denied to him he had made possible, by the sweat of his brow, for this gifted son.

As James Wallace finished his oration and the applause began, a shower of bouquets thrown by admiring friends fell upon the platform. Members of his Sunday-school class in the country at McBride's Schoolhouse came forward with much ceremony and presented their beloved teacher a bunch of colored wax flowers enclosed under a glass dome.

Little did James Wallace then know *where* Providence would place him in the world struggle, how the struggle would tax his mind and heart and physical strength, nor did he know *when* he would see the causes to which he would dedicate himself come to their triumph.

III

Beginning with Aesop

O that's the lassie o' my heart,
My lassie, ever dearer
O' she's the queen o' womankind
And ne'er a ane to peer her.
ROBERT BURNS

T H E brilliant record that James Wallace had made in the college, his maturity, dignity and poise, led the president of Wooster University to offer him the position of principal of the preparatory department and instructor of Greek in the college. Big, jovial, strong, scholarly and devout, he won the hearts of the boys and girls under his care, and he saw to it that they received an adequate training to fit themselves for matriculation in the college.

In the fall of 1875, Janet Morris Davis appeared in his Greek class. She was the daughter of the university librarian, the Reverend T. K. Davis, who was a graduate of Yale College and of Princeton Seminary. The family had come from Chambersburg, Pennsylvania, to Wooster. She was friendly, an easy conversationalist, loved books, read much, had a keen mind that sparkled in repartee, and was simple in taste and chaste in demeanor. She admired the tall young instructor with the big nose and friendly smile. She liked his scholarly approach to problems. She decidedly liked his attitude of disapproval of both smoking and drinking. Tobacco smoke made her sick and she looked on its

37

users as persons who defiled their mouths. One day she stopped by James Wallace's desk. He showed her Aesop's *Fables* in Greek and translated the fable of the wolf for her. She was delighted. He admired her bright dark eyes, her white teeth and regular features. Her interest in Greek led to frequent conversations on Greek construction and on classic literature. Soon he was calling at the librarian's home and finding pleasure in conversation and games with Janet and her older sister Miriam Maude. Frequently he would be asked to stay for a cup of tea with the family. Afterward he would mount his horse, Poderchers, and ride out to Belvidere for the night.

When Janet Davis was fifteen years old she started a secret diary. She wrote as to a dear, confidential friend. To beloved "Diary" she poured out the deep longings, ambitions, and perplexities of her life. She promised to tell it at a later date all the free, happy days of her early childhood. Just now she was excited over the new experience of going out with young men. She led up to this by telling of an earlier experience with two cousins. She wrote:

I have heard and have suspected that I have a sympathy with boy-life which enables me to be more agreeable to gentlemen and boys than most girls. That evening I found myself in the parlor with my two boy cousins, J. and E. They were in one corner on a sofa where they evidently intended to remain silently. A sudden desire seized me to show these boys that a little girl could think and talk with boys. I wheeled around on the organ stool and tossed a couple of light remarks into their corner. No response. I commenced again: What a fine creek they had, did they boat or fish? Yes!—Oh that was charming, and did they improve the shining hours in the woods? How pleasant it was to collect specimens, leaves, stones, etc.! That was enough, the Keynote of their pleasures had been found. They showed me the butterflies they had caught, blushing at my praise. Then I wandered to books, Robinson Crusoe? Too old! But we found books of mutual pleasure and profit and they showed me what volumes were their favorites. I had succeeded—I had two eager interested friends who looked sorry when bed time arrived.

She then told of the trip that she and Miriam made to Hays-
ville, Ohio, to attend a reunion of the graduates of Vermillion
Institute. They had graduated from this school and their father
had taught there. They were guests at the home of the principal,
Mr. Armstrong, whose daughter, Emma, was a schoolmate. After
the noon meal the girls went to their rooms to dress for the afternoon celebration. She wrote "Diary":

> I came down stairs very happily dressed in my fresh, pink
> cambric and my hair in its soft dark curls. Ah—Vanity Fair!
> No. No. Miriam (Maude) looked very beautiful in her laven-
> der, soft grenadine, and snowy polonaise, and with her abun-
> dant hair, braided back from her pure, sweet face. I had
> intended to go in our buggy but Frank claimed me so per-
> sistingly that I laughingly acquiesced. Soon we were flying
> over the road. We went about a mile in every direction.

After the reunion exercises,

> Frank drove me over to Ettie's. That evening was the gayest
> of my life. I was excited, my cheeks burned, and I never
> laughed so easily.

She noticed that throughout the evening, Frank had his eyes on
her and she wondered what was in his mind. About eleven o'clock
she and Frank decided to walk back to the Armstrongs' under the
starlit sky. That night she lay awake a long time reliving the events
of the day.

Sammy Bellman had given her a picture, "The Evening Star."
She hung it on the wall of the upstairs room which she and her
sisters occupied. Sammy had been her childhood playmate. There
was a mirror on her west wall. She described the mirror por-
traits of herself and her sisters thus:

> For Maude it reflects back a rosy-cheeked countenance with
> regular features and firm but gentle lines: a high forehead
> and a wealth of short dark hair, laughing blue eyes, and a
> cherubic mouth. For Bessie an oval face, light hair, blue eyes,
> fair complexion, graceful neck and pleasing expression. For
> me a colorless face, lighted up by dark eyes and scarlet lips:
> white teeth, comical nose, broad brow and soft, dark curls
> falling nearly to my waist.

On another wall hung a large painting of a river scene done by a great-uncle, Thomas Officer. It awakened in her the desire to be a painter. She wrote:

> How I long for the power of thus detaining the tints of the sunset, the pose of the bird, the glance of the water, the smile of friendship and beauty of love! . . . I have no higher ambition than to be constantly learning, learning the while I am doing all in my power to make home happy, and benefit and assist all mankind . . . But it may be my duty to have a dozen children call me mother, and to spend my life in helping those immortal souls to do and be good. My heart leaps at the thought! And to have *one* soul knit with mine in life-long noble love! . . . I cannot help wondering, smiling, if I have an *unknown husband*. He is in college now, or no, he has been graduated (if he is living). He must be twenty-five years old at least—I am sure I will never marry a boy. My husband must be ten years older than myself. Is he living, longing, hoping, striving for great things? But even while thrilling with these blushing wonderings I think I would be relieved to learn that God would let me live on earth for self improvement and His ministry alone . . . I think I *will* strive to fit myself for His ministry as a Missionary and writer.

Dr. and Mrs. Davis were concerned about Janet's health. It was arranged that the two daughters, Miriam and Janet, with Aunt Beckie as chaperone, should go for six weeks to the sanitarium at Dansville, New York. They went by way of Niagara Falls. Sammy Bellman had heard that Aunt Beckie was coming and wrote that he would meet her at Buffalo and then take her over to Niagara. Janet confided to "Diary":

> He knew nothing of Maude and me coming. My heart gave a great leap! Was that manly looking youth my golden-haired playmate, Sammie? The moment Sammie heard the sound of my voice, he sprang forward crying, "Jennie"!

The next morning they took an early train for Niagara. At the Falls Janet was deeply stirred. She told "Diary":

I enjoyed the rocks at first more than the water, but when we stood almost literally beneath the Falls, wet with the foam (to think that I have been baptized in the spray of Niagara!) I realized the majesty of Niagara Falls. We seemed to be intruding upon Nature, for Oh, how solemn it was! How vast the silence even through deep calling unto deep! I never felt God as much, as I think everyone *feels* prayers there, even if they do not say them.

From Niagara, Sammy accompanied the party to Dansville. The more Janet saw of Sammy the more she admired him.

At the sanitarium, however, she met a Mr. D. and there developed a warm friendship. Sammy returned home. The six weeks passed quickly. On the night before they left, there was a dance, of which she wrote:

Mr. D. and I danced most of the time and had a long philosophical talk on the present state of society. After a bonnie "Scotch Reel," "Virginia Reel," "Double Quadrille," etc., we, for the last night, gazed from a window at the never-to-be forgotten Hillside at Dansville.

Listening to the lectures at the sanitarium she had become convinced that a vegetable diet is nature's food and leads to a healthy body. She confided to "Diary":

I firmly resolved weeks ago that I would never touch meat, butter, cake, white bread and pastry of any kind, as food. Ah, to live so purely, simply and naturally as to have that physical health God meant us certainly to have—we must learn to live as a child learns to love the sunlight and avoid the fire.

At length Janet and Miriam were back in Wooster. The trip to Niagara and to Dansville had been a deeply spiritual experience. Before going to bed that night Janet wrote the last words that her "Diary" records:

. . . Our visit is over. But oh, thou loving, helping Father, help me to love Thee for all Thy tender mercies and loving kindnesses: and grant that all the lesson-seeds thou hast been planting in my heart during these weeks may take root and, in Thy sunshine, blossom into fruit to Thy honor and glory.

With these lofty aims and dedication of life, Janet returned to her studies. She advanced from the academy into the college. Her Greek instructor was showing a more than mere professorial interest in her. One day he remarked that he had an apology to make and would come around to her home to make it. Janet seemed surprised and replied that he had no apologies to make to her. A little later she found this note from him.

Miss Jennie:
    I want to make that call whether my apology is to be received or not. Thought you were so accustomed to liberal translation that you could readily see that only a pretence for calling was sought. Sometime in the neighborhood of 7 P.M. tomorrow the door bell will ring and I will be glad—recipi a te.

                                                     Very truly,
                                                         James.

Since apology in the Greek means "To speak in behalf of," the young instructor was apparently preparing to plead his case.

In July 1876 he attended the convention of the National Educational Association in Baltimore and from there he wrote his first letter to Janet. He began:

Dear Jennie! That's affectionate for a first letter isn't it? Well you know this is intended for your indulgent eyes and not for the acumen of a critic. If, however, your great modesty in any measure revolts at this use of the above tender address we will understand it in a somewhat religious sense . . . You know we are exhorted to treat each other as brethren and sisters and to *love one another* . . . yet after all I really don't want to whittle down the meaning of that precious adjective—dear—If I could muster up courage I would hint that the understanding of that word in its usual unlimited sense would do very little injustice to my feelings.

He told of his visit to Washington and the White House, and of the boat ride on the Potomac to Mount Vernon. He wrote:

The place seemed sacred to me and I could not help feeling serious and sad as I examined the various relics of that illustrious man. Saw among other things a short business letter in which he asks how much he could get for his barley delivered at his own landing. But the sentence which struck me so forcibly was, "It is mixed, in some small degree, with oats. I mention this for the sake of fair dealing!" Often have I thought since I left there how strange that we are so slow to acquire those simple virtues which the Bible urges upon us and upon which so largely depends the blessed immortality of our nation's fathers. Am very glad I went. It stimulates to right and noble action.

Very truly,

J. Wallace

He was disappointed in the convention in Baltimore because there were few college men present; most of the delegates were from high schools. He took pains to ridicule the speech of a man from Kentucky who predicted that in a few years men would travel in balloons and with much greater speed than by any means now afforded. He wrote:

Though possessed of considerable scientific knowledge I think it would be quite correct to say of him that "he is flighty."

He could not visualize the fantastic development of air travel in the not distant future.

After his trip to Mount Vernon, James Wallace went on to Philadelphia to see the World's Fair. The effect of the displays upon him there was overwhelming and he wrote:

Whatever may be said of the weakness and imbecility of man, the aggregate of his ingenuity can not but excite the most profound wonder.

He signed himself "Yours, Prof. James."

In August of 1876 Janet and Maude had gone with their father and others to the fair in Philadelphia. Janet wrote James Wallace addressing him as, "My Dear Teacher." She wished that he were with them so they could see the displays together. She expressed pleasure at the prospect of having him as an instructor in the fall, and closed with the words:

> If you really care to hear from me, you can signify it by writing soon. Whoever thinks your letter will not be welcome differs from your scholar—(not scholarly) friend.
>
> Jennie

When college opened in the fall of 1876 Janet enrolled as a freshman and again signed up for a class with her favorite professor, James Wallace. He, in turn, was using his daily contacts in the classroom, intervals between classes, and visits at the Davis home to cultivate the affection of the vivacious brunette. Frank and Sammy and Mr. D. were fading away into the past.

In May 1877 some exhibits from the Philadelphia Centennial were brought to Wooster. Evidently James's courtship during the winter had made good progress. He sent her this note:

> Dear Jennie:
> Think it would be pleasant for us to see that part of the Centennial to be exhibited in the Opera and so unless *notified* to the contrary I will expect the pleasure of your company. As a substitute for prayer meeting you may prepare some remarks on the morals of courtship and give me the benefit of them while on the way. In that department of ethics you know I am very inconsiderate. Very truly, James.

One night he spoke to her seriously of his affection and of his desire to marry her. She frankly admitted that she had grown to love him. He accepted her modest admission with satisfaction but did not sweep her into his arms and kiss her. He did steal a kiss once, but in a very unexpected moment. Janet thought it proper to wait for kisses until the marriage vows were spoken. She wanted to be able to say to her husband, "I have reserved my kisses for you—the lips of no other man have touched mine."

James Wallace had been developing a deep desire to study the Greek language and literature in the land of their origin. He wished to see with his own eyes the famous relics of Greek art and architecture. He wanted to follow the footsteps of Socrates, Plato, and Aristotle as they moved about sunny Greece, discoursing on the great realities and meanings of human existence. He wanted to see Mount Olympus, the home of the gods; the Aegean Sea, Thermopylae and Salamis. He wanted to live in Athens, go down to the Piraeus, climb the Acropolis, and see the Parthenon. What a thrill it would bring to stand where Demosthenes once stood to deliver his immortal oration on "The Crown," and to stand on Mars Hill, where the Apostle Paul delivered his great sermon on the Unknown God!

He believed that from a year in Greece he would bring back to his Greek classes new enthusiasm and some originality: he could become an authority on classic Greek, would also be able to converse in modern Greek and read Greek newspapers to his classes; someday he could put the results of his research into book form; he could simplify the study of Greek and make it attractive and interesting to students. He set aside as much of his monthly salary as possible to build up a fund for this trip abroad. Janet had a secret desire to accompany him. He did not ask her to go with him, for several reasons. First of all he wanted to test the strength of their love by a year's absence. He also wished to be free to devote himself to intensive study and he feared a honeymoon trip might interfere with this.

Summer school over—he had been asked to be principal— James finished his preparation for the year abroad.

The passport that James Wallace had applied for in the summer of 1877 arrived. It gave the following description of its holder:

Age 28
Stature 6 ft.
Forehead high and receding
Eyes gray
Nose aquiline
Mouth large

Chin   medium
Hair   light brown
Face   sharp featured
*Signature*_____(James failed to sign it.)

IV

The Year in Greece

For we had fair resource in store,
In Classic, and in Gothic lore:
We mark'd each memorable scene,
And held poetic talk between;
Nor hill, nor brook we paced along,
But had its legend or its song.

SIR WALTER SCOTT

EARLY in September, James Wallace bade his family good-by. His father was now seventy-seven years of age and his strength was declining. James fervently hoped to find him still on earth when he came back from Greece. From New York on September 7, 1877, he wrote to Janet:

In every way I have no doubt there are more devils in this densely crowded thoroughfare than in Hades itself. Maybe that it is rather emphatic but you would hardly think so if you saw the multitudes of men and horses running in all directions as if they were crazy . . . After some inquiry I concluded that the best terms I could obtain were a round-trip ticket to London for $100.00. This is a reduction of $20.00 on their advertised rates and secures very good accommodation, I think. It is on the steamship *Australia* of the Anchor Line. It is a Scotch line. Scotch crew, Scotch everything . . . I have bought considerable of German gold and some English also . . . Will go to London, then to Bremen, thence to

Hanover . . . In order that I might be certain of the ship and to avoid hotel expense I will go down to the vessel tonight. Went to second hand store in Baltimore and was offered a rather small copy of Donnegan's Greek Lexicon for seventy cents. I jewed him down to sixty and took it. I wanted one of that kind and this was a stroke of economy.

A week later, from mid-Atlantic, he penned a second letter to Janet.

My dear Friend:

We have been on the deep, deep sea just one week—my wish has daily been that you could participate with me in these pleasures . . . Perhaps in the lapse of many years we may have these same pleasures in common . . . this trip will but lay the foundation for another. [Then he tells of his struggle with sea sickness.] Hang it! I wouldn't have been as sick as a dog and as weak as a cat if the weather had not got on a pout and the sea a swell, the very first day we left port . . . The good-byes were said, the gangway removed, the whistle blown and the *Australia* steamed out for the sea . . . The North-east wind was blowing boisterously and the sea rose high. I leaned over the railing and watched the tossing billows and at the same time looked anxiously for symptoms of sea sickness. The vessel rolled from side to side, rose and fell with the huge waves like a duck upon a wind-tossed pond. This seemed to make no impression upon me! In fact I enjoyed it very much and felt sure that my break-fast was perfectly safe. At 12 they rang for lunch and, as my breakfast was still in loco proprio, I resolved to be present. Then was I soon aware of the subtle and mean approach of the sea disorder. Two bites of beef were all I found it possible to take. Everything in the cabin was swinging, the old tub would rise slowly and pleasantly to the summit of a huge wave and then fall so rapidly that one could feel the very seat leaving him . . . I hastened to my state room . . . This over I crawled into my bunk, painfully conscious of my mortal-ity . . . But was I going to give up all at once and be de-prived of the pleasures of the deck! Not a bit of it! After resting awhile until my equilibrium was restored, with a good strong resolution I got up, put on my shoes and was *about* ready to leave my room, when alas! . . . Back into my nest I went . . . I actually reached the deck but in such a condition of [infirmity] that down to my resting place I was obliged to go . . . I was in my bunk almost all the time till Tuesday afternoon.

The weather cleared up and James was able to go to the deck and the dining room for three meals a day. In this letter he told, also, of his cabinmate, a New Englander of a different outlook on life, and of a pious Scotchman with whom he struck up a warm friendship:

The young man who shares my state room with me is about my age, much better looking, polite and agreeable—Have found him to be a worldling, living for money and pleasure and of low morals . . . The more I learn of society the more thankful I am that I have had the advantages of leading a more secluded life . . . How little do we appreciate the advantages of a quiet, Christian home if God dwells there!
. . . The best friend I have on board is an old Scotch Illinois farmer, an elder in the Presbyterian Church, and as he himself says, a regular old blue-stocking—He is a thorough Scotchman, radical in all his views—We have discussed psalmody, foreordination, secret societies, close communion and all the points of Calvinism and differ but very little . . . I greatly admire his faith and fearlessness. If a man swears in his presence *he* will correct him.

A second storm at sea drove James to his bunk for another two days. Again the skies cleared and the voyage was pleasant as they neared Southampton. James did not stay long in London but moved over to Hanover, Germany. There he found letters from Janet and Jonas and Margaret. He was profoundly moved at the account Jonas gave of Benjamin Wallaces's behavior when he learned that his son James had sailed. He wrote Janet:

The longer I live the more do I feel the power of his example. How often and how often has the first sound I have heard in

the morning been his voice lifted up in prayer! and with what
fervency and frequency have I heard him commit his children to God . . . As these few lines have already cost me
tears . . . this little spell has unfitted me for writing and
so I will close with the reflection that it is comforting to
know that if these bonds of affection, so old and so strong,
must ere long be broken, God has wisely and mercifully ordered it that usually ere this sad event takes place other bonds
may be woven which will bind us closely to younger hearts
who will feed our souls with their love, and help us to bear
the severance of older ties.

James had studied German in college and believed that he
would be able to acquire a speaking facility in the language with
little difficulty. He engaged a teacher and wrote Jonas to send
him a money order to cover his expenses in Germany. He found
that acquiring a good accent and a knowledge of the colloquial
took more time than he had anticipated. Since his chief goal in
Europe was to develop greater facility in Greek, he decided to
push on to Athens. However the failure of his money to arrive
promptly held him in Hanover for a month. He left by train for
Athens on November 7. On December 2, he wrote of his daily
routine in Athens as follows:

> After breakfast I take a walk among the ruins nearby, then I
> study modern Greek until about 12:30, when I have dinner. I
> then have a recitation in translating into Greek, after which
> my teacher and I take a walk, he talking in English and I en-
> deavoring to talk Greek—They do chatter it off so rapidly
> that I sometimes fail to recognize the most familiar words. I
> find my ear which seemed at first as dull as a meat-ax growing
> in power to distinguish the sounds, and I live in hope that
> ere long I will have Greek ears.

In a letter written in March 1878 one sees that this daily routine had been somewhat varied:

> Rise about 7 and, after dressing, study New Testament a lit-
> tle—breakfast of coffee, milk and one biscuit only; then a
> short walk down street to get a morning paper. Return to

study, read newspaper, and translate from *Uncle Tom's Cabin* in Modern Greek. From 9–10 or 10–11 hear a lecture in the University. At 12 have dinner, at which we usually spend 1½ or 2 hours. Then a short walk and, on return, study. At 4 go about ¾ mile to recite to teacher. He corrects my exercises and hears me translate from a newspaper. Have a new paper every week; thus I become acquainted with the different papers and get the political, religious and literary vocabulary. After lesson then walk till supper at 7. Then after a little exercise, study or write to my lady love, or to other less important folks till about 11 P.M., when I close the day with a short study of the Greek New Testament.

One notes his frequent walks. Evidently he was realizing the danger of a sedentary life to physical health. He wrote to Janet:

The great difficulty with me as also with *you*, as you must confess, is that I do love books and study passionately. It is a wonderful source of pleasure, but the body is ever in danger.

James Wallace boarded at the home of Mr. Chrisikopoulos, a former librarian in Athens, who developed an interest in and affection for the young American and sought to further his practice of Greek by introducing him to his own circle. James met other American students who were in Greece to study the language, to examine its ruins, or to paint its landscapes. Christmas 1877 was spent on the island of Aegina with Mr. Davidson, a Scotchman; Mr. De Forest, an artist from New York; Mr. Leonedus, a young Greek; and Miss Russell, a German woman from Vienna. There were others whom he met or with whom he sometimes tramped the hills or plains of Greece, a Mr. Carr, "a young spoiled chap, celebrated for his blasphemy," and an American spinster with whom he crossed swords.

Miss L. is from Virginia and still favors slavery . . . sees no justice in our dealings with the South—even defends the treatment prisoners received at Andersonville and Libby. I did hold my tongue until she came to this and then we both grew angry.

Athens itself, had he seen no more, would have made James Wallace feel his trip worth the cost. By the end of December he was writing back:

> With the Acropolis crowned with buildings which were once and even yet the finest embodiment of architectural and sculptural art the world has ever seen; with the theatre in which sat thousands of Greeks listening in rapture to the immortal plays of Sophocles and Aeschylus; with the Bema, from which Demosthenes addressed not those of his own age simply, but hundreds of generations then unborn; with these and many other places of almost equal interest, almost before my eyes, how could I say aught but that my highest expectations have been far more than realized. To walk along the banks of the Illisus and Kephissus, where Socrates, Plato and Aristotle talked to a listening world; to hear a people using many of the words upon which man put the honor of conveying God's latest will to man, has been to me a pleasure which I could ill define. . . .

In January 1878, however, he was lamenting his lack of progress:

> Everybody seems to speak two or three languages but, alas, I am tied to English. Of course I can now speak the Greek well enough to travel through Greece alone, if need be. I could tell them what victuals I want, and when they charge too much, etc. Yet I know that there are very many persons who would have learned twice as much in half the time . . . Tomorrow I will go to see the battle-ground of Salamis and sit where Xerxes sat. Today I traced the old walls quite a distance about Piraeus . . . Heard a Greek sermon—*Thus Saith the Lord*—and understood most of it.

The excursions to historic places with his fellow students were delightful. Much of their travel was on foot. On one occasion they hired a rig and driver. The horse balked, and no amount of shouting or beating made him budge. Suddenly James Wallace leaped from the driver's seat onto the animal's back, dug his heels into the horse's sides, with the command "Get up!" The startled creature lunged forward and pulled his load without

In Greece in 1877: James Wallace, DeForrest, Davidson, Carr, Leonidas.

further resistance. James Wallace was putting his farm knowledge to use. Another time they came upon a shepherd. They had him catch a ewe and, holding out half of an orange peel, they let him fill it with warm sheep's milk, which they drank. He and his companions were relishing these new experiences.

In February James wrote from old Sparta:

> I looked on the so-called tomb of Leonidas day before yesterday utterly unable to feel that I was in the death place of that old hero . . . The people of Lacedaemon had two city walls . . . The valley is very fertile—full of orange, and citrus trees now laden with fruit, a beautiful sight! . . . I have visited Aga, with its fine large old theatre and lofty-walled acropolis—crossed the mountains getting the glorious prospect to Mantinea . . . We go hence to Messene and Mt. Ithome and Olympus.

On the way they passed the old temple of Artemis. James described the view from the summit of a range of mountains:

> We reached the summit just at sunset, and such a sunset I have never seen before. In front of us . . . were dense, dark rain clouds which extended far to the South over the gulf of the sea. Below lay spread out the broad, beautiful valley of Messene with its lemon, orange and fig trees. Now the sun hidden wholly from us turned the atmosphere in all the upper part of the valley into a bright golden yellow. Soon the great red disk was seen drawing near the horizon and drawing his golden ether after him far to the West over the mountains. Thus he went down. The valley with its many villages, the sea, the river, the lake, the mountains, the clouds, the rain, the gold ether, the great red disk of the sun, all thus brought together, furnished a scene which no pen or brush can ever put on paper. I thought then and think now it was *divine* beauty and man can not imitate it.

Again he described the beauty and fertility of Tenos and the image of the Virgin that through a dream had been discovered underground. After it was unearthed it was believed to have delivered a captain and crew from shipwreck. In gratitude they brought gifts. Many costly gifts were also brought by others who attributed to her the power of healing, and, eventually, a splendid church was erected to house the image.

During the Easter season he attended the ceremonies of the Greek church. He told how on Thursday evening they read the Gospels leading up to the crucifixion. They brought out a cross with the figure of Christ on it. On Friday evening they buried the image with great ceremony, and on Saturday night they raised it from the tomb with much rejoicing. On Easter Day every family that could afford it had a lamb for dinner. James was learning something of the religious customs of modern Greece.

In his last letter from Greece on June 23, 1878, James reviewed the year spent abroad. He was conscious of his mistakes. One was his inadequate preparation at home. The other was the month spent in Germany, which cut down the time in Greece. Nevertheless:

> I have labored diligently and, besides traveling and the study of antiquities, can use the language in conversation pretty well and write it with a good degree of accuracy.

He had come to some general conclusions. He was convinced that the usual way of studying Greek and Latin injures the memories of most students. He felt that he had obtained an insight into the practical life and everyday beliefs of the Greek church and had discovered a clue to the understanding of this important phase of church history. He had not entered deeply into the studies of antiquities believing that he could learn what he needed from books on the subject. Through the year his health had been on the whole good, but now and then an attack of indigestion had plunged him into a spell of blues.

From Rome he told of his visits to all of the major points of interest. From there he went to Pisa, and from Pisa headed for Paris by way of Geneva and Turin.

After a few days' sight-seeing in Paris, he went to London, hoping to reach there by the Sabbath so that he could hear Spurgeon preach at the City Temple. This he failed to do, for the great preacher was ill. In London he made the usual rounds, adding Smithfield, where Sir William Wallace was executed.

From London he went to Edinburgh. From there he wrote Jennie on July 28, 1878:

In the good providence of God I have reached the land of my fathers . . . I have looked upon this most interesting land and people with no ordinary pleasure . . . I *feel* that it *is* the land of my fathers: that it is one of the homes of civil and religious liberty. In view of past history—what it has done for the human race, I can not but love its people, yes its very hills and brooks.

And I do assure you, coming from the East and from the Continent—where there is little but formality in religion, I have with glad heart witnessed their strict observance of the Sabbath and heard their earnest sermons from the pulpit. No rattling street cars and drays mar the sacred day. All is quiet— except at times one hears a cab and that is probably carrying some sick or feeble person to or from church . . . I did not hear Horatius Bonar. I went to his church, however, heard them sing from the old metre version of the Psalms. I saw many gray-headed fathers and mothers and such are the good fruits of piety . . . Bibles abounded in the Church and were well used. I noticed many good old mothers engaged in secret prayer before the service began. In all meetings I notice that women considerably outnumber men . . . The Christian mothers of Scotland have done quite as much for her and the world in my judgment, as her great men. They used no organ but a chorister stood forth in front of the pulpit and led the congregation . . . I do like the earnestness of these people. They have grave faults. They are fond of drink, strong drink, and are not free from sensuality, but religion with them is a real, living power.

From Edinburgh, James made excursions about Scotland, visited the birthplace of his mother at Airth, went to Falkirk, where the family had worshiped, saw Stirling and the field of Bannockburn, and reveled in the beauty of mountain, stream, and loch.

At length he arrived in Glasgow. There he went to inquire about his trunk, which he had shipped from Italy by boat to Glasgow; he was told that the boat had sunk off the west coast of Spain. His trunk with his precious notes on Greece and his gifts and souvenirs, painstakingly selected, were now at the bottom of the sea. There was no insurance. He could have sat down and wept.

From Glasgow he went to Belfast. In County Tyrone he visited the early home of his grandfather and then he went to Moville near Londonderry, boarded the steamer of the Anchor Line, and headed for home and his loved ones.

At length he arrived in New York, gazed with a thrill on the Stars and Stripes, and saw the buildings and landscape of his beloved country. He breathed a prayer of thanks as he went down the landing steps and found himself once more among fellow Americans. At the earliest possible moment he boarded a train and headed for Wooster, Classic Hill, and Belvidere.

The year in Greece added prestige to his standing as a teacher of the Greek language and literature. But what effect did the year of absence have upon the budding romance between him and the vivacious daughter of the Wooster College librarian on Classic Hill?

V

Separation

There's not a bonnie flower that springs
By fountain, shaw, or green:
There's not a bonnie bird that sings
But 'minds me o' my Jean.

ROBERT BURNS

J A N E T had refused to kiss James before he left for Greece.
Their engagement was as yet a secret save as James had confided
it to his brother-in-law and sister. James, himself, though often
self-reproachful at what he deemed his own "coldness," wrote
later:

> I have little faith in that love which is all emotion and devo-
> tion, and perhaps I ought to add, commotion . . . I believe
> a lasting attachment rests on a knowledge of the merits of the
> objects loved.

He had intended this year of separation to be a test of their love,
yet by December 2 he was saying, "I wish to wed you as soon
as I return," and was complaining that between letters "time
drags slowly and wearily on."

By the end of December he was so sure that his love for Janet
had stood the test that he wrote to Dr. and Mrs. T. K. Davis
formally asking their consent to his marriage to Janet. He explained why he had not spoken before; but since absence had
rather increased their mutual affection, he felt that Janet's par-

57

ents should know from him that each had found in the other
a kindred spirit and that a fervent attachment had sprung up
between them, and this had

> grown in intensity until it had led to a desire on the part of
> both that we may be united in the most solemn of all com-
> pacts.

At the same time he pointed out to them certain difficulties.
Janet's father was a minister in the Presbyterian Church, U.S.A.,
and she had been reared in its teachings and practices. He was,
moreover, librarian at Wooster, a Presbyterian institution, and a
member of the executive committee of its Board of Trustees!
James Wallace was the son of an elder in the United Presbyterian Church and had been reared in its doctrine and forms.
Though the fundamental creeds were the same, there were real
differences in emphases, traditions, and usages. Both felt that
there were special reasons demanding that they be loyal to the
church in which they were reared. He explained his dilemma:

> My elder brother . . . went with his wife to the Presbyte-
> rian Church and sister will doubtless in time go with her hus-
> band.—Father looks to me rather to assume something of the
> responsibility which hitherto devolved upon him and in this
> I desire very much to gratify him . . . Of course if dear
> Jennie would willingly consent to go with me I should be
> but too glad, but I earnestly wish you to advise and she to act
> in this matter from a sense of right and not from constraint
> put upon her by me.

On the same night he wrote Janet also:

> This is New Year's Eve—the last of 1877. I desire to spend
> some of its closing moments with you . . . For several
> years—three or four at least—it has been my custom, as the
> year draws to a close and as the new one is beginning, to pray
> with all the faith I could that God would direct my steps
> through the year—I thank Him tonight for you, for your
> life, for your Christian heart, which, I believe, will stand the
> test of troubles, cares, and disappointments. . . .

As the closing year contains a record of our love, culminating in an agreement to lead our lives together, so let us pray that God will grant that the coming year of 1878 may record our entrance upon that joint life, and that meantime, He will prepare us for each other.

Dr. and Mrs. Davis were pleased over the developing romance between Janet and the promising young instructor, but they felt that she should finish college and build up a strong physique before undertaking the duties of married life. If the young couple were bent on marriage in the near future, they must make their home with them so that Janet could have the training to fit her for wifehood and motherhood. James Wallace was willing to accede to their demands in the latter respect and wrote to them:

I wish to request that you not only receive me into your home with open hearts but that you will extend to me much of that parental affection which you have and exercise toward your own children.

But he could not bear the thought of postponement. On this he wrote his "dear Jennie":

Now to spend another year in Wooster visiting you every week, as I should certainly wish to do, will inevitably make us the subject of any quantity of gossip among the students and as a consequence in a large part of the town . . . I know very well that very *grave* reasons may be urged against your marriage at so early an age but they are not of necessity valid—if they appear to you to be of great force I should almost feel like abandoning our project until those reasons cease to have any force.

A little later another letter from Jennie told him that she and her mother agreed that it would be better if the marriage were postponed for a year and that in the meantime he could spend another year abroad and visit Egypt and Palestine. To this he replied decisively:

Father has kindly given me all the opportunity he could to get an education. By industry and economy he has accumulated considerable property which he now leaves to his children. He offers me, if I desire it, the property on which he now lives. On the strength of the prospective aid from him I have been more willing to risk the time and money spent in Europe. Now in his old age I wish to show what gratitude I can, and I *will not* stay away another year. Perhaps, as I have said, I should not see him more.

Once he had written of dreaming of his father, who appeared greatly changed and seemed to be withdrawing from him, and he had awakened weeping.

He concluded:

I do not wish to be absent a year more . . . O Jennie, I feel that God has given you to me and I wish to receive His gift.

Both of them recognized certain differences in their thinking. She had once chided him in a letter (while he was in Athens), for attending a theater, and he had replied, begging her pardon but suggesting that

. . . when we are married we will realize as we cannot now the sacredness of that relation and we will be drawn to each other with an affection and interest which will cover our imperfections.

Evidently she was still trying to argue him into leaving his beloved United Presbyterian Church, for he wrote on one occasion:

You are so firmly set in the Presbyterian creed I almost fear at times lest we may have some unpleasant differences. I think it will be wise for us neither to read specially upon these topics, nor discuss, for I am sure if you win me to your *entire* faith it will be by your love rather than your logic, and so I expect to be at no pains to change your views.

At another time after reading Bulwer-Lytton's *Maid of Lyons*, he expressed the belief that he and Jennie would never encounter the heartaches there depicted:

We will never quarrel about the merits of our respective families—the blood, the stock, I mean. We are *both noble born*—never quarrel on politics, we are of one mind there; never about our pursuits, our tastes are all for books of the same kind, full of wholesome truth; on all the great questions of religion we are one, and nothing left to quarrel over but close communion and Psalmody, and if we are such fools as to quarrel over these points we ought both to be sent to the mad house. . . .

I sometimes fear, Dear, that you *are* very ambitious and will be disappointed if I do not rise to a position of considerable influence. I wish to do my utmost—but if I never rise higher than I am now I believe we can live a very pleasant, happy life.

Yet there was no lack of ardor, for in the same letter, after having just received three from her, he addressed his "beloved Jennie":

. . . last night I could not control that throbbing heart of mine and for two to four hours I lay awake thinking only of you while my heart was full of joy.

And again he wrote:

. . . Sometimes when I am diligently studying something reminds me of you and my *heart* says, "you should take another look at her photo." But my mind says, "Oh, no matter! you have seen that a thousand times." . . . the heart always triumphs and the photo must be gazed upon.

And she was equally sure:

God has denied me many pleasures, beauty and perfect health, wealth and the luxury of life, but he has given me something better than them all—yourself, and I thank Him with a gratitude I never knew before . . . Think of me as your very plain but loving, Jennie.

If you teach me everything else as thoroughly as you have taught me to love you, I shall be well-educated indeed.

Janet's health was indeed something of a worry. In the spring of the year she was not well, her studies became a burden, and her parents would have been glad to have had the wedding, planned for the fall, postponed. She wrote James of the weakness of her eyes:

I know it would be better to stop school before my examination, but I cannot think of doing so, altho Mama wishes it.

One notes, however, that she had won an oratorical contest at the college during that year.

James himself had certain reservations about his own future, which troubled him no little. One of these was the challenge to him of the ministry. He sometimes felt, especially when he heard Christianity questioned, "I must study theology and I sometimes dream that I might be eloquent." As late as May of his year in Athens, he wrote:

Of course should I teach in the U. all my life I would have great opportunities of doing good and yet much of my time would be spent in the classics.—When I reflect on the delightful fields of study in the ministry and the work to be done there, I often long to be in that work and feel that there I could work more with thoughts and less with words and roots. Yet for the sacred office I feel so unworthy, and what failure is worse than a failure in the Ministry? So there is still this struggle going on in my mind and heart . . . I feel sure that you would be an excellent minister's wife. You could so nicely help to select material for sermons and criticize my style, delivery, etc.

Both of them worried, too, whether James's position as principal of the academy at Wooster would be open to him on his return. Janet had heard rumors that others were seeking the position at less money than the thousand dollars paid James. But eventually word came that James Wallace had been re-elected and made also adjunct professor of Greek in the college.

Now that the threat of loss of position was removed, they could go ahead with their wedding plans that had been somewhat tentative. James wished that they postpone any wedding trip; after this year of travel he preferred a quiet time at home with his Jennie to any trip. He asked her opinion as to what kind of suit to order from the tailor, blue or black. He wished the wedding to be at eight o'clock in the evening, and he wanted it to take place immediately after his home-coming, if possible on August twenty-seventh. He hoped to arrive the twenty-second. Janet evidently suggested an attendant, but quickly withdrew all thought of bridesmaids when James wrote concerning the one she had named:

> You know some of my good old Scotch friends think they know the character of the leading families, and those which have not a standing in your church or my own, would hardly be thought worthy to furnish a bridesmaid for James's bride. As I think much of them I wish you to be highly esteemed by all.

Would he have any objection to a *small* company at the wedding? she asked.

As the summer approached, James urged Janet not to overwork during the vacation lest the rush of preparations interfere with the wedding. "I would rather marry you in your *rapper* this year," he said, "than in silk next. So do not work too hard." He expressed the hope that she could build her ninety-five pounds to one hundred by the time he got home.

Both were growing more eager as the weeks passed. Janet wrote on the twenty-eighth of June to her "dearest friend":

> I heard the other day, that married people grow into a resemblance of each other. Think of it! You may dwindle down into a mere Jennie-size and bless me! my nose may yet be of respectable length. Do hurry home . . . I shall be the best of wives because I shall have the best of husbands . . . Do you know, I appreciate you more and more as I discover your real character . . . To think how simple are your tastes! Here I have been worrying over my dry goods and grumbling because, not being exactly a millionairess, I cannot possibly have as nice clothing as, under the circumstances, I

should like, when my Apollo answers me and prefers me in my "rapper" this year to silk in the next . . . And, Dear, I would very much prefer marrying you in your linen duster to not doing it at all. Dear Gift of Heaven to me, God speed the ship that brings you home to her who is in heart if not in name your loving ——.

As to his clothes Janet had words of caution:

Do be particular, my dear, about the fit of your clothes. It is just as easy to have them without wrinkles. For Sweet Pity's sake, avoid light navy blue. Your business suit, you know, will not be admissable within the borough . . . You will infer from the above, that I have not a very exalted opinion of your judgment in dry-goods affairs . . . I cannot assure you that your inference is incorrect, as Mrs. N. has been enlightening me somewhat. Be comforted. Papa is a jewel of a man and yet *he* never knows what coat he has on, or what he is eating, unless his attention is called to it.

By this time he had put all arrangements into the hands of Jennie and her "Pa and Ma" to do as they thought best. Then he exclaimed,

In a little over a month you and I will, God willing, be joined in marriage. Oh! what a relation that now seems to me! We will go out and come in, we will lie down and rise up together during all our lives. The same joys will gladden, the same sorrows sadden our hearts, and melt them together. We will kneel in prayer together and, whether the prayer is expressed by you or by me, it will be that God will bless us both as one.

When he got home Jennie was all he had dreamed her to be. The wedding day had been set for September 2.

On that Monday night the relatives and friends of the T. K. Davis and the Benjamin Wallace families crowded the rooms at the Davis home on College Hill. The ceremony began with the singing, in which all the guests joined, of the 100th Psalm:

> All people that on earth do dwell,
> Sing to the Lord with cheerful voice.

*Janet Morris Davis (1877) married James Wallace,
September 2, 1878.*

Him serve with mirth, His praise forth tell,
Come ye before Him and rejoice.
Know that the Lord is God indeed;
Without our aid He did us make:
We are His flock, He doth us feed,
And for His sheep He doth us take.

O enter then His gates with praise
Approach with joy His courts unto:
Praise, laud, and bless His name always
For it is seemly so to do.
Because the Lord our God is good,
His mercy is forever sure;
His truth at all times firmly stood,
And shall from age to age endure.

As the organ began to play, Janet descended the stairs, but at
the foot she hesitated. The singing was off key and her trained
ear would not permit her to advance to the marriage altar to
discordant notes. As soon as the singing became harmonious, she
proceeded, in white, unattended, to take her place beside James
Wallace. Her father was the officiating clergyman and he was
assisted by the Reverend A. A. E. Taylor, president of the university, and others, among whom was James's uncle, the Reverend William Bruce of Xenia Theological Seminary, who delivered to the bride and groom an exhortation on marriage. So began the wedded life of James Wallace and Janet Davis. It was,
as James had once written he wished it to be, "the union of two
of the gladdest hearts that ever beat," and it was to continue
through joys and sorrows, through struggles and triumphs, for
thirty-six years.

VI

Father, Professor, Crusader

For hym was levere have at his beddes heed
Twenty bookes clad in blak or reed
Of Aristotle and his philosophie,
Than robes riche, or fithele, or gay sautrie.
GEOFFREY CHAUCER

T H E year's study abroad gave James Wallace a new feeling of confidence as he began his Greek classes once more in Wooster in the fall of 1878. He had planted his feet on Greek soil and walked the paths of the Greek masters and had looked upon the ruins of the great civilization whose literature he taught. His new rank of adjunct professor gave him a sense, also, of security of tenure and standing with the faculty. He had received his Master of Arts degree from Wooster and was now enrolled in the graduate school as a candidate for the degree of Doctor of Philosophy. Greek language and literature was his major, Greek history his minor. He planned to work up a specialized vocabulary of the words in Xenophon's *Anabasis* for his doctor's thesis. He had blocked out for himself a full schedule, with teaching, graduate study and church activities. Besides, a vivacious young wife demanded a good deal of his attention.

It was his hope that Janet would continue in college until graduation. But in the fall her eyesight still would not permit her to resume her studies. Instead, she gave her attention to housework, to learning to cook, and to helping her husband.

She continued her vocal lessons and practiced on the organ. She memorized the whole of Scott's *Lady of the Lake* and recited it to her husband. In the spring of 1879 she learned that she would have to put college aside and begin preparation for the arrival of her first child about the beginning of the new year.

At the close of 1880 James Wallace began to keep a journal of the principal events of the year gone by. This annual summary, he believed, would lead to self-improvement, and he hoped it would provide interesting reading in his old age. From this we learn that he taught beginning Greek, the *Anabasis*, Herodotus, and Lucian, Cicero's *Orations*, and an outline of history. Evaluating his work for the year of 1880, he concluded that he had been fairly successful in teaching but had neglected his students in favor of his own studies. He was making a thorough analysis of words found in Lucian, listing their roots and derivatives. Someday he hoped to put the results into a book. His personal reading, beyond the limits of his classroom or his studies, included such books as Wine's *Laws of the Ancient Hebrews*, Murphy's *Commentary on the Psalms*, Pascal's *Provincial Letters*, and Philip Smith's *Ecclesiastical History*. He also dipped into the literature of the ante-Nicene Fathers. For the next year he was proposing to himself a careful survey of early church history, and the memorization of John's Gospel. He still hoped to take a course in theology someday, as the matter of a call to the ministry was not yet settled in his mind.

On the more personal side we learn from this record that for the next year he resolved to take more exercise, more scrupulous care of his diet, and to economize his strength for a life of activity and usefulness. All his debts were paid except a balance due on some lots he had bought in Wooster. His worldly possessions, he estimated, amounted to about fifteen hundred dollars.

The great event in his family for 1880 had been the birth of Miriam Gabrielle, called Gay in the family, on January 6. He recorded:

She proved to be a large, healthy, active child, affording us much pleasure by day, and me, a very great vexation often at night. In the training of it Janet has shown very great patience, and I have shown very little. I can easily understand now why literary men are often very poor husbands: for I find it exceedingly hard to leave a good book to entertain a baby. I am resolved to have but a small family—say four or five—but whether my resolutions will be kept is uncertain. Janet and I have lived very harmoniously despite my loss of patience occasionally.

In May of 1880 the little family left the Davis home and moved out to Belvidere with Father and Mother Wallace where there was more room. After some months, however, they returned to the Davis home so that Ma Davis could keep an oversight on Janet, as the time approached for the arrival of her second child. Helen Margaret was born on the evening of July 29, 1881, while James was at his father's farm. He wrote:

Greatly to my relief and pleasure Helen proved to be a healthy, happy and contented child. This increase of cares was not according to program when we were married and I greatly regretted it but I found comfort in the old woman's scripture text "Grin and bear it." I was ill prepared, too, at this time for additional cares for I was wholly devoted to my work in Greek etymology.

He recorded in the journal also that "the cares, expense, and responsibilities of married life were much greater than I anticipated." His salary at this time was one thousand dollars a year and he still owed five hundred dollars on two and one-half acres on Beall Avenue, known as the Cherry property.

On December 16, 1882, Janet gave birth to her third child, Benjamin Bruce. The growing family made it advisable for the James Wallaces to have a home of their own. Accordingly James let a contract for a house to be built on his property on Beall Avenue. It was comfortable and the children had plenty of space in which to play. There, in a stable behind, they kept a horse and buggy, a cow, and a good-sized flock of chickens.

By the spring of 1883 James Wallace felt the strain of long hours at the college, intensive study, and responsibilities at home.

He had difficulty with his digestion, resulting in spells of depression. Janet urged him to go, during the summer vacation, for a few weeks to the sanitarium at Clifton Springs, New York. She assured him that they could manage in his absence. Before long she had lost her servant and she found it necessary to move in again with her father and mother, taking Gay and Benjamin with her. Mother Wallace volunteered to take Helen to her home. While there, the child fell down the back steps and broke both bones in her left arm. Of this Janet wrote her husband:

> Something always happens when I misspend my Sabbath. Yesterday I read too much in Finch.

James answered that he blamed himself for Helen's accident, for he should have put a railing on those steps "long ago." His absence led him to examine his conduct as husband and father. Three lively children in the house and frequent calls away from his books had given rise at times to angry remonstrance. In a penitent frame of mind, he wrote:

> I shall be very glad to get home once more. My wife and family seem dearer to me than ever, and I have much regretted impatience and words spoken unadvisedly with my lips. Hope that you will not remember those things. I hope to be more worthy of my good wife.

And he signed the letter, "Your erring husband."

In the summer of 1884 James Wallace went to Chicago to study Hebrew under William R. Harper, president of Chicago University. It was a profitable summer. He wrote that he was getting up every morning at five to study, a remark which drew remonstrance from Janet.

> You distress me. It will be *so* cold and dark at five o'clock next winter . . . It is your bounden duty to be in bed by ten o'clock until six.

She urged him also to keep up appearances, for "apparel oft proclaims the man," and when a number of the students, he among them, became ill, she sent him a cure for "sun-cholera":

The country home of Benjamin Wallace and Janet Bruce Wallace, three miles southwest of Wooster, Ohio. Here the two youngest children were born and here all grew to manhood or womanhood.

Equal parts of Cayenne pepper, Tincture of opium and Rhubarb. Add a little Essence of Peppermint and spirits of Camphor. Take 15 to 20 drops in a little water, repeated every 15 or 20 minutes.

James wrote toward the close of the summer session that he was sure that his work in his classes the following year would show the effects of his study in Harper's school. He said:

If possible, I would like to spend one month every vacation in some profitable study away from Wooster. In this way I can keep awake and abreast of the times . . . We chant the Lord's prayer in Hebrew every day after chapel.

Dr. Harper had gained a favorable impression of the work of James Wallace. As editor of a series of textbooks designed for the study of the classics in college, he now proposed to the young Wooster professor that he make a thorough study of the *Anabasis* of Xenophon and write a college text to be published in his series. This seemed a providential opportunity. Dr. Harper was well known and highly esteemed as teacher, author, administrator. A book published in his series would at once have prestige and sale. So once more James Wallace resumed his study of Greek roots and derivatives and dug back into Greek history for relevant material. This study was to continue for the next four or five years.

In the fall of 1884 two events were significant in the life of James Wallace. One was the birth of his fourth child, Robert Sinclair. The other was the registration in the academy at Wooster of Harry Thaw of Pittsburgh, son of William Thaw, wealthy banker, railroad stockholder, and real-estate dealer. Both Mr. Thaw and his wife were Presbyterians well known for their philanthropies. Harry Thaw was an eccentric boy of fastidious tastes, always getting himself into difficulties with other students and with the administration. He did not like study and spent much of his time seeking pleasures. James Wallace befriended the boy and did his best toward directing his energies during his two years at the academy. James Wallace did have a way with boys, a warmhearted, half-bantering way, characteristically Scottish, that got behind a suspicious boy's defenses and won him. He understood young people, was sympathetic—up to a point—with their desire to play. His approach was not that of a grownup anxious to save their souls, but of an equal who loved fun, too, and could on occasion play with them. Mrs. Thaw never forgot this kindness to her son, and in later years when the Wallaces were fighting for the life of Macalester, she came several times to the rescue.

The interest that James Wallace took in politics in his boyhood had grown more intelligent and purposeful as he exercised his franchise as a citizen. He realized that democracy can function successfully only when the people are intelligent, informed, and motivated by justice. He saw that an ignorant citizenry and a corrupt political machine would bring about the doom of a republican form of government. He therefore thought it his duty to enter the struggle and throw his influence toward the forces working for good government. Already in 1879 he foresaw that the national elections in 1880 would be crucial. The Democrats in the South were regaining a commanding voice in the policies of their party, and there was danger that a slave economy might be reinstated should former slaveholders come to the helm. The Ohio election in 1879 would, he believed, have large influence on the national election, and it behooved Ohio Republicans to set up strong candidates for the local offices of governor and lieutenant governor.

At this time a local postmaster who had resigned, Captain A. S. McClure, was Republican candidate for nomination as lieutenant governor, along with Judge William H. Taft, candidate for nomination as governor. The political enemies of Captain McClure had conceived the idea of buying a local newspaper to oppose his election, and they were trying to interest some of the college faculty in taking shares in what came to be known as The Wayne County Herald Publishing Company. The idea appealed to three young professors, one of them being James Wallace, who bought two shares for fifty dollars. The others were his brother-in-law, J. O. Notestine, and his cousin, W. W. Wallace. An editor and business manager were employed; the professors became contributing editors. A well-edited news-

*Mrs. James Wallace and her three oldest children, Benjamin,
Helen, and Robert (the youngest in the group).*

paper, they thought, could be a potent force for the right. Besides, as one of them put it, writing for a newspaper would allow them to give expression to their superfluous talent. They had no personal ill will toward the former postmaster but regarded him as a political opportunist unworthy of the office to which he aspired. Judge Taft they opposed because he had ruled against the use of the King James translation of the Bible in the public schools.

The three young professors organized a movement to appoint tribunes throughout Wayne County to educate the people on political issues and so guide the selection of delegates to county, state, and national conventions. They succeeded in placing 747 of these. When Taft and McClure were defeated at the state convention by only four or five votes, they believed that their efforts had tipped the scales. At home, however, Captain McClure deeply resented their activities.

When the national Republican convention in Chicago nominated James A. Garfield for President of the United States, James Wallace threw himself into the campaign with enthusiasm and vigor and made addresses in various parts of the county. The first returns on election night showed Maine going Democratic; the three professors were plunged into gloom. But when Indiana reported a majority of five thousand for Garfield and Ohio a majority of twenty-two thousand their despondency turned to jubilation. Again they felt that their efforts in the *Herald* and on the speaker's platform had been useful. Reviewing the events of the year later, James Wallace concluded that his participation in the campaign had been personally valuable in giving him a more intelligent view of our American institutions and in acquainting him with the political views of such men as Roscoe Conkling, Ulysses S. Grant, John Sherman, Carl Schurz, Benjamin Harrison, James G. Blaine, Robert Ingersoll, and others.

The election campaign over, the three crusading professors turned to the problem of temperance. All three were ardent advocates of prohibition of the manufacture and sale of alcoholic beverages. In this cause the Wayne County *Herald* came once more into bitter conflict with the *Republican*, of which Captain McClure was the editor. In the course of the controversy the latter published what James Wallace regarded as a scurrilous attack on his brother-in-law and faculty colleague, and he could not sit still complacently. The Wallaces, his sister Margaret had once said, were inclined to be blunt and outspoken. This time James Wallace answered invective with invective. He did not hesitate to cross swords with a seasoned politician and former congressman. It was a day when no holds were barred; and he was young. After saying that McClure's personal attack had been "only the filthy scrapings from the depleted locker of a debauched pot-house politician," he went on to list unsavory incidents in the life of the latter. He charged him with being a failure as a lawyer, as a man, and as a politician. (He had been overwhelmingly defeated for a second term in Congress.) He wrote:

> He has packed conventions, manipulated executive committees, winked at the enforcement of the unit rule and practiced all the schemes of the adept politician. They know that he has no settled convictions on any moral question and that today he represents the worst tendencies in American politics. While we sincerely regret the necessity of writing this article we can truly say that no malice flows from our pen— We try to follow Paul's advice and, "as far as possible live peaceably with all men," but when that is no longer possible then we take our own part.

Throughout his life the cause of prohibition lay heavily on the heart of James Wallace, and he welcomed every opportunity to lift his voice and his pen against the evils of drink. He believed that the triumph of prohibition could be secured only through united political action, and he saw no possibility of this within the framework of either the Democratic or the Republican party. The reasonable and logical course was for the leaders in the movement to unite in a new, the Prohibition, party, the dominating purpose of which would be the destruction of the American saloon system. The saloon, he held, promoted only misery and want, and in the interests of justice the state must abolish it.

Once, much later, he published a pamphlet analyzing the

teachings of the Bible on the use of wine and strong drink. He insisted, however, that the use of liquor today could not be decided by what the Hebrews did in biblical days. Concubinage and slavery were also tolerated in biblical days, but had been outlawed because we have discovered that they have proved injurious to society. So, he argued, since we have discovered that liquor is a menace to our social order, its manufacture and sale should be prohibited.

And so with speaking, writing, teaching and study, with church activities, family duties, and household cares pressing upon him, with growing friendships taking their toll of his time as well, the years at Wooster since James Wallace's graduation had been gathering momentum. In the summer of 1886 his father and mother went to Iowa to visit the other four sons who had settled there, two on farms, two in business. There the eighty-six-year-old father was stricken with paralysis and died on the last day of July. He had been a patriarchal figure in the community, throwing the weight of his influence back of every worthy cause. He was a substantial citizen, owning a farm of five hundred acres in the county and another home just north of town where he had retired. Between him and his scholar son there had been a special bond of understanding and affection. Not the eldest son, James Wallace was in a more subtle sense the heir of Benjamin Wallace and of all those other Scottish men, his forebears in North Ireland. With a surge of memories and deep emotion, he laid his pioneer father to rest in the family plot in Wooster cemetery and went again about his work, adding now new duties to his old. He must first settle his father's estate, must aid his widowed mother and her daughter to adjust themselves to their new life.

Up in Minnesota still other events, of which he knew nothing, were shaping themselves, to challenge through the years every ounce of James Wallace's faith and courage and endurance.

VII

A Pioneer Goes North

Come, my friends,
'Tis not too late to seek a newer world.
ALFRED, LORD TENNYSON

ONE early December day in 1886 James Wallace was surprised to receive a letter from Macalester, Minnesota. It came
from Francis B. Pearson, a graduate of Wooster, now teaching
at Macalester College, a young Presbyterian institution between
St. Paul and Minneapolis. He informed Professor Wallace that
Dr. Nathaniel S. McFetridge, professor of Greek, Anglo-Saxon,
and modern languages, had recently died and that the college
was looking for his successor. He wrote:

> Waiving all compliments that I would be perfectly willing
> to give you as a scholar, teacher and man—let me ask you
> if you would consider a proposition to take the chair of Greek
> here if it ever should be offered?—Furthermore, could you
> not take the Anglo-Saxon, and have you not had the German
> so as to teach a little "Dutch," in an emergency . . . The
> salary of the professors is $2000 . . . I believe in you and
> should be glad to do you a favor if opportunity should be
> present.

Soon after Pearson's letter came one from Dr. T. A. McCurdy,
president of Macalester College:

Are your relations in Wooster University so permanent, that you could not and would not, entertain the proposition of a professorship in Macalester College? Please advise me as early as possible and hold in strictest confidence this inquiry.

A second letter from Professor Pearson rejoiced at Professor Wallace's interest in the vacancy, and described the situation at Macalester:

I can't pile up figures to prove that this is a rich, well-endowed college—for such is not the case. Its endowment is rather in the men who are back of it . . . There is no discount on these men and they will never let it want. Besides there is a constantly growing sentiment among the people, and that because the college is proving itself so much better than the people anticipated.

The building . . . on the ground is paid for and there is $10,000 and possibly $15,000 in hand for the other part, which will be begun as soon as spring opens, I think . . . The President's chair is endowed in the sum of $30,000 as also the chairs of Dr. Neill and Dr. Rice for the sum of $25,000 each. The income from those chairs accrues to them though they are not actively engaged in the work. A bequest of $25,000 has been made and papers all signed by an old lady of Minneapolis. A man that I know very well has set aside $15,000 for a library building, with plans all complete. Now this doesn't count up very much, but you must not forget that this is a new college—as also a new country—and business men would far rather give a few hundred dollars each year to keep the college going than to endow a chair—for in that way they can have the use of their money and can make more out of it than the college could, most likely. There is no *petty* business here, and men give hundreds where they give tens in Ohio, say.

I believe in Macalester most firmly—and its developments will certainly be far more rapid than Wooster, and that is saying much.

He assured Professor Wallace that two thousand dollars in St. Paul would be better than the fifteen-hundred-dollar salary in

Wooster. These enthusiastic letters interested Professor Wallace.

On December 16 President McCurdy wrote James Wallace that he was ready to place his name before the Board of Trustees as soon as he was assured of his acceptance, if elected. In the college proper, he said, there were eight sophomores and nine freshmen. The rest of the eighty-three students were in the preparatory department. He would like to have a personal conference on the subject and would be in Wooster December 24. On December 18 Professor Pearson wrote again, this time at the request of the president, urging Professor Wallace to come to Macalester at the earliest possible moment. He pointed out the danger of employing someone to take over classes on a temporary basis; such an arrangement could cause complications; there were already a dozen men who would like to step into the vacancy. In a still later letter he assured Professor Wallace that he need have no misgivings about the courses in Anglo-Saxon and German. He would find it more agreeable, also to be teaching Greek on the college level at Macalester. Anyhow the salary paid him in Wooster was an injustice to his ability. He mentioned Professor Wallace's former students at Wooster now at Macalester, Sam and Will Kirkwood, Ben Irvin, Will Lee, and J. C. Hambleton; they would all throw up their hats with joy at his coming.

On January 7, 1887, James Wallace received word that he had been heartily and unanimously elected to the chair of Greek and modern languages at a salary of two thousand dollars and a house free of rent. In his letter President McCurdy spoke hopefully of the future of the college:

> The Board are going forward in the erection of the central portion of the College building. Plans are adopted, estimates are in, and I expect the work of excavation, and foundation to be well under way before your arrival.

In response to the official notice of his election, Professor Wallace answered:

> While I cannot bring to Macalester the ability and scholarship I would gladly possess yet I accept the trust fully resolved to

put into the work all the energy and enthusiasm I can command. While my work will doubtless need the charitable judgment of your Board yet I hope and pray that in loyal devotion to Macalester and the great cause she represents, I may be found in some good degree worthy of this proffered trust.

President Scovel and members of the faculty urged James Wallace to remain at Wooster. Wooster was his alma mater; his family and that of his wife lived in the community and he had many friends there. Macalester was a new adventure and was destined to go through the usual struggles of a new institution. Wooster, they argued, was, on the other hand, now well established and had a high rank as a Presbyterian college with a bright future. In the course of time there he would move up to the headship of the department of Greek; he would have leisure for literary work, and he would have a comfortable salary, with secure tenure.

But both James Wallace and Janet were imbued with a missionary spirit. They saw the need of Christian leadership for the rapidly developing Northwest. If the Presbyterian Church was to shoulder its share of responsibility, it would have to establish a college to train leaders from among the youth of the area. So the call to Macalester seemed to them the call of God.

President Scovel at length gave reluctant consent, and announcement of James Wallace's resignation was made. He would leave Wooster at the close of the winter term. From the president, the faculty, and the students there were many expressions of regret. As the end of the term approached, the pupils of the preparatory department presented him a handsome French clock as a memento of their esteem and affection. Professor Karl Merz, head of the music department, wrote them: "I desire you to regard next Saturday's recital as a farewell performance in your honor."

The Wallaces had recently built a new home and were not now able to finance a move. But in view of the urgency of Macalester's situation, it was decided that James Wallace should go on ahead and prepare for the coming of the family later. In the meantime, with the help of Jonas, perhaps Janet could secure a buyer for the house, and so provide moving expenses for the family. Early in March, in the midst of the excitement of winding up their work, Gay took sick with what was called malarial fever. On the ninth she died. Her father believed her death due to incompetent medical attention, but Janet found comfort in the assurance that God had but mercifully removed her from the cares and sufferings of this life.

At length the examinations were over, grades turned in, books packed, desk drawers cleared out, and ties that had bound James Wallace to the college at Wooster since 1870 were severed. He reached St. Paul at night, the first week in April, 1887, and went at once to a hotel. The next morning he boarded an inter-city train connecting St. Paul with Minneapolis ten miles up the river. In fifteen minutes he arrived at Macalester station at what is now the junction of Snelling Avenue with Marshall. A walk of three quarters of a mile south brought him to the edge of the campus. This plot comprised forty acres of rolling fields including a wooded area. At the intersection of Snelling with Summit he saw four frame buildings up on the terrace on the south side of Summit. The first, he was to learn, was the president's home. The one next to it would now become the Wallace home. The third was occupied by Professor Pearson, and the last by Dr. W. R. Kirkwood, professor of mental science and logic. On the north side of Summit Avenue several other residences were either built or in building. Looking south, James Wallace saw on the far side of Grand Avenue a three-story red brick structure on a high stone foundation. A small cupola topped the building. This, he supposed, was Macalester College. The boiler room, he discovered later, kitchen, dining room, and reception rooms were in the basement. The chapel and classrooms occupied the first floor. The second and third floors were being used as a dormitory for men. A windmill, perched on a high steel tower, pumped the water for the furnace and the bathrooms. All around on the front campus, dry and wind-whipped cornstalks still bore witness to last summer's crop.

James Wallace was given a cordial reception by Dr. McCurdy, Professor Pearson, and Dr. Kirkwood, all men he had known. Dr.

Thomas McCurdy had been the pastor of the First Presbyterian Church in Wooster, had served for three years on the Wooster University Board of Trustees. Francis B. Pearson had been a student of his at Wooster University and William R. Kirkwood had been the fiscal agent there for a short time. The Wooster transfer students at Macalester had petitioned the trustees to call James Wallace to the vacant chair of Greek, and they joined in the hearty welcome given him.

Macalester College had opened its doors to students on the St. Paul campus on September 16, 1885, barely two years before James Wallace arrived. Its origin, however, goes back to February 26, 1853, when Edward D. Neill, now senior professor on the faculty, secured from the Territorial Legislature a charter for Baldwin School, from which Macalester College evolved.

Neill had had a distinguished career and had for Macalester College the feelings of a father for his child. He had founded two important churches; he had helped mold the public-school system of the state as the first superintendent of public instruction and the first chancellor of the University of Minnesota in its formative days; he had been the chaplain of the 1st Regiment of Minnesota in the Civil War; he had served as a secretary in the White House under Lincoln and under Johnson and had been consul to Dublin, Ireland, under Grant. He was the author of a widely used *History of Minnesota* and had written many historical pamphlets. He carried himself with the dignity that he felt.

Neill, an Amherst graduate who had been a student at Andover and a reader in theology under Albert Barnes of Philadelphia, on April 23, 1849, with his bride, stepped off of a Mississippi River boat at St. Paul, then a town of about eight hundred, to begin missionary work among the settlers streaming into the territory. By the end of 1849 he had established the First Presbyterian Church, and in 1855 he had founded the House of Hope Presbyterian Church.

Seeing the need of a college to develop leaders for the rapidly developing Northwest he secured aid from friends in the East, among whom was M. W. Baldwin, the locomotive builder, and erected Baldwin School, a two-story brick building facing Rice

Square. In December of 1853 the building was ready for occupancy, and on the twenty-ninth of the month it was dedicated with a big banquet and speeeches and prayers by notables. Governor Gorman was one of the speakers. Ex-Governor Alexander Ramsey was a member of the Board of Trustees. The students were largely girls and young ladies. In 1855, aided again mainly by Mr. Baldwin, he built a three-story stone building on the Mississippi River bluff at the end of Wilkin Street and opened St. Paul College for Men. The depression of 1857, the development of a free school system, and the outbreak of the Civil War brought Neill's educational ventures to a halt. In 1861 he left for the battle front as chaplain of the 1st Minnesota Regiment. In 1864, when he was a secretary in the White House, he had the trustees in St. Paul secure a charter amendment changing Baldwin School to Baldwin University in the hope that Mr. Baldwin would underwrite a broader educational program. St. Paul College was absorbed by Baldwin University. Unfortunately Mr. Baldwin died suddenly in 1866 and left nothing for the university. While Neill was away from St. Paul the trustees sold the two school buildings. Much of the money was lost by bad investments.

In 1872, after an absence of more than ten years, Neill was back in Minnesota eager to push his early dreams of a men's college patterned after Amherst to completion. He rented Winslow House, a fine tourist hotel on the east bluff at St. Anthony Falls, now a part of Minneapolis and opened Jesus College. He hoped that the students at the nearby state university would enroll for classes in Bible and related subjects and also take advantage of the boarding opportunities in Winslow House. Baldwin School was the name of the preparatory department. By 1874 Neill had persuaded Charles Macalester of Philadelphia, the wealthy and prominent owner of the building, to deed it to the trustees of Baldwin University with the understanding that the school would be named Macalester College and that twenty-five thousand dollars would be raised for an endowment. So on March 5, 1874, by charter change, Baldwin University became Macalester College with the provision that two thirds of the trustees must be Presbyterians. Jesus College ceased to exist. Baldwin School continued as the preparatory department of Macalester College.

In this same year, 1874, Neill secured from the presbytery of St. Paul a letter dismissing him to the Reformed Episcopal Church. He liked its ritual and believed its broad views on the validity of ordination by other communions gave a good basis for the reunion of divided Protestantism. He continued with this church as a clergyman until 1890 when he returned to the Presbyterian fold. When Neill left the Presbyterian Church he cut himself off from his best hope for students and funds. Even though Macalester College had a board of trustees largely Presbyterian, Synod gave it no official recognition.

By this time the major denominations in Minnesota had their own colleges. The Methodists had founded Hamline in 1854; the Lutherans, Gustavus Adolphus in 1862 and St. Olaf in 1874; the Congregationalists, Carleton in 1866; and the Episcopalians had their own schools at Faribault. The Presbyterian Synod also had plans for a college of its own. Several towns were offering inducements to have the college located in their midst, notably Albert Lea. The friends of Macalester urged Synod to adopt it as Synod's college, pointing out that two thirds of its trustees were Presbyterians. Neill offered to resign to make way for a Presbyterian president provided that thirty thousand dollars be raised to endow the office. At long last, in 1880, Synod accepted the offer of the trustees and commended Macalester to the churches of Synod for speedy and liberal endowment. At the same meeting Synod approved a woman's college to be located at Albert Lea, near the Iowa border. The Reverend Daniel Rice was appointed to lead a drive to raise thirty-five thousand dollars for Macalester and fifteen thousand dollars for Albert Lea College for Women. Two colleges were a great burden for seven thousand Presbyterians. Funds came in slowly.

In the meantime, industry had crowded in on the Macalester campus at St. Anthony Falls. The trustees bought the Holyoke farm of one hundred sixty acres in the Midway District, now in St. Paul, blocked off forty acres for a campus, and sold the rest to real-estate syndicates. The college property at St. Anthony Falls was sold for a hospital and the proceeds used in the summer of 1884 to erect what is now the East Wing of Old Main.

In response to the request of the trustees, Synod, in the fall of 1884, nominated a candidate for the presidency of Macalester College. The trustees confirmed its nomination of the Reverend Thomas S. McCurdy, of Wooster, Ohio, and invited him to come and look the situation over. McCurdy was not impressed. The new building stood in what was an old cornfield, alone and unfurnished. There were no water or sewer connections with the city systems. No streetcars came out to the campus and the depot for the inter-city trains was three quarters of a mile to the north on a dirt road. There was no church, no school, no shopping center and no post office near. The endowment drive had bogged down, but the trustees assured him that one hundred thousand dollars could be raised in six months. McCurdy accepted the challenge with grave misgivings. He moved to the Twin Cities and pushed the endowment drive through the fall and winter. The spring of 1885 arrived and little money was in sight. Since the trustees had announced that the college would be opened in the following September, they felt obliged to push ahead on faith, trusting that the Presbyterians in the state would rally to the support of the college when they saw it in actual operation. A house for the president and three houses for faculty members were built on Summit Avenue on borrowed money.

President McCurdy determined to build up a faculty that would compare favorably with that of any competing institution. He offered two thousand dollars a year and a house to prospective professors. This was a good salary in that day. He secured Francis B. Pearson for the chair of Latin and, temporarily, for mathematics; he chose Nathaniel S. McFetridge for the chair of Greek and Anglo-Saxon; Charles Forbes, M.D., took over the chair of the natural sciences and acted as college physician; Daniel Rice became the lecturer in biblical literature; Edward D. Neill took the chair of history and political science and acted as librarian; and President McCurdy added to the duties of his office the chair of apologetics and ethics. He was a man, to quote the *North West Presbyterian*, "of fine scholarship, majestic appearance, faith in God and Presbyterian pluck."

This was the situation and these were the personalities on the campus when Professor Wallace arrived in the spring of 1887. He had been already introduced to the students as a "natural teacher" in an article written in January by Professor Pearson in the college *Echo:*

> In addition to his high rank as a linguist he is a man of fine qualities, his modesty and sincerity often being the subject of remark . . . The college authorities are certainly to be congratulated upon securing the services of a man in whom scholarship, teaching force, sturdy manhood, and earnest Christianity so happily combine for this responsible position.

Professor Wallace engaged a room at the home of Mr. and Mrs. Hampton on Snelling Avenue and took his meals also with them until the health of Mrs. Hampton failed. Then he boarded for a while at the Pearson home. He was alone now in a new environment and he reveled in his opportunity for uninterrupted study. He had, of course, a busy life, teaching, reading papers, attending faculty and committee meetings, teaching in the Sunday school, preparing talks for the Wednesday-evening prayer meeting, which the students were expected to attend, showing an interest in the various student activities, and finally, putting what he thought were to be the finishing touches on his text of the *Anabasis* of Xenophon.

Instead of fraternities, which had not been permitted on the Macalester campus, there were several literary societies. Every student was expected to become a member of one of these in order to cultivate his talents in declamation, essay writing, delivery of original orations, and in debate. The professors were welcome guests at these meetings and usually were asked to take part in the program. From the beginning, Macalester students entered upon their studies with seriousness and seemed to realize that the success of the institution lay as much in their hands as it did in the work of the faculty and trustees.

The athletic spirit, too, of the college was at a high pitch. On the afternoon of Macalester's opening in 1885 the boys had organized a baseball team, walked to the neighboring St. Thomas

College, played them and won. Indeed during the first four
years of the team's existence it was to hold the lead in the college
conference. Out of forty-three games played, they won thirty-
nine. James Wallace entered into the athletic life of the college
as he did into its literary and religious life, with zest. His favorite
sport was baseball, and one of the pictures of his first years at
the college shows him in baseball uniform with his trusted bat
in his hand. He was skilled also in pitching horseshoes and often
won over his faculty opponents. The students sometimes saw
him, too, racing with professors, or sprinting up the road to his
meals.

With friends James Wallace was cheerful, full of quips and
stories and easy badinage. But at times, alone in his room, financial
worries fell like a pall upon him and things "took on a dyspeptic
tinge." This gloom was reflected in some of his letters. Where
would they find the money for moving expenses and household
equipment? He observed that Mrs. Kirkwood had put down a
very handsome piece of matting in her parlor, which she planned
to cover with a rug in winter; that she had a body Brussels in
her front hall and sitting room, and that the Forbeses had their
parlor nicely furnished with Brussels, pictures, etc. He added in
comment, "But that is no reason why we should have the same.
We must cultivate a lofty independence."

Janet, on the other hand, had her own difficulties but found
comfort and strength in her faith that God was but leading
them through a period of discipline and struggle. She wrote:

"Is it like God to call us to Macalester and forsake us in the
moving and getting settled?"

We have certainly been highly honored in receiving such a
position of usefulness as the one in Macalester. It gives me
more confidence in ourselves that God has put us there. Now
let us do our very best, with entire self-consecration to the
good we *may* do.

She was busy planning for their new home. She asked her husband to put a mahogany stain on the floors of their house, and,
if the floors had cracks, to paint them a dark, rich, reddish brown.

She hoped to make her home not only a haven of peace and joy for the family but also a place where she could invite students and faculty and do her bit in adding to the pleasure and culture of those living in the college community.

> I am filled with more ambition than I ever felt before to make ours a delightful home. Alas! that bread and butter and muslin and coal cannot be procured "without money and without price."

James had suggested that it might be well when they got settled to take in Dr. and Mrs. Rice as boarders. They were an elderly couple. Mrs. Rice was not strong enough to do her own work, and they were benefactors of the college. Janet rose at once to the defense of the home.

> I know too well from bitter experience that where there are boarders the chief thought and care must be for them and the home almost ceases to exist for the children. They must be suppressed in a thousand ways, and their plans and tastes kept severely in the background, and the younger the children the more they must suffer from being subordinate.

She never allowed the welfare of her children to be forgotten.

James and Janet Wallace felt the separation keenly. Letters passed between them every few days. He wrote:

> My dear little Jewell:
>   What sort of conduct is it to get one in love with you so that I am not satisfied unless I am writing to you almost every day?

And Janet wrote: to her "Dearly Beloved and Longed for":

> If I had half an hour a day to myself, you would get seven letters per week at least . . . I have been up and down twenty times while writing this.

And again:

> This taste of widowhood makes me pray that you may long be spared to us, as I could not have prayed before.

And toward the end of May she wrote:

> If within the next twelve days I can only get my arms around
> your blessed neck, I shall be satisfied.

Another time, weary from a heavy day, she gave vent to her
feelings:

> I am weary, a worn-out old woman on the threshold of life's
> usefulness. But a letter like yours of last Sabbath does much
> to rejuvenate me. It is like balm to a wounded spirit to hear
> you say you *need* my love.

Janet indeed was feeling the strain of having borne four children in less than six years.

There was to be no commencement at Macalester that year,
since there had been no seniors enrolled. James Wallace was
free to return to the Wooster commencement, there to receive
his Ph.D. degree. Janet had planned for him a full summer of
domesticity. She wrote:

My dear *Big* Earthly Companion:

> It is very important that the drive be made for a dozen
> reasons, but it cannot be done until you come . . . The fence
> ought to be built around the section planted with trees. An
> earth closet must be made in the buggy shed. The barn ought
> to have a coat of paint. There are not nearly enough hooks
> in the closet—the cellar must be fixed so the water can get
> out. The cellar partitions ought to be finished and the garret-
> bannister made. There are many urgent reasons for your
> reaching home at the earliest possible date . . . so I do hope
> that you can arrange to come by the close of the second week
> in June . . .
>
> I wanted to write to you last night after receiving your very
> strengthening epistle of last Wednesday and Thursday but
> my sense of duty and neglected Bible conquered, so I read a
> number of chapters instead . . . Some of your sweet flattery
> has aroused enough self-confidence in me to make me deter-
> mine to make you a sweet and noble wife *yet*.

James Wallace left for Wooster in early June. He felt that he had earned his degree by hard, honest toil. It had cost him

> . . . a year of hard study and travel in Greece and six years in connection with my teaching, in the study of Greek philology as a major and Greek history as a minor. My thesis was the complete working up of the vocabulary of Xenophon's *Anabasis* from various points of view. It cost an enormous labor.

During the summer his time was devoted to his immediate family and their wide connections and to getting the home and premises in good condition to attract a buyer.

VIII

Again Alone

Around me scowls the wintry sky,
Blasting each bud of hope and joy;
And shelter, shade, nor home have I;
Save in these arms of thine, Love.

ROBERT BURNS

THE summer wore on. Still the house on Beall Avenue was unsold. James Wallace once more bade his family good-by, regretfully indeed, and took off for St. Paul. Janet and the children would remain in Wooster till April. Pa and Ma Davis, Miriam, Bess, and Alice would move in with her. This arrangement would reduce expenses for both families and give Janet help in the housekeeping and care of the children.

In Macalester, James proceeded at once to set up housekeeping on Summit Avenue. He made a deal to have a Mrs. Crulman, a widow of fifty-eight, take over his house and operate it as a boardinghouse until Janet should come. She was to pay him seventy-five dollars in rent for the time and he would pay her three dollars a week for his boarding. He was to retain one room for a study and another for living room and bedroom. In this way he could have some of the comforts anyhow; he would be able to have hot water to drink when he wished, and Mrs. Crulman was used to serving adequate meals with meat three times a day. James Wallace would preside at the table. He would pay his share of the fuel and he agreed to take care of the furnace. Mrs. Crulman had a maid to help with the work. James felt that he had made a good bargain, that except for fuel he would really be getting his living without expense, and that he would have congenial companions at meals.

Anticipating some such arrangement, Janet had packed for him not only his trunk but a barrel and a box of books. The trunk with his personal effects he unpacked at once. He was distressed to find there an old overcoat of Janet's father's, but not his own new coat. Already the September nights were getting chilly and he wrote Janet at once that he feared he might have to buy a coat. She, too, was disturbed, but assured him she had packed it. His barrel and box he had brought over to the house from the terminal by one of the student roomers who kept a Texas pony and a buggy in the Wallace stable. From the barrel he got out the carpet and spread it on his parlor floor. It missed fitting by only a few inches on each side. This did not worry him greatly; he could cover the bare edges with furniture. The fine old walnut bed that Mrs. Crulman had lent him he put against the north wall, her walnut bureau on the east side, and a washstand on the west. The trunk fitted into a corner. A large rug he put beside the bed, a smaller one in front of the washstand. Janet had sent splashers, and a sewing kit for mending and darning. At the windows he hung two new shades which he had bought downtown. Later he was to buy a sofa for his after-dinner nap, and on his bare walls he hung a Greek calendar and a chart of English literature. This done, he surveyed his quarters with satisfaction. Other adornments could wait till Janet came—but his overcoat still was missing. He went downtown and bought heavy woolen underwear.

On the campus Professor Wallace noted several changes. The brick walls on the new section of the college building had risen twenty-five feet and gave promise of an imposing structure. The small new library, gift of Henry L. Moss, a trustee, had been completed, the books installed, with Dr. Neill as librarian. It was rumored that Summit Avenue would be graded to the Mississippi, and that a bridge would connect St. Paul with Minneapolis and the boulevard running to Minnehaha Falls.

But he was aware also of a feeling of increased tension between the president and the faculty. Even last spring James had been writing Janet that he wished Dr. Kirkwood were president, that he was "a stronger man [than McCurdy] in every way."

> Dr. McCurdy surprises me almost daily with some want of judgment. We have been working off and on for two weeks on the catalogue. He is not consulting a single other catalogue . . . I have gathered up three or four and have sent for some others. I want to know what the northwest colleges are doing. He has only four recitations weekly now. Yet you would think, to hear him talk, he was half to death with work. The faculty mean to see that he gets about 10 or 12 recitations a week next year. There will be music then no doubt.

Dr. McCurdy, he wrote, announced hymns and read notices in chapel while sitting, and he had a bad habit of running into houses and rooms without knocking. Incidentally, he told Janet that Mrs. McCurdy and Mrs. Forbes read little except the newspaper and added, "I want you to beat the whole of them as I am sure you easily can."

The strain between faculty and president was more fundamental than those incidents suggest. Several of them felt that President McCurdy was assuming dictatorial powers and that he was attempting to deal with faculty and students on a high-school level. They all, they felt, had a share in the administration of the college and were not employed as teachers alone. They resented his frequent, unannounced appearances in classrooms where he would sit and listen and then move on to another room. They felt that he lowered his dignity by rushing into the hall between bells and acting as if he was expecting disorder among students. They thought he should be out trying to raise funds to pay the college salaries, which were in arrears.

The immediate subject of discussion was the formulation of a set of rules for the government of the college. Professors Pearson and Kirkwood intimated that even though they drew up a set of rules for the students, the president lacked the courage to enforce them. Dr. Wallace took the position that it was the duty of the whole faculty to enforce rules, and not that of the president alone; that if the president failed, then the faculty should petition the Board to dismiss him; and if the members of the faculty failed, they should likewise be dismissed. He assured President McCurdy that he meant no disrespect to him but was speaking on the principle involved.

The trustees finally took a hand and defined the powers of the president and of the faculty. This was done supposedly under the influence of the president; the document put nearly everything into his hands. There followed caucuses and stormy faculty meetings. To Dr. McCurdy the faculty presented their objections "in an able document" that he was to present to the trustees. He was pale and his voice faltered as he finished reading it. In all of this James Wallace took an active part, and he told the president frankly what he thought the root of the trouble. A joint committee of faculty and trustees was set up to consider the matter. Eventually the Board sent in a modified set of rules, and made it plain to both faculty and president that it was the final court of appeal in disagreements between the two. Of this all Dr. Wallace wrote Janet:

He [McCurdy] was beaten at every point, as we all think and, I hope most earnestly, that our hitches are now at an end. I am fearfully tired of them and do want to live at peace and brotherly love. I am not quarrelsome if let alone.

James Wallace was really enjoying his work at Macalester, especially his advanced classes in Greek with the mature junior and senior students. He wondered that he had been so long content to do "gerund grinding" at Wooster. "We have some fine boys here," he wrote, "and I find myself getting more and more interested . . ." He was proud to record that a Macalester boy had won the state oratorical contest. He spoke of his fine Sunday Bible class of college boys, and of the satisfying Sunday services in the small college chapel, more intimate than that at Wooster. The ministers of the faculty preached at these services, Dr. Kirkwood being, in Dr. Wallace's opinion, the best of the lot. The aging Dr. Neill sometimes came out from St. Paul to take his turn. His sermons were always thoughtful and pleasant to listen to. Then there were the Wednesday-evening prayer

meetings, led by members of the faculty, that stimulated his
mind and warmed his heart. He himself had spoken once on
"whatsoever a man soweth," and again on "rejoice in the Lord,"
a subject he had chosen "partly because," he wrote Janet, "I need
to be stirred up on that subject as my letters clearly testify . . .
If only our hearts could be flooded with divine fervor all the
time, that would burn out every sin."

To the public the twinkle in James Wallace's eye bespoke a
man who found life good indeed, yet in his letters home, it is
true, he was often troubled. "I often wonder," he wrote Janet,
"if anything but death will free me from this accursed financial
thraldom," and again he exclaimed, "What unspeakable fools men
are who marry without accumulating several thousand dollars
first." The house on Summit Avenue was proving to be "a white
elephant." Even the staining of the floors that Janet had requested had cost twenty-five dollars.

> Think of it! It cost only $56 to paint our house outside [on
> Beall Avenue], two coats and the kitchen beside . . . My
> bills on this house run thus far to $108.00—these big bills
> make me pretty sick . . . I have promised to pay off a note
> of 100 dollars next month. With the infernal paint bill, that
> will nearly exhaust my income for October—I am sick enough,
> I am sure, with this hand to mouth living, but I suppose
> there is little hope for anything else on this sin-cursed foot-
> stool. Still we always have Mother's comfort, "It might be
> worse."

He was watching jealously every penny, and did not think they
could live any more cheaply.

> We have lived much like work people all the while. We only
> received 1000 for a year or so after our marriage, then 1200,
> then 1300, 1400, and the year before I came away, 1500. Of
> course on 12 and 13 we could save but little. Life Ins., Herald,
> building, etc. has kept us where we are. Possibly a better day
> is coming. We can still pray for it anyway.

His trousers wore thin, and he ordered a new pair, hoping to
wear them first to a meeting of the Presbyterian Alliance in Oc-

tober, but when the time came, he said, "I dislike to get them tomorrow, for I have not money enough to pay for them." In the spring he wrote Janet that he was out at the elbows. It would cost him thirty dollars to go home for Christmas, and he debated whether he might better stay away, but in the end he decided that he would be healthier, happier in every way if he were to go.

This was a bitterly cold climate. When the wind blew—and this was a country of heavy winds—the furnace would not heat the house. He had put storm sash on the windows, yet often he had to stand or sit on the register or wear an overcoat in his room. He had found his overcoat in his box of books. The total coal bill, he figured, for heating this house even inadequately would run to $200–$250. The only solution, as he saw it, would be to put in stoves, and these would cost $125. The fuel for these would probably be $100 to $125 a year. He prepared Janet for this, prepared her also for closing part of the house and using the parlor or study as a bedroom, and for the simplest possible furnishing:

> One thing I want to impress on your mind and that is to set up no ideal as to how our house is to be furnished. We will simply do what we can with our money and then stop. We will add nothing to our debts to fix up to a certain standard. I will probably then be distracted or nearly that and want to be kept from stark madness.

By the end of February he was "sick, sick, sick, of these bankrupting coal bills," sick of firing the furnace, of having to chop the thick ice off the top of the cistern to draw water; the pump was frozen. He had looked at a snow-covered ground for four months. When would there be a spring? The roomers in the house had given up the struggle to keep warm and had gone elsewhere. Only Charley Murray had stayed to keep him company; on cold nights he slept with Professor Wallace for the warmth of both of them. Charley Murray had other virtues, too; he played the mouth organ, old familiar tunes like "Home, Sweet Home" that Dr. Wallace enjoyed. Naturally, when her boarders left, Mrs. Crulman had had to give up, too. Dr. Wallace had to

find another place for his meals. In the meantime he and Janet
had postponed the date of her moving the family to Macalester
until the next summer. There were advantages in the new date:
she would have more leisure in Wooster for the training of the
children, for her music, and for all the sewing she must do before they left. During the summer James could once more push
the sale of the house. With stringent economy he hoped that
possibly they could save $684 by August.

All through the winter they had been faced, too, with another
threat. Dr. Rice, who represented the Board on the faculty, had
already spoken of a possible cut for faculty salaries. When he
had talked with Dr. Kirkwood as to whether the faculty would
accept such a cut, he had got no encouragement. Professor Wallace had his speech ready when he should be approached. On
May 13 he wrote Janet that Dr. Rice had had a frank talk with
him on the subject:

> He thinks poor as the college is, 2000 and a house is too much,
> that these houses will rent for 500 and that the profs should
> pay the rent . . . He does not think that the Board can re-
> duce them honorably without the consent of the profs, and
> that it should be a last resort . . . The Pres. has not pushed
> the canvas in these cities at all but allowed it to drag. He has
> not raised at all what was hoped. If the canvas now to begin
> in Minneapolis goes on in the same way, then retrenchment
> will set in and it will fall on the President first. It seems to me
> more clear that he will not be here beyond another year. At
> the same time or later it will fall on us. I am not worrying over
> this and feel confident that no change will be made for three
> or four months anyway and probably not then. One thing is
> settled, I will not pay 500 rent for this house—never. I would
> rent a decent little house in St. Paul first and ride out to the
> college on the train. Dr. Rice said of course they were pleased
> with the Professors and did not want them to leave but
> thought something would have to be done or there would be,
> ere long, a financial crisis. I am getting tired of this buzzing
> about my ears about the reduction of salaries and I am re-
> solved to do what I can to get some rich pupils in these cities

this vacation so that if the salaries are knocked down I can find refuge, if need be, here in these cities from starvation at least.

Accordingly Professors Wallace and Boyd and Pearson decided to stay in Macalester for the summer and conduct a tutoring school in Greek, Latin, and mathematics. They sent out a printed card to about two hundred parents, but no pupils came. Janet had all along disapproved the plan. "I believe," she wrote, "that if God means to help us financially, and I am strong in the hope that He will, He will not give you any pupils."

Her reaction to the threat of a salary cut came from the angle of a professor's wife vitally interested in students:

. . . the danger of a reduction in our salary sounds the death knell of *my* hopes. I want to have time to entertain the students often. They must have recreation, they ought to find much of it in the refined, attractive homes of the faculty. A Professor's wife should have time to read, that she may keep up with the news and be able to talk with the students. She ought to have leisure to practice new music, that singing may be a part of the recreation in social gatherings. But an insufficient income always means a quiet, tired wife weary with endless patching and mending and trying to make a little go as far as possible . . . In the course of time, refreshments cost no little. Living where we do must also have quite a bill for carfare. And Professors are not ministers, there will be no "Relief Fund" to keep the wolf from the door in our old age. We must save at least two hundred a year if possible . . . I think it would be cruelly unjust to Professors who, instead of being pinched and hampered and depressed, should have the carefree, genial manner that attracts the young and, most unjust to the wives, who being educated Christian women, should wield a powerful influence for good over the students. In your case especially, it seems to me it would be dishonorable to propose a reduced salary. You had just built here. With the difference in living, your income here was nearly what it is in Macalester, and you had the assured prospect of Dr.

Black's place. Now we shall probably lose our property and must spend hundreds of dollars in moving and settling. A heavy tax will be laid on us for doing our shopping in the cities, and we can hardly persuade a servant to come out where we live and any workman feels justified in charging us ruinous rates . . . If those rich men up in the two cities, really love Macalester, have they any right to say, "We trust you to build up the college and win the hearts of the students so that the Alumni shall be generous to their beloved Alma Mater, but you must pinch yourselves, your wives, and your children to do it"? Surely the Board will not act in so unbusiness-like and unjust a manner. But we ought to know soon and either look out for another place where you can give yourself up gloriously, heart and soul, to your work, or continue here where you are so much missed and where so many are determined to have you back . . .

He, indeed, when things grew rough, played with the idea that he might someday go back to the college at Wooster.

Other things worried Professor Wallace. President Harper of Chicago had been pleased with the manuscript of the *Anabasis* text. In fact, he had written: "I am amazed at the work you have done," had reported that the book was partly in the printer's hands, and had suggested to Professor Wallace that he prepare a second volume in the Greek series to include the remaining books of the *Anabasis*. But there were delays and delays, and Professor Wallace began to despair of the book's publication. He wrote Janet:

I have debated much whether to throw the whole enterprise overboard . . . it has been such an unending vexation . . . What I most confidently expect is that before my work reaches print some one else will have the same thing out. So my work will be time and labor wasted. So it goes. The philosophy "All things work together for good," etc. is excellent but the hardest in the world to apply. I have hardly grace for it. If I had let this abominable stuff alone what could I not have read and done meantime.

All year, too, he had been unsettled as to whether he should present himself for licensure, and, if so, whether in Minnesota in the Presbyterian Church or in Wooster in the United Presbyterian Church, which would greatly please his mother. He saw many opportunities to preach in needy churches in Minnesota, and his colleagues there were favorable. "To be a powerful preacher," he felt, "is easily the greatest gift bestowed on man." But he feared his own "lack of spirituality," and "besetting sins." He feared also that he could "never speak with sufficient animation to arouse interest . . . Not that my convictions are not deep enough—but somehow at prayer meetings I cannot speak with force or enthusiasm. I do wish I knew just what to do." He asked Janet to pray that he might be guided in this decision. All year he had been making clippings toward future sermons and in the spring he began seriously to study Hodge on theology to prepare for the licensing examination. He had made it a habit to do much devotional reading, spending his Sunday afternoons and evenings thus, after his dinner and customary nap. At the end of the evening, in his usual letter to Janet he would tell of spending the evening with his Greek Testament or the *Harmony of the Synoptic Gospels*, or of reading an essay on immortality or prayer. Once he mentioned the ninth chapter of *Ecce Homo*, recommending it to all the adults of the Beall Avenue home as "one of the most satisfactory and convincing evidences of Christianity" he had ever read.

As the anniversary of Gay's death on the ninth of March approached, he found himself thinking much of her. "That sad event," he wrote, "has had a softening and subduing effect on me and I think has been quite a means of grace and I do hope will ever be while life is spared." Three days later he forgot his own birthday till noon. Then he wrote:

Today I am 39 years old . . . How can a man live so long, know and do so little? I am ashamed of myself. Life is not a total failure. I have an A.M., Ph.D., a wife, four children and a library . . . yes, and a salary of $2000 a year and need of every cent of it too. Well it is discouraging but I am not without hope that even yet I may get out of debt and do some good.

If he could have talked his troubles over face to face with Janet, no doubt James Wallace would have found life easier, but the strain of separation was hard for both to bear. Janet wrote:

I am always in a feverish state of excitement hoping for a letter from you . . .

She had her doubts whether "this way of half-living is consistent with our marriage vows . . . May it be our last long separation!" Her "whole woman's nature rebelled" against "this forlorn way of living."

. . . that last word [home] has grown inexpressibly sweet to me, sweeter than ever in my life before. And I very much fear that I am so completely spoiled that a palace without my dear God-given husband would be but a dreary prison. My one absorbing idea is to get out of debt and get snugly settled for the remainder of my life-work . . .

She had once seen their old friend Mr. Brown lay his head on his wife's lap to have it caressed, and she said:

A lump came into my throat and—but won't I make up in the future for lost time!

And again she wrote:

Have I laughed over your injunction "to be dressed to receive" you? I laughed all the more gleefully because I had just hung up in the closet one of the prettiest dresses you ever saw, to be inaugurated the night of your arrival.

On his part he was writing:

It sometimes seems a grave question whether I can stay here or you there till June.

And again, addressing her as "My dear Comforter," he remarked:

It is very hard to keep from writing you even when I ought not.

In June, a few weeks before he was to see her again, he said:

Now if you were here to count my hairs, kiss me, and do all your conjugal duties toward me I could be in a very complacent frame of mind. The feeling grows on me that I married a most sterling wife—one having all the qualities of Christian womanhood and more than worthy of my love and admiration.

Long before he had asked her to "put on her silk" and go down and have her picture taken. He wished photographs also of the children. When he had her picture before him he admitted gazing at it with as much ardor as in his days in Greece.

Yet at long distance Janet was nettled to hear that Mrs. Crulman always had breakfast on time.

I am rejoiced that Mrs. C. is so faithful, but I cannot but reflect that she can retire when she pleases and does not need to be up during the night.

When he wrote in the early fall of his comfort on Summit Avenue, she showed some dudgeon:

Are you not sure you would not rather continue the present arrangements indefinitely? You see I am a trifle sore that you are so comfortable and happy without me. I wish I were more essential.

Sometimes, too, letters were misinterpreted, and brought unneeded pain. Janet wished more than all else to be a "noble" and "worthy" wife, but when she teased him about his spelling and laughed with her parents over his blunders, she struck a sore point. His spelling, he admitted, had been a "thorn in my flesh ever since I had awakened in me some ambition to be a scholar."

Better unconscious ignorance than to be stung to death with the everlasting perpetration and remembrance of blunders.

And when he was feeling sorely the financial burdens of married life and wrote of this quite candidly to her, she wept, "in agony" thinking he regretted his marriage and his family. Separation was indeed a cross to two persons as truly lovers as when they married.

Janet was so sure that "the Lord knoweth you have need of these things" that she could cheerfully lecture her husband, a "Christian troubled with debt and indigestion," on his want of faith.

> If you could only look forward a year and see us nicely settled in our Macalester home, you would fairly blush at our present distrust of Providence! Is it like God's dealings with his children to give us a beautiful home, and then not help us to move and get that home in ship-shape?

Having to pay the bills each month, James liked to feel the hard cash in hand. It was not that he did not have faith; it was rather that he knew the demands upon him, and he was Scotch and a worrier. He had gone to Macalester in good faith as a pioneer. Now the promised salary was in arrears, and every cent of it spoken for before it came.

Yet he was not always wrestling with depression. He had fun, too, and pleasant companionship. For a while after Mrs. Crulman gave up, he boarded at the dormitory with several of the faculty and two of the students. He took time off even for Haliburton's *Sam Slick*. With James Boyd of the faculty, he went over to the city to see Edwin Booth in *Hamlet* and *Julius Caesar*. Since he had to teach a course in English, he felt that seeing a play was equal to half a dozen or more readings. Janet reported that she was secretly delighted that he had done so, but added ". . . but surely you will not go to the T. again." With Professor Pearson he visited also the State Fair in October and was present at a sham battle, of which he wrote:

> It was immense, especially the "sham" part of it. To see men—hundreds of them—firing at each other in close quarters and no one falling was "too thin." If they had actually killed and wounded a couple of hundred I would probably have enjoyed it . . . I hate shams, even sham fights.

He attended Synod, in October at Stillwater, Minnesota, and was greatly heartened by its decision to raise two hundred thousand dollars for endowment, two thirds of this for Macalester. He watched the parade for President Cleveland and his wife when they came to the Twin Cities. And in the spring the beauty of Minnesota's fields and woods and lakes drew him outdoors. With Pearson and Boyd he spent one afternoon in early June fishing in Snail Lake seven miles to the north. They caught 257 fish, chiefly crappies and pickerel. "If we all live to next summer," he wrote, "we must all go out to some lake and camp out awhile and fish, read, and sleep." Perhaps by that time the workmen would have finished the extension of Summit Avenue, and they could take delightful walks down to the Mississippi. He was looking forward now. Next year his family would be with him—and the sky would be a brighter blue.

IX

Postmarked Wooster

There's nae luck about the house,
There's nae luck at a'
There's nae luck about the house
When our gudeman's awa'.

ANONYMOUS

B A C K in Wooster, Janet was carrying half the load. In the house on Beall Avenue she was on call twenty-four hours a day, caring for three lively children, feeding them and comforting them, punishing them when they were naughty, listening to their prayers at bedtime, kissing their bumps, doctoring their sore throats, seeing that they always had something to do or make, mending their clothes, and answering their questions. Her sense of responsibility for their welfare seemed at first to release day by day the physical energy she needed.

If I were not so sleepy it would be *funny* to lie awake in the dead of night singing "Baby-bye, here's a fly" and "Good morning, merry sunshine!" But it's like medicine to me that they need me so much, otherwise I would probably be in bed myself . . .

The necessity for guiding them with a sure hand nevertheless weighed heavily upon her. "I feel very deep anxiety about our little ones," she wrote James, "and I beg of you to pray most earnestly for them." She was sometimes reduced to tears over a spell of contrariness or unreason, but always in the end the naughty child came around with hugs and kisses for its mother; they were all affectionate and demonstrative. She rose at five in the morning; the children must be dressed and look well for the family breakfast at six-thirty. Helen was comparatively little trouble, but the boys kept her always on the run. Finally she took the two oldest, Helen and Ben, to Miss Pettibone's kindergarten for the mornings.

> The simple fact is I have not the strength to have the children with me all day. We spend the afternoons generally together in the nursery and I am fagged out long before they are snugly tucked in bed for the night.

James was always sympathetic, but there was little he could do at long range. Occasionally, to be sure, he would write to them a story-letter, as of the chickens he heard persistently clucking "or chuckling" in the cellar, just under his study, it seemed. Yet he could not find anywhere the source of the noises, and he began to wonder if he were crazy. Then he let a student down into the cold-air chamber and still there were no chickens. So he went in beside the furnace, lifted a board, and craning his neck peered underneath the firebox, and there walking about in the ashes, quite unconcerned, were a rooster and a hen. And he took them out and fed them. Presumably, he explained, a dog had chased them into the yard and they had tumbled down the fresh-air duct and from there had found this place of refuge. Surely children familiar with the tale of Shadrach, Meshach, and Abednego, must have relished this story. So while Janet, back in Wooster, kept them ever mindful of their "precious Papa," James himself was, by such stories on occasion, making the home waiting for them up North come alive to his children. Once indeed, Benny, asked if he did not wish to go to heaven, answered quickly, "No, I want to go to Macalester."

And that was where Janet wished to go, as soon as it was reasonably possible. Where James was, that was her home. There she could make him comfortable. There she could do her share for the students. He wrote her in detail of student activities, of the games they won, even of his own triumphs over fellow professors in pitching horseshoes. As early as November she was writing her husband, "I am astonished at my own interest in Macalester students."

She had sent James off in the fall with many little things to help transform his rooms into a likeness of home. Most of them he had not even used.

I thought your taste and all would show better if I would let things alone. So, of those fancy things you sent, I tucked them all away carefully in my trunk . . . the head-rest for the rocker I used for a day or two but like all such stuff it had an ungovernable propensity to fall on the floor so I stowed it where it gives no further trouble. On general principle I am opposed to much of modern housekeeping appointments. One can hardly sit down any more lest some mat or what not is knocked out of place and one feels that he is a transgressor. Pillow shams, for example, what an unspeakable fraud they are!

She was responsive, too, to his actual physical needs. When she found he was "sleeping cold," she ordered him to town at once to buy a good wool mattress in two parts, a pair of scarlet all-wool blankets, and a soapstone for his feet. Planning for the home, for carpets, draperies and furniture, she asked James for floor diagrams and measurements upstairs and down. She wanted a large cookstove, thinking no doubt of the entertaining she would do. A friend had found for her an organ which she might purchase for sixty-five or seventy-five dollars, and she wrote James of it. When he replied that they must be honest and pay their debts first and that the organ must wait until they had sold the house in Wooster, she was bitterly disappointed. Once she even asked James to pray that one of the children might become a good violinist.

Janet resented the idea that a woman's job was just in bearing and rearing children. She felt that a woman had a responsibility for the community in which she lived and for the world. She regarded herself as a person and wished to be so regarded. In her early married life she even rebuked her husband for addressing his letters to her as Mrs. James Wallace. "I am Janet D. Wallace," she had said—though later she withdrew her objections. She was proud of having helped James, even in a small way, on his *Anabasis*, and liked to talk of it as "our book."

As her eyes grew stronger, she rejoiced that she could read more

at night. She wanted constantly to be improving herself, particularly her spiritual life, for her own sake first and so that she might
be of greater assistance to her husband.

> I have just finished reading Professor Drummond's address at
> Northfield on Holiness . . . Don't you suppose the great trou-
> ble with me is I have read my Bible so little for years, have read
> so little of anything indeed that I am nearly starved.

In much the same vein she wrote later:

> I am growing in grace . . . it makes me very thankful and very
> humble . . . Ah my Dear, give me a few more years and see
> if I cannot help you.

During the long year, however, her frail body often seemed un-
equal to her tasks, and finally in the spring she wrote her husband
of her discouragement:

> I acknowledge that the most bitter ingredient in my cup has
> been the consciousness that if I had had a little more leisure and
> strength I might have been a more attractive, agreeable, and
> lovable wife. This world must always be a dreary prison to a
> woman whose husband does not love her, so it is the hardest
> part of duty that its performance saps the life and lighthearted-
> ness and vivacity that perhaps first attracted the husband. But
> then no woman wants her husband's love half so much for her
> own sake as for his. She can never make him a happy home un-
> less he is really attached to her and she knows it. So I am glad
> I am feeling stronger and can perhaps do more to make home
> pleasant for you . . . I find myself often wondering why God
> ever gave *me* such a noble husband. And I thank Him most
> fervently that, even if occasionally some thoughtless words of
> yours would cost me a night of scalding tears, nothing has
> ever made me love you less.

She was always trying to bolster his morale. His digestion was
never good, and she knew that he was subject to the blues. When
he despaired of the publication of the *Anabasis*, she reminded him
that he had already received "a liberal reward in your own scholarship." She was well aware of his financial burdens, but she did not

believe in dwelling on them. "Just forget it," she would often say.
She continued to talk faith to lift him out of his gloomy view of
their financial state. She never doubted, but wrote:

> When we need that money for moving, it will be supplied.

And again:

> What makes me happy is the confident assurance that an easier
> time financially is coming. So don't let us despond.

Having had a visit in the spring from a Macalester boy on his way
home from the national oratorical contest, she had learned that
her husband was "jolly and as full of life as can be." She rejoiced
that he was "showing a radiant face to the world."

Like most wives, she was always eager that he should put his
best foot forward. For this reason she had teased him persistently
about his spelling. After all, had he not teased her often "to within
an inch of my life"? He was a tease, had always been. "Sometime,
somewhere," she wrote, "you will know me well enough not to
take offense at anything I may do or say." She exhorted him evidently about many things, for in a letter to Wooster, when he
was anticipating a trip home, he remarked:

> My weight is 166 . . . I mean to take care of myself so that
> when I go home in vacation I will weigh not less than 175. I
> do want to be a man physically even if I am not mentally, and
> can't spell, nor remember a dozen things to be brought home
> when I go down town, nor hold my head so high that I can see
> the zenith and a half dozen other things thought necessary by
> a certain young girl whose photo I have sitting up beside my
> clock on my study table. [James Wallace was notably absent-
> minded. He had once been so absorbed in his own studies that
> he forgot altogether his class in Anglo-Saxon.]

Janet tried to be critical of herself as well. She analyzed what
she termed her extravagances, wondered whether by rising earlier
and doing more she could dispense with a sewing woman. She
papered the wall of the nursery with a twelve-cent paper, "close
imitation of a forty-cent paper," and did the work herself. She
scrutinized the food budget to see whether the kinds of food they

bought were real necessities. She wrote James that on next year's budget they must include ninety dollars for milk, a sum that scandalized her husband. At his remonstrance she was ruffled:

> With our income it would be a *sin* to say we could not afford our children plenty of suitable nourishment . . . When you remember how much I have sacrificed—willingly—for my children, you can hardly wonder, my Dear, that a thrill of indignation went through me, at the thought of giving $100 to a College and then putting the little ones God has given us on a short allowance of milk!

At the Beall Avenue home they had been keeping a cow, and her husband was not yet used to reckoning milk in dollars and cents. Flossie had always furnished an adequate supply. Now, in the spring, Janet had arranged for her sale in preparation for their leaving. The money from this was to go toward moving expenses. The day before she was taken away Janet herself went out and curried her, "the only cow in the world," she remarked, she was "not afraid of."

When spring came and Janet began to think seriously of the move in the summer to what seemed the far Northwest, she also began to wish she could first go East to Pennsylvania to visit relatives, uncles, aunts, and cousins, who had long been asking her to come. Maude would go with her and they could time their visit so that they could attend the Presbyterian General Assembly, meeting that year in Philadelphia. It would be her last chance for such a trip, she felt; once in St. Paul, she could never hope to go so far East again. In fact, Wooster would be very far away. She and her mother had indeed made up their minds that they would not be seeing each other again after she left. James did not share that view at all. But he also wished she could make the trip East, regretted only that he was not a rich man to finance it adequately. However, Janet had resources. Without a word to him she carefully composed a letter to Mrs. William Thaw of Pittsburgh, whose husband was a railroad man. Could Mrs. Thaw get for her a pass between Pittsburgh and Philadelphia? She would then somehow find the money for the fare from Wooster to Pittsburgh. Mrs.

Thaw was most gracious. Of course she'd provide a pass; not only that, but she would also furnish the round-trip fare between Wooster and Pittsburgh, and she would send a carriage and have Janet come out and have dinner with her the night she was to spend in Pittsburgh. James, when he heard, was distressed at his wife's "cheek," but she justified herself; she had acted not just for her own pleasure but also for her sister Maude's and Helen's, whom she could take along on that pass.

Janet was disturbed, however, as the time drew near, and the pass came but not the fare. She feared her expenses might run to fifteen or twenty dollars more than she had counted on. Possibly she could not go after all. James hoped that she would not "be so terribly afraid of spending a few cents that you will have no pleasure at all when you go." She was still distressed when one night, with others of her household, she had the opportunity of looking through the telescope in the college observatory. "We had a fine peep," she wrote, "at Mars and Jupiter . . . Jupiter's belt was distinct and his moons bright." At that she got to thinking of the "many mansions" above prepared for those who love the Lord, "and I thought if we are to go there some day I won't fret if we do *not* see everything in Philadelphia and New York." Then the miracle happened. To Janet miracles were never a surprise. Uncle Robert Wallace, who had bought Flossie, heard of Janet's proposed trip, surmised she might need money, and brought twenty-five dollars to her, first installment on the price of Flossie. Surely the Lord did provide, though sometimes at the last moment, to test their faith. The next day Janet, her sister Maude, and little Helen entrained for Pittsburgh. The boys were left at home with the Davises.

It was a wonderful trip, dinner at Mrs. Thaw's, a visit with Aunt Rebe in Mechanicsburg, the town where Janet had been born, and then the General Assembly. There was the "great meeting" in commemoration of the one hundredth anniversary of the organization of the Presbyterian Church, and Dr. Cuyler's address. Mrs. Grover Cleveland occupied a box seat at the meeting, and Janet thought her lovely. She and Maude had found a room near the auditorium at a dollar a night for both of them. At the Women's Christian

Association they got a "very satisfying dinner for eight cents"; they were trying to keep their expenses for meals down to twenty-five cents a day. From Philadelphia they proceeded to New York. There they had engaged "a charming room" at a boardinghouse for five dollars a week, including meals, "though possibly not dinner." They visited the Lenox Library, where Maude reveled in first editions and old parchments. In the Historical Society rooms they looked at paintings by Titian, Murillo, Guido Reni, Tintoretto, Velásquez, Rubens, Sir Joshua Reynolds, and others. They visited hospitals and churches, heard Dr. Parkhurst preach, saw the Statue of Liberty from the Cyrus Field block, and the view of the city, its environs, and Castle Garden Island. (Janet was not sure about the wisdom of allowing all this horde of immigrants into the United States.) They rode the "L," and took a train to Coney Island. There they were thrilled to look out over the ocean from a height of three hundred feet and to feel the cool breezes blowing their hair and tugging at their skirts. The sight of many young lovers made Janet homesick:

It hurts my feelings no little that I always have my pleasure trips apart from my husband.

On Saturday afternoon they took a horse-drawn stage up Fifth Avenue toward Central Park as far as the Mall. There they stopped and watched the procession of men, women, and children move along in holiday attire.

We lingered until tea time and then found that the most magnificent part of the pageant was to be seen on the main drive. We waited for a few moments for the throng of glittering carriages to pass, but they kept coming round the curve on and on and on . . . until at last we realized that we were seeing not merely scores of these fine equipages, but hundreds and hundreds and hundreds of them, and no buggies, remember, nor plain carriages, nor even Hansom cabs, but two-horse carriages, with liveried coachmen and often a footman too. We agreed that all the palatial buildings we had seen had failed to give us the impression of wealth and princely state conveyed by those countless costly equipages.

While they were in the East they went also to Princeton, and to the battlefield of Gettysburg; then back they went to Mechanicsburg to pick up Helen, and then home. James they found already there, to their surprise; and "one of the prettiest dresses you ever saw," in which she planned to greet her husband on his return, was still packed away.

X

Settling In

Wi' cantie wee things all about
An' wife to gie him solace,
He watched the rampin' storm without
An' made his hame his palace.

ANONYMOUS

T H E summer of 1888 was a busy one for James and Janet Wallace. The house and lot on Beall Avenue had to be made ready for a buyer, the household goods to be packed for shipment. No buyer appeared. But the family, they decided, must, whether or no, be united and the move to Macalester made. The Davis family planned to continue in the Wallace home and pay rent. Miriam Maude, inseparable companion of Janet since childhood, accepted an invitation to go with the Wallaces and make her home with them.

In early September they arrived in St. Paul, took the little train through the stump fields to Macalester station, made their way to 1596 Summit Avenue, and brought life and cheer to the big frame house on faculty row, next to the president's home. Summit Avenue had become a beautiful, well-graded street. The main boulevard ran between grassy stretches now planted with small trees, and on either side were smaller service roads. The public had discovered it, and elegant turnouts now drove past the college campus. Nevertheless, to the children, seven, and six, and four, respectively, the campus had many of the attractions of the country. Over to the south were some open woods. Not far away there was a ravine, too, Shadow Falls, that was later to become a popular picnic grounds. And there were uncluttered fields. That, out in front of the main building, the students used for ball; out behind there was still another. Behind the house there was a stable; they were used to a stable in which to play. In the house there was a cellar —where the "chuckling" chickens had been found, and an attic with a tank into which with great labor their father could pump water. However there were no water connections yet with the city, and on Saturday night, which was bath night for everyone, water was heated on the kitchen stove and the big washing tub brought into the kitchen for their ablutions. Just as at Wooster, their light came from kerosene lamps, which had every day to be cleaned and trimmed. There was a windmill on the campus, too. They liked that. At times, their father told them, when the wind went down it would stop, the water tank would be empty, the boilers could not be fired; then the students clad in overcoats and blankets would shiver through their classes.

The main feature of the campus, the college building, was impressive with its stone carriage porch, its gables and dormer, and its stone trimmings. The new central unit measured 104 feet wide by 55 deep. Its cost was reported as $62,000, of which about two thirds had been borrowed. It had a modern heating and ventilating system—depended on the Minnesota winds. The basement was given over to a gymnasium with baths. The three floors above provided ten classrooms, a museum, and a reading room. The members of the faculty, in the order of their names in the catalogue, were allowed to choose their classrooms. President McCurdy and Dr. Edward Neill had theirs on the first floor, furnished with Brussels carpet, desks, chairs, pictures and curtains, and Dr. Neill's also with busts of Webster and Clay. Professor Wallace chose his room on the second floor, and there carried on his work in severe simplicity.

For the new family in Macalester the opening of college and the fall held much of interest. Janet was settling into her house and being called upon. There were special events, too. While it was still warm James hired a carriage and drove them all to Minnehaha Falls, scene of Longfellow's *Hiawatha*. Field Day delighted everyone. James Wallace had been chosen by the students as referee. There were muleback races, three-legged races, egg races, potato races. Prizes had been donated by merchants of the Twin Cities. And boys and girls from Hamline, a few blocks away, had come up the boardwalk to attend. Then in October the Synod of Minnesota, meeting in St. Paul, visited Macalester College. Twenty-five double carriages drove the delegates to the campus. Dr. Maurice Edwards, the moderator, declared, "It is a place beautiful for situation, a place where every prospect pleases and only funds are scarce." That fall, too, James gave a public lecture on his travel in Greece; and the College *Echo* commented: "One of the most interesting and scholarly lectures given at the college." Janet was pleased at that.

James, too, went once to Buffalo, Minnesota, to preach. In the summer in Wooster he had passed his licensing examinations in the United Presbyterian Church, much to his mother's delight, and that of an uncle, too. In Buffalo he had so pleased the congregation that he was asked to supply them while they were without a minister.

By Thanksgiving they were pretty well settled in their new home. On the day before, a surprise awaited them. The class of 1889 had begun the custom of presenting a turkey to one of the members of the faculty. "Aunt Miriam" wrote her mother of the occasion:

We are really going to have turkey tomorrow. We had decided to have one chicken. Yesterday Prof. came home from school —he was soon called on by the Senior Class and Mr. Lee in a very good speech—plentifully interlarded with Greek—presented him with two turkeys—about ten pounds each and just ready for stuffing. Janet couldn't find enough feathers to need singeing . . . Yesterday there was two weeks' washing—and today we ironed and made pumpkin pie, and one mince, and cranberry jelly, and stuffed the turkey . . . We got grapes at 25 cents . . . Turkeys are down to ten cents a pound dressed . . . I hear Prof. and Janet cracking our 75 cents a peck hick-

ory nuts for dinner tomorrow. It is late for they were out taking
a pumpkin pie to Mrs. Rice.

There was as yet no nibble for their property in Wooster, and
the Wallaces were keenly conscious of their poverty. The first
Christmas in the north called for a tightening of belts. Of this,
on December 22, Aunt Miriam wrote again to her mother:

It fairly wrings my heart to write a letter to you today merely
to say "Merry Christmas," instead of the little Christmas pack-
age I have been thinking about for months . . . Prof. has been
penniless for some time past until Papa's rent came which bill
has been saved to give Annie tonight as she starts home for her
vacation . . . The only good thing is that "Faculty Row" is
all alike in the lack and I think all the children have been told
there will be less Christmas than usual . . . Two days before
Christmas . . . not a stitch done (except part of a doll dress)
nor a cent spent. I did think our first Christmas away from home
should see something nice sent home . . . Janet is now busy
with mince pies. She has engaged a pair of wild ducks for
Christmas dinner, they are cheap here . . . More festive than
chickens. What if we should not like them? . . . Janet bought
a doll for Helen two or three months ago . . . we must dress
it by Monday . . . Last night we had a very pleasant entertainment for the children of the neighborhood . . . A half-
dozen of the older girls got it up. They popped corn, made
bags and bought the presents—a house was thrown open to
the company. Each child got a ball of corn, a bag of corn, nuts
and candy and a little present. Benny is happy with his tiny
locomotive and cars which he is dragging all around this morning . . . Robin very proudly takes out his watch . . . and
Helen has a doll set of high comb, necklace and earrings . . .
I am glad the children saw a Christmas tree as they will not
have one at home this year.

Meanwhile James Wallace was busy with his teaching and his
scholarly activities and was fast making a reputation for himself.
Advance sheets of his *Anabasis* had been circulated among college

teachers of Greek and had brought favorable comment. He kept before him an ideal of the competent scholar. Of this he wrote in the *Echo:*

> As in carpentry, and in mechanics generally, careful attention must be given not only to construction but also to the finishing, so in education every student who deserves the name, will seek to give a fine finish to his scholarship, indeed it is this more than anything else that distinguishes the real from the nominal student.

He felt, too, that this type of scholarship, this enthusiasm for learning, and competence might as often be found in the small college as in the large, and quoted James Bryce in *The American Commonwealth* to enforce his point:

> They light up in many a country town what is at first only a farthing rush-light, but which when the town swells to a city, or when endowments flow in, or when some able teacher is placed in charge, becomes a lamp of glowing flames which may finally throw its rays over the whole state in which it stands. In some of these smaller Western colleges we find today men of great ability and great attainments; we find students who are receiving an education quite as thorough, though not always so wide, as the best eastern universities can give.

He was himself such an able teacher. According to the *Echo* he had "few if any superiors and was making Greek a pleasant as well as a profitable study." Under his inspiration several students had subscribed to and were reading Greek newspapers. In the classroom, he believed, the teacher is in constant danger of talking too much, of explaining things which the student should be required to master for himself. But he was also a very human person. When the class of 1890 was graduated, they went out of their way to write him a letter of appreciation. They wrote:

> You have been a friend indeed. We feel that time spent in your class room has been to us most enjoyable and profitable. We

felt that we could not separate without first thanking you for your endeavors in our behalf.

In the small college the relationship between students and faculty was necessarily close. Janet, herself, in giving a birthday party for her husband in the spring, asked, surprisingly, not his colleagues but the senior class to tea.

There was a dignity to be observed, but it was a dignity of the spirit, not usually of age or position, or outward trappings. When there was work to be done on the campus James Wallace and other members of the faculty could be found in work clothes along with students nailing down a new boardwalk or planting trees. Macalester was poor.

A fiscal secretary had, this year, been engaged at $100 a month to raise money for the college debts and deficits in current expenses. In three months he had given up; he had raised only $205. Dr. Daniel Rice, trustee and professor, had died in early April, bequeathing property valued at $50,000 to endow chairs of biblical literature at Macalester and Albert Lea. This property, however, made up of 150 residential lots, was entailed with a mortgage and was subject to taxes and the costs of street improvement and the installation of sewers and water pipes. Instead of being an asset to the college, it became a liability. The outlook was bleak. In the face of this the secretary of the Board of Trustees wrote each member of the faculty sounding him out on a proposed salary cut of 25 per cent.

James Wallace had been anticipating such action. He answered, offering to contribute from his salary $200 toward the current deficit, and to make at his own expense all ordinary repairs on his house. But if this offer were not acceptable, he tendered his resignation to take effect on September first, asking only that he be given a statement as to why his services had been cut short and as to the acceptability of those services. He asked for an immediate decision.

Mr. W. M. Tenney, secretary of the Board, replied that the matter of salary reduction had been postponed till June. There had not been a quorum. He assured Dr. Wallace that all present hoped that he would not feel compelled to resign. It was the expectation of the Board, he added, that the faculty would be willing to make some sacrifices for the institution "in which we all feel so deep an interest."

This crisis focused the spotlight on President McCurdy. Both faculty and trustees were murmuring at his inability to raise funds, and held him responsible for the situation.

Professor Wallace, fearful of the outcome, began to seek other work. Of course he would prefer to teach, and so wrote various friends who might know of openings. Yet he did not overlook other possibilities, and applied to the Mutual Reserve Fund Life Association of New York to be appointed one of their agents. To Dr. A. A. E. Taylor, former president of Wooster, he unburdened his heart. Dr. Taylor strongly advised him to stand by the college but to protest vigorously and persistently against a salary cut. He urged that Dr. Kirkwood, who was a bold critic of McCurdy, also "stick." He hoped the trustees would meet the situation by strong, decisive action and remove the president.

At their meeting in June the trustees did take drastic action. Dr. Wallace summarized this in a letter to his father-in-law on June 19:

> The Board was unanimous on the need of a change but was charitable as to time. A committee was appointed to inform the President that he should begin at once to seek out a new field and it was hoped he would be successful in finding one soon. *But* they would not force his resignation or limit his time till June of '90, one year . . . The Board did not reduce salaries but accepted our subscriptions to the deficit . . . But how the monster debt will be raised I am sure I can not see, though there is much wealth in the Board and may be, to get a new president of suitable dimension, they will subscribe liberally. On the whole the outlook seems much better.

After commencement, at which Macalester's first class had been graduated, James Wallace took Bennie and started for Iowa and Colorado to visit his brothers. Janet remained at Macalester preparing for her fifth baby. The pot of rumors boiled in the community. Nerves were taut and feelings hurt. Dr. Gregory, formerly of Wooster, and now head of Bennett Female Seminary in Minneapolis, it was said, would be Macalester's next president. Mrs. Mc-

Curdy even thought that her husband was being pushed out in order to put Gregory in. Another story told by the president of the Board said that Dr. Wallace and Professor Pearson were the chief instigators on the faculty of the action against President McCurdy; the most alarming rumor of all was that Dr. Kirkwood was to be dismissed. To all of these rumors Janet tried faithfully to listen, to report them to her husband on his vacation, and when she felt it wise she sought to pour oil on troubled waters.

Only the third of them proved to have any truth in it. On July 12 Dr. Kirkwood received notice that his services would not be needed after September first. The Macalester community was incensed. They all had great respect for his preaching, aside from his work in teaching. A petition was at once circulated, signed by eighty persons, asking for his reinstatement. Students and alumni protested. After some delay, the trustees, hating to seem to yield to pressures, did nevertheless reinstate him at a salary of one thousand dollars with the understanding that the church community should raise additional funds to make it possible for him to live comfortably.

Through all this summer of turmoil the faculty wives kept going back and forth. Janet, quietly at home, received them all. Mrs. Kirkwood came early before the rumor was a fact. "Oh well," she said with reference to it, "we are only travelling through this world. At some hotels we are treated well, but over the Alps lies Italy." Mrs. Neill added her ounce of bitterness, saying that the trustees always did what her husband advised them not to do. Mrs. McCurdy gave away her hand. She it was, Janet now saw, who was so persuasive with the trustees. Her earnestness, her tearful logic, her almost irresistible tributes to her noble and stainless husband threw a flood of light for Janet on the situation. Mrs. McCurdy had really believed that the trustees had wished to have Dr. Gregory instead of her husband. Furthermore, it was reported that she had said that professors who had spoken against her husband should be paid back. Possibly, Janet feared, James, too, might be asked to resign.

Then Dr. Neill, returning from the East, came also to see her, and reassured her. Mrs. McCurdy could not do Dr. Wallace any harm. The battle was really won. Possibly even the agitation had done good by drawing attention to the college.

It was good to find anyone so serene. All summer she had been trying to keep her husband from jumping into the fray—

Now keep cool.—It is better that you are not here.—Do not do anything rash that you will regret for years.

Later while everyone was awaiting the outcome of the petition for Dr. Kirkwood, she wrote again:

Don't hurry home. I want this settled before you come. It is fortunate that four of the faculty were absent.

In answer to his question about herself, she had said:

What am I doing? In the first place, *enjoying your absence* . . . Of course there is a fearful blank in the house, but there is the reassuring consciousness that it is only temporary . . . You are better away from this agitation.

James, even at long distance, was near the boiling point. When he heard of Kirkwood's dismissal he wrote his father-in-law:

It is utterly astounding to us all and a most egregious blunder. How long McCurdy is yet to be here I cannot tell but it is amazing that they have not kicked him out at once, that they are so merciful toward him and so summary in their dealing with Kirkwood. My feeling is that the college is going to collapse utterly. How can a young college recover from such an incubus? But how some men ever brought it to such a pass it is hard to see. I am trying to keep serene. But I pity poor Kirkwood. I hope if you know of any good vacant church wanting a pastor you will recommend him. . . . What a struggle life is and how much better not to be born into it.

To this Dr. Davis replied:

My dear boy, I am afraid you allow yourself to be too much affected by the "rough places in life." . . . Is life worth living? Yes, a thousand times, yes! The disappointments and troubles are not only worth minding, but they are among the good things in life; among the very best. Borne bravely and cheerfully they develop the highest and best style of character and they work out for us an exceeding and eternal weight of glory. Let Dr. McCurdy and the Board of Trustees go to grass like Nebuchadnezzar: you have a charge to keep, a work to do, a glorious, a magnificent mission to fulfill.

But James could not be so easily appeased. He came back:

I am so disgusted with the management of Macalester College —hope when I get back there we can go camping so as to be out of the road—I have not time to discuss whether life is worth living. I suppose we ought to live it on the supposition that it is, but there seems to be such a surplus of devil on our little globe that one often feels like emigrating. No wonder Paul felt that it was better to depart.

James Wallace in later life was known to express himself in much the same terms as his father-in-law. If life had really not been worth living to him, he never could have stood what he did stand in the next ten or fifteen years.

Dr. Neill had in some respects been wrong in his prognosis. When college opened there were fewer students by ten. However, the valiant souls on the faculty determined to drive ahead and trust the outcome to the Lord. Dr. Wallace, apprised of an opening back at Wooster, chose to remain. He felt that Macalester was fulfilling a great need and had a future full of promise.

Thanksgiving 1889 found the Wallace family rejoicing over the safe arrival of the new baby, a boy, on November 12. Janet was in excellent spirits and full of hope. Since the nurse had had to leave, Aunt Miriam had become nurse as well as housekeeper, was looking after the baby and sleeping with the children at night. Janet could not come downstairs for the Thanksgiving chicken dinner, cooked under her sister's competent supervision, but in the evening the family assembled in her bedroom and ate together. Of the baby, a few days later, James wrote to Grandma Davis:

The baby sleeps well and does not cry much. Janet thinks it a very superior baby, while I am quite non-committal on the subject. It is too soon to formulate an opinion . . .

This vicinity is the most remarkably fruitful this season I have ever seen on this mundane sphere. Nearly every night marks the arrival of a new-born. If a woman is not at church or prayer meeting the chances are that she is at home giving birth to "an addition to the family." Thus the good work goes on.

We have not named the youth yet. Janet wants to call him James, but I object . . . I favor plain John Wallace without any middle name or any other 19th century varnish. But Janet does not endorse this. So I guess we will call him Anonymous for a while.

Later he was to be called DeWitt, after a favorite uncle of his father's.

James was deeply humiliated that he could not pay his sister-in-law adequately for her invaluable services to his family. In September he had written to Wooster:

. . . even to make ends meet, one has to practice a close economy and can never show the generosity that he has in his heart. It mars one's self respect not a little.

At the end of November there had been no money from the college for a long time and James had had to borrow some. There was no sign of the president's leaving.

But two weeks before the holidays the faculty did receive almost half their overdue salaries. As a result on the day after Christmas James was able to write to Janet's family:

We had a lovely Christmas . . . Janet had taught the children that the baby was all the Christmas gift they should expect . . . Still we had stockings and all the forms of Christmas any way. Janet and the baby were downstairs for the first time. We had a good dinner, plain but excellent, oranges from Italy, hickory nuts from Ohio, walnuts from Indiana, pecans from Louisiana, grapes from California, apples from New York, tea from China, sugar from Cuba, bread from Minnesota, pepper from Brazil, hazel nuts from Wisconsin—I drank tea out of a handsome cup, beautifully painted by an accomplished lady from Ohio [his sister-in-law] . . . I can not enumerate all the presents except that I got a bag of nuts, candy, etc. The gifts were not expen-

sive but contained much good will . . . College matters are
much as before. The Presbyterians here have built a new church
and elected Dr. Kirkwood Stated Supply till June 1st . . . The
college service will be discontinued and all will worship in the
church. This means that we will not hear Dr. Mc. very often
here. No tears . . . They are raising no money but borrowing
more. I am really certain the salaries will be reduced very low
at the end of the year.

In February 1890 the Board of Trustees attempted to initiate a
drive to raise $125,000 to clear off the debt of the college, but little
was actually realized. February did mark a material improvement
in their lives. The long-awaited extension of the Grand Avenue
electric-streetcar system was opened on February 22. No longer
was it necessary to walk three quarters of a mile to the interurban
train. Streetcars now passed through the campus and one could
reach the loop in St. Paul in twenty minutes for only a nickel. Of
the celebration Aunt Miriam wrote her mother:

Yesterday they ran 7 double cars—crowded with men—all invited guests, from the Governor of the state down to all the
Faculty of Macalester and gentlemen hereabouts . . . All Macalester turned out—every man, woman and child. Three big
flags moved from the college,—each student had a little flag—
cannon had been brought from the fort—we made quite a
noise and quite a show and quite a crowd as the cars whizzed
by. The first four cars were unloaded here—the Governor made
a short speech to the students . . .

As spring came on, James became greatly interested in a proposal
to come before the Presbyterian General Assembly in May, the
revision of the Confession of Faith which had been formulated
by the Westminster Assembly in the seventeenth century. Some
of the ultraconservatives were totally opposed to any tampering
with the sacred document. Some wished to make changes here
and there to tone down the harsher aspects of Calvinism. Others
of the more liberal group wanted the whole creed rewritten to
conform to present-day thinking. When the discussion began,

James Wallace was pretty strongly in favor of revision. He prided himself on his open-minded approach to the Scriptures, but he could not align himself with so-called "higher criticism." The Shorter Catechism, which he had memorized as a boy, formed the warp and woof of his theological thinking. He believed that the "higher critic" approached the Scriptures with preconceived notions of the truth and accepted or refuted biblical statements according as they fitted his system. "The whole Revision movement," he said, "is intensely interesting as showing how strong is the tendency to sugar-coat the hard doctrines and sayings of the Bible." When the General Assembly decided to retain the Confession in its historic form but change words here and there, delete objectionable statements, and add clarifying clauses to avoid misunderstanding, he was pleased. Yet three years later when Charles A. Briggs of Union Theological Seminary, New York, who spearheaded a liberal tendency in biblical criticism, delivered a series of lectures in Minneapolis, Dr. Wallace went to hear him and came away impressed. "They were able and interesting," he wrote to his relatives in Wooster, "but it will be years before all his positions concerning the Bible will be accepted."

As commencement approached, there was a growing restlessness on the campus. The students wondered whether the college would be opening in the fall and whether a diploma from Macalester would have any worth in years to come. Members of the faculty chafed under the delay in the payment of their salaries. Some of them had to borrow money or give notes for their groceries and other necessities of life. It was with distress, therefore, that they received notice that the Board at its June meeting had cut salaries to fifteen hundred dollars.

Dr. McCurdy preached the baccalaureate sermon significantly from the text: "Except a corn of wheat fall into the ground and die, it abideth alone but if it die, it bringeth forth much fruit." His resignation was announced at the closing exercises. A few weeks later he accepted a call to Peoria, Illinois. Early in the summer the faculty began to disintegrate. Professor Boyd went off, on leave of absence, for a year of graduate study in Europe. Dr. Forbes resigned in favor of public-school work. Kirkwood and

Pearson were looking for other positions. Professor Wallace agreed to supply a Presbyterian church at Fisher, three hundred miles to the north, for part of the summer. He was hoping to earn enough money to pay for his life insurance. Again he was wondering whether he should leave Macalester and seek work with more financial security.

XI

Dean

But in his duty prompt at every call,
He watched and wept, he pray'd and felt for all:

. . . .

He tried each art, reprov'd each dull delay,
Allur'd to brighter worlds, and led the way.

OLIVER GOLDSMITH

WHEN James Wallace heard, in the lonely town of Fisher, of the appointment of the Reverend David J. Burrell to the presidency of Macalester he was greatly disappointed. This did not seem a wise choice. Dr. Burrell was the eloquent and persuasive pastor of the Westminster Church in Minneapolis, but he had not been asked to give up his pastorate but only to take on, in addition, the administration of a college ten miles away. It was hoped, of course, that with the help of the newly appointed fiscal secretary, the Reverend David E. Platter, he would be able to lift from the college its crushing load of debt. Yet the record showed that Burrell had done nothing for Macalester in the past among his wealthy parishioners, and though he was himself receiving six thousand dollars a year, he had urged the recent cut in faculty salaries.

James Wallace was bitter about this cut; he felt it a breach of contract, and he expressed his resentment to his father-in-law then visiting Janet and Miriam at Macalester:

> I told McCurdy when at Wooster that if the salary was to be reduced I would not go, that I would not move my family

hundreds of miles on an uncertainty. So I insist that they have no right to break their contract with me . . . There are some as incompetent men on it [the Board] as you can find, and men of great wealth who have given nothing to the college and yet insist on reducing salaries.

. . . .

So I regard our reduced salary as simply due to the lack of interest and to the illiberality on the Board's part. Lewis and Cochran are to be excepted . . .

If they would only quit electing each other and put some new men on the Board there would be more confidence inspired, but it is literally *self*-perpetuating . . .

He was tempted to resign, but both his sister Margaret and his father-in-law urged him to stay, and the always optimistic Janet sought to soothe him and hold him to the path of duty and opportunity. In a letter on July 26, 1890, she wrote:

. . . It is a miserable policy for a man to get out of a position. It decreases his chances immensely for receiving another call . . . You are out of sorts now. You are not yourself. You know you do have sincere regard for this college . . . I believe you will be astonished next winter, to see how, with God's blessing, our money will last like the widow's oil . . . Wait till he [Dr. Burrell] makes a powerful plea for Macalester in some of the churches.

She had recently forwarded to him a letter from Mr. H. K. Taylor of the Board of Trustees, asking his decision; would he accept the cut and stay? She had clearly feared for his answer, for she had herself written to Mr. Taylor to prepare him for whatever might befall:

Yours of the 19th is forwarded to Professor Wallace. If he has not yet answered you definitely, it is not that he does not love our college, but is feeling depressed. He is in a lonely place, trying to make enough to pay his insurance, though he had hoped to devote this vacation as his publishers urge, to editing his Greek book. And allow me to add, lest you should for a moment, think him mercenary, that he is hampered now, mainly because for some years he *voluntarily* drew a small salary! as Wooster was *then* in debt.

What her husband might say to this interference she did not know, but she wisely sent him a copy of her letter, saying that the original she had sent without compunction, the copy she feared might vex him. She asked him to forgive her and to remember that her epitaph was to be, "This sinner is a loving one."

What James actually thought we do not know. Nor is there any copy of his letter to Mr. Taylor. But Janet was his loyal helpmate and he knew it. He was pleased at the way she had entered, in these two years, into the life of the college, and proud of her ability. That fall he was to write home often of how she had handled a public missionary meeting in the church:

> They all did well, Janet especially, who won much praise . . . I knew she would do us all credit. There are few ladies in the church who can make a better missionary address than Janet can or could do if she were put forward. She must take her place and put her talents to more public use. She is a first class wife, a no. one mother and a first rate woman generally and if she would lay aside the idea that she is a mere girl and assume the place she can easily command, she would reach great usefulness.

It was Janet's turn to be tempted when in August a letter came asking James Wallace to accept appointment as professor and head of a school for the training of Christian workers in São Paulo, Brazil. It had been one of her girlhood ambitions to go as a missionary. He, too, felt that

> A good college there, could be a missionary center and if prosperous would be of immense influence.

But there were problems. The salary was meager, and there was opposition on the part of some missionaries already on the field, who felt the emphasis should not be on college training but on evangelism. Dr. Wallace mulled the matter over; he still loved Macalester, was still convinced that it was meeting a real need in the Northwest. But he procured a Portuguese grammar and began to study. The Presbyterian Board of Foreign Missions was disposed to give him time to make his decision, to sell his property in Wooster, and settle his affairs before leaving the country.

With this offer before him (he was not to turn it down completely until the following spring), he faced the opening of college in September. Only three members of the old teaching force were now on the campus. Faculty leadership fell on them, the brunt of it on Pearson and Wallace. There were five new instructors, some of them on a part-time basis.

In spite of faculty limitations and financial worries, a hopeful spirit pervaded the campus. Dr. Wallace wrote of this to Dr. T. K. Davis:

> We will have about 35 new students, more than at any time before. Nearly all the old ones are back. One of our Juniors went to Princeton and entered Senior without conditions. We are all pleased at this and this speaks well for poor, despised Macalester . . .
>
> The tide has turned, I think . . . If McC. had left a year sooner we could now have 50 more students . . . The Board has ordered water put in Pearson's house and ours. This is due I suppose to the fact that we have stood by them this vacation . . . My dear people at Fisher where I preached 3 Sabbaths paid me 50 dollars!!! This was a profit of 25 dollars which greatly surprised me. Pray for Macalester. Her star may yet rise high and shine brightly.

This fall everyone seemed willing at least to plug for Macalester. The students gave a banquet for trustees and faculty. One of the trustees sent out a load of lumber for a boardwalk, and a dozen students, with the help of the faculty, set to and built it. Someone gave matting for the dormitory corridors. The senior preparatory boys carpeted one of the professor's rooms at the college; the junior preparatory boys planned to put up the window shades. The students dismantled the toboggan slide back of old Main, hauled in loads of dirt, built a skating rink on the front campus, and filled it from a fire hose. (There was a fire alarm now near the campus, the key kept in the Wallace house.) The college engineer had extinguished a blaze from an exploding kerosene lamp in the dormitory, and then had gone out and solicited funds for an electric-light plant for the college buildings. It was, gossip said, "one of the best plants in the city." There was a kind of blessed contagion around that cheered the heart.

To be sure, students had their fun, which sometimes called for disciplinary action. Earlier they had tied up one of the maids and raided the dormitory kitchen. This year on Halloween they had carried off gates and outhouses in the community, and, worst of all, had led a cow into the basement of the main building and left her there. Dr. Wallace liked nothing better than tracking down such culprits and bringing them to justice. He could be stern and filled with righteous wrath; he had no patience for wanton abuse of property. Often he wished that he could take the boys, like six-year-olds, over his knee and soundly spank them. Yet long afterward, remembering these occasions, he would tell about them with that mingling of annoyance and merriment that his friends had come to recognize as characteristic.

The Reverend Mr. Platter, meanwhile, was meeting with an encouraging response in his appeal for funds. By November about $50,000 had been subscribed toward the debt. This rose to $75,000 a few months later. During the year the Macalester community subscribed $4000. The House of Hope Church in St. Paul contributed another $4500, making their total $25,000. Dr. Wallace wrote Mrs. William Thaw of Pittsburgh, whose son he had befriended at Wooster, setting forth Macalester's financial plight. She sent him a check for $5000. This gift at once increased his prestige among students, faculty, and trustees. Minneapolis was still lagging behind in its quota of $40,000. The Minneapolis *Evening Journal* in an editorial spoke for the college:

> It has proven itself the peer of any like institution in the Northwest—an honor to the church that founded it and to the state of Minnesota . . . It would seem that the Presbyterians in this state would wipe out that debt in a week, or a day.

The president in a chapel address was confident that his city would yet rise to the occasion.

Then in March President Burrell accepted a call to the Marble

Collegiate Church of New York City. His resignation seemed a severe setback to the hopes of Macalester. In April another blow fell. A faculty house, next to the Wallaces', burned to the ground, and the Pearsons, whose home it had been, lost nearly everything. Thoroughly discouraged, Professor Pearson promptly accepted a pending offer from Ginn and Company, textbook publishers, and on the twentieth of the month left Macalester, to the great regret of everyone.

In early May the trustees met. Dr. Wallace had urged them to put the burden of administration on the faculty and save the salary of a president until the financial crisis should be over. In consequence, they created the office of Dean of the College with a salary of $1800 and offered him the position. He demurred because of Dr. Neill, who was an older man and one to whom the college owed its existence. Assured, however, that Dr. Neill, who lived several miles away, would find it impossible to give the necessary supervision to the college, Dr. Wallace accepted. The additional $300 a year would fill a big hole in his family budget.

His first act was to suggest that Professor E. C. Downing of Toulon Academy, Illinois, be invited to take the chair of Latin on a trial basis. Professor Downing was a graduate of Wooster of the class of 1884, and the son of Judge Downing of Wooster, Ohio. (Judge Downing had been James Wallace's teacher in Plain Township.) He arrived to begin his work in May of 1891.

By June, Mr. Platter reported that $90,000 had been subscribed toward the college debt. However, the subscriptions were conditional on securing the full $125,000. "The situation is very grave," he said. The trustees, meeting on June 2, thought so too. The running expenses of the college plus the interest on the debt for the coming year would amount to $18,000. A motion was made

> . . . to suspend the college work until such time as the funds of the college and the interest of the Presbyterian Church will warrant us in opening the school again.

Such suspension was to take effect after commencement unless the subscriptions should reach the necessary $125,000 by that time. Strenuous efforts the next two weeks brought the total to

$112,000. Then Judge Vandenburg pledged over $5000 and Mr. J. J. Hill raised his subscription to $15,000. From out of the state, besides that from Mrs. Thaw, subscriptions came from Mr. Stinson and Cyrus McCormick of Chicago. At commencement there was great rejoicing over the lifting of the debt. Mr. Platter, Dean Wallace, and Thomas Cochran of the trustees were given credit for spearheading the successful drive. The campaign had produced a total of $130,000 in subscriptions, all earmarked against the debt. It had made no provision for meeting the annual deficit in running expenses.

It was the understanding that subscribers could pay their pledges within a five-year period. Money already received was used to reduce the debt to an even $100,000. This the St. Paul Trust Company then assumed and took a first mortgage on the college property. It issued bonds for the amount and sold most of these in the East. The Episcopal Diocese of St. Paul bought $15,000 worth of them. The college property was valued at $350,000 and the Rice legacy at $60,000.

When Dr. Wallace handed the graduating class of five seniors their diplomas, he closed his farewell address to them by saying:

> The cloud that has so long hung over your Alma Mater is now breaking and the sun is coming forth with the promise of a long and glorious day. So while your diploma does not admit you to a long line of illustrious alumni we are confident it *does* admit you to the van of an army of alumni, that, as the decades and centuries go by, will increase not only in numbers but also in honor and in the brilliancy of their achievements.

With commencement over, the dean prepared for a busy summer. First he pared down the budget to $10,500 and urged a rigid economy in all operations of the institution. Then he recruited new members of the faculty. Professor A. W. Anderson, another graduate of Wooster with a high scholastic rating, he secured for the chair of mental science and English. The Reverend George W. Davis, who had received his Ph.D. at Yale in Semitics, he engaged to teach Hebrew and Bible history and literature. Dr. Samuel M. Kirkwood of Macalester's first graduating class, son of the former professor, was appointed to teach the natural sciences. Professor James H. Boyd returned from his year of study in Europe. The Reverend Niclaus Bolt came to teach German.

The appointments made, with the new Professor Downing as assistant, Dean Wallace toured the state to secure new students and round up old ones. Nevertheless college opened in the fall with a loss of fifteen students. No juniors returned; this meant no graduating class of 1892. The faculty went on with its work with a spirit of determination and hope that Providence was on their side. On his part James Wallace was busy teaching, administering the college routine, soliciting funds to pay faculty salaries, preaching on weekends, seeking new students.

At the end of the year in his first annual report to the trustees, he reviewed the situation he had found when he took over his duties as dean:

> I need hardly remind you that last year so uncertain were we whether the college would be opened this year that the catalogue was not published before commencement . . . Meantime through the year the impression became so general that the college was hopelessly involved financially that it could not be easily or speedily corrected.
>
> After Commencement the catalogue was published. There were four vacancies in the Faculty to fill. The dormitory was to be put in order and a canvas for students made—It was a serious problem to fill up the Faculty with competent instructors and at the same time materially reduce the running expenses of the College. The responsibility devolved practically on one. The senior professor was busy with his affairs in the library. Professor Boyd was in Germany . . . There remained but the Professor of Latin to give assistance and he had been connected with the College but one month. There was no president or recognized head.—It was not strange that the college opened with an enrollment of about 15 less than on the year before . . . However average daily attendance was greater . . . a more hopeful spirit has prevailed.

He made several specific recommendations, among them that a new president be chosen at the earliest possible date. He pointed out that from the beginning the college had had an annual deficit of from five thousand to seven thousand dollars. He advocated that the land left by Dr. Rice be sold, that the proceeds be invested and the interest used toward the annual deficiencies in running expenses. He laid before them this ultimatum:

. . . my own duty seems clear to me. I am not willing to remain in the institution and see it sinking deeper and deeper into debt. Much as I am attached to the College and deeply as I am interested in this effort to establish a much-needed Presbyterian College in the North West I have made up my mind fully to tender you my resignation one month hence if there is not by that time a hopeful prospect of speedily putting the finances of the college on a self-supporting basis.

In June, Macalester received another jolt when Judge Kelly handed down a decision that the college would have to pay taxes on all of its campus except the twelve acres actually in use for educational purposes. The trustees planned to appeal the decision to the Supreme Court.

By fall they were ready to recommend a president to Synod. He was the Rev. A. W. Ringland. A graduate of Centre College and McCormick Theological Seminary, he had done a notable work as pastor of the First Presbyterian Church of Duluth. There he had built up the membership from 109 to 434 and had inspired them to erect a splendid stone church. Synod gave its approval to his election by a rising vote. Dr. Ringland agreed to assume his duties the first of the new year. He came to Macalester with high hopes and deep enthusiasm, feeling that he was called by God to the work. The Duluth *Herald* predicted editorially that he would speedily make Macalester one of the strongest and best educational institutions in the country.

The new college year had opened with an increased enrollment as the result of a vigorous canvas for students. But the event of the fall was the building of Edwards Hall. Dr. Wallace had succeeded in interesting W. C. Edwards, a lumber dealer living on Summit Avenue, in the need for a house where students of meager means could have a co-operative boarding club and so reduce the cost of their education. Mr. Edwards, with the aid of Frederick

Weyerhaeuser, R. A. Kirk, and some others, furnished the
materials. Faculty and students did the building. Among them
was a trained young carpenter, Hugh Alexander, a former student whom Dr. Wallace had prevailed on to return to college.
He and Dr. Wallace together nailed shingles on the roof. By New
Year's, 1893, a three-story frame dormitory, able to accommo-
date thirty-five students, was completed. It was named Edwards
Hall and was immediately filled.

At the beginning of the year 1893 Dr. Ringland and his family
moved into the president's house next door. Professor and Mrs.
Wallace were happy indeed to welcome them, and relieved to
have some of the financial burdens of the college shifted to another's hands. A few days later they entertained the faculty to
meet the president and his wife.

For a year and a half Dean Wallace had carried the load of administration. As he thought things over he was not displeased
with his experience, and so wrote his father-in-law:

> This interregnum has been most trying. It has cost me unre-
> mitting toil, great cares and at times tears but I am heartily glad
> I remained here. If I had left last summer I think the college
> would have closed and perhaps, indeed probably, forever. I was
> determined that the college should never perish through any
> dereliction in duty on my part. I feel that I already have great
> reward, not in money of course but in growing influence, in
> an approving conscience and in greater maturity of character
> . . . alas how immature even yet with all these years of dis-
> cipline.

He had recommended to Synod that a committee study the
advisability of merging Macalester and Albert Lea College for
Women. The committee was at work and he hoped the union
could be consummated within a year. His own strength as a public
speaker, he recognized, was growing, and some of the larger
churches were inviting him to fill their pulpits. He remarked:

> I am slowly growing in confidence in the matter of preaching
> and hope ere long to have some leisure to prepare some fairly
> creditable and I hope useful sermons.

The continuing financial stringency in the college, and in his own household, kept his thoughts on ways of making money to supply the necessities of life. He was still searching for a buyer for his house in Wooster. He wrote:

. . . I mean now to devote more attention to my finances. I will not voluntarily and willingly die a beggar. It would be a disgrace with all the chances to make money.

The arrival of a new president enabled Dr. Wallace to give more attention to the academic aspect of college administration and gave him more leisure to pursue his scholastic interests and to finish his book, which during the last few years he had been able to work at only off and on. Letters, proofs, telegrams, passed between him, Dr. Harper, and the American Book Company. Much of the summer vacation in 1893 was devoted to giving the finishing touches to the manuscript. Dr. Harper wrote a preface and the book was ready for the printers. A letter from Dr. Harper, dated October 3, 1893, said:

It is finished at last and it is a fine piece of work. I am very glad that it is through, and am glad that you have finished it for your own sake.

The book came out under the title, *Xenophon's Anabasis*, by W. R. Harper, Ph.D., D.D., and James Wallace, Ph.D. An introduction of about sixty pages contained a description of Persia, an account of the arts of war in different countries, biographies of Cyrus and Xenophon and other relevant material. Charts, pictures, and pen sketches, some Dr. Wallace's own work, illustrated phases of Greek and Persian life. The book was well received and adopted as a text in many schools throughout the country. It remained longer in use and enjoyed a larger sale than any other of the books in the Harper series. Some years later the publishers were urging him to prepare a similar text of Lucian.

President Ringland began his work with dedicated energy. He studied the Macalester situation and came to the June meeting of the Board with an ambitious plan of action. He proposed that a canvas for funds be made to clear the college of all debt; that men students be recruited for the college proper and that a wealthy

sponsor or sponsors be found to underwrite the cost of maintenance; that the doors of the college be opened to women students
and funds be raised to erect a women's dormitory; that a seminary
be established in connection with the college to provide ministers
for the growing Northwest. Dr. Ringland was not disposed to
argue the principle of coeducation: he claimed that it was necessary for the very life of the college. The trustees split with a
tie vote over the proposition that coeducation be tried for a period of five years as an emergency measure. Dr. Ringland cast
the deciding vote and coeducation was adopted on an experimental
basis.

At the end of the preceding May (1893), Dr. Edward Neill
had felt it necessary, because of a heart condition, to leave St.
Paul for a rest. Dr. Wallace wrote him in care of his daughter,
Minnesota Neill, informing him of the action of the trustees on
coeducation. He justified the action by saying:

> By the present arrangement we are steadily losing our con-
> stituency. When a Presbyterian daughter goes to Carleton or
> Hamline, we not only lose her but we lose her brothers as well,
> if she has any. I know of case after case of this kind.

To the daughter he added,

> I hope he will not take the temporary admission of ladies too
> much to heart. Personally I have not a particle of doubt about
> the wisdom of the course . . . The real question for two or
> three years has not been this or that system of education but
> whether the college can be saved at all.

Dr. Neill, greatly disturbed by the action, wrote the trustees:

> As the founder of Macalester College, who expended several
> thousands of dollars in its establishment, I must therefore most
> earnestly protest against your late action by which you have
> thwarted the design of the founder, and all the donors to the
> fund . . .
>
> For twenty years it has been announced by the Trustees that
> Macalester College was a college for young men . . . To it,
> as a college for young men, I gave a library of about 1000 vol-

umes, valuable manuscripts of William Penn, George Washington and other illustrious men, as well as many articles to the museum of History, and also procured more than two thousand dollars for the purchase of books for the reference library.

Dr. Neill concluded his letter with the hope that the trustees would reconsider their action.

The signs on the economic horizon proved to be ill omens for Dr. Ringland's administration. When Grover Cleveland again "took office, on March 4, 1893, he found that the nation's gold reserve had reached the danger point." When it "fell below the $100,000,000 required to safeguard the nation's credit, fear seized the business world and the great panic was on. Within six months there were over 8000 business failures, involving the huge sum of $285,000,000. Four hundred banks [thirteen of them in the Twin Cities] closed their doors. Fifty-six railroad companies fell into the hands of receivers. The depression lasted from 1893 to 1897." *

In spite of the determination of the young president of Macalester, the attempt to put on a canvas for funds proved a failure. Friends of the college were battling for their own financial lives. Debts continued to pile up against the college and the arrears in the professors' salaries grew larger month by month. It was touch and go whether the college would be able to open its doors in September. President Ringland decided that a drastic retrenchment was necessary. Without consulting his dean or other members of the faculty, he dropped Professors Davis and Downing from the teaching staff. Dr. Wallace, in Wooster for his vacation, hearing this, hurried back. The college, he urged, could not be saved by destroying the confidence of the students in the adequacy of the teaching force. He was able to restore Downing, at a reduced salary, by taking also some reduction in his own. For Davis all seemed unavailing. The juniors and seniors petitioned that he be restored so that they could have courses in Hebrew, but Dr. Ringland held out. Dr. Wallace suspected that the conservative president regarded Dr. Davis as too liberal and wished a good excuse to drop him from the faculty. However, when President Ringland heard that Lake Forest College in Illinois was

* Hicks, *A Short History of American Democracy.*

offering to admit Macalester students to corresponding courses in that institution without examination, he yielded to pressure and reinstated the popular professor.

Not until September 8 did the trustees, after long deliberation, vote to reopen the college, with the understanding that it would be kept open only as long as current expenses would be provided. On the opening date, September 20, an even one hundred students enrolled. Three women were entered in the college, four in the academy. On September 23, President Ringland wrote Dr. Neill welcoming him back and inquiring when he would be able to meet his classes. Dr. Neill replied:

> Believing that there ought to be in the great state of Minnesota at least one college for young men, I established it . . . The Trustees may be derelict of duty but I shall never resign, and whenever they notify me that they have reconsidered their action, I shall resume instruction in my classroom.

On September 26, 1893, following a visit from President Ringland, he suddenly collapsed at his home from a heart attack. With his death, opposition to coeducation at Macalester faded away.

Despite the announced intention of the trustees not to go on without money for current expenses, the college continued and the faculty members tightened their belts. James Wallace wrote his kindred soon after college opened, ". . . no money yet on salaries, do not see any prospect." A little later in the fall he was still writing:

> There is no financial deliverance yet and not likely to be soon. If the way was open I think I would leave and yet I do not wish to embarrass the college and disappoint the students after so much service. So I shall have to work along as best I can until spring anyway. Perhaps I shall have to try the water diet. That is about all I will be able to buy soon.

The widespread use of the *Anabasis* in colleges encouraged Dr. Wallace to undertake the preparation of a second Greek text for college use. He spent much of his extra time in his study. He said:

I am studying every moment I can get. I am determined that
. . . the Winter shall count for more thorough education if it
doesn't in dollars and cents. I have several grave objections to
this world and the general constitution of things. One is that
money plays too important a part and is too hard to get. The
other, that old defunct, putrid, nauseating political parties have
too much vitality.

There had been a Republican landslide in the November elections. Dr. Wallace, still a confirmed follower of the Prohibition
party, expressed his attitude toward the two major parties in a
letter to his relatives:

The only justification for a Republican victory was that the
Democratic party was upon a careful examination one or two
degrees meaner and more worthless than the G.O.P. so-called
. . . while it is true that the Republicans are "darn" fools it is
no doubt equally true that the Democrats are "darnder" fools.
This language is very shocking to me as it is to you but the
justification of it lies in the general "cussedness" of the subject.
Ordinary terminology does not meet the case at all. In speaking
of the old parties I see no objection to using language that sug-
gests brimstone and the bottomless pit.

By winter the college administration was in desperate need of
cash to pay salaries, delinquent interest and taxes, and to meet the
cost of city improvements adjoining its large property holdings.
An attempt was made to get rid of some of the property, but it
could be sold only at staggering losses. As the college headed
toward bankruptcy, Dr. Wallace thought again of his old friends
in Pittsburgh, the William K. Thaws. He wrote to Mrs. Thaw
telling of the college's financial crisis and asked if she would be
willing to buy some of the lots in the Macalester addition on
Randolph Street, or a piece of the college campus facing St. Clair
Street. She replied promptly that she would consider the purchase.

A special meeting of the trustees was called for March 2, 1894.
They approved a motion that the south ten acres of the campus be
sold to Mrs. Thaw for not less than $25,000. It was also voted that
Professor Wallace go to Pittsburgh at once to confer with her.

Mrs. Thaw received Dr. Wallace graciously and the deal for the sale of the ten acres was consummated. She agreed to pay $15,-000 in cash and $5000 a year for two years. Not long after this Mr. Thomas Cochran of the trustees met Mrs. Thaw in New York and persuaded her to pay the whole $25,000 at one time. Dr. Wallace returned to Macalester with a feeling of triumph. He felt that he was the instrument in the hands of God for rescuing the college from certain death and preserving it for future generations.

The $25,000 was used to pay the accrued interest on all outstanding bonds, delinquent taxes, and assessments for city improvements, and a large number of miscellaneous bills. In addition $10,-000 worth of bonds were redeemed. The major part of the college debts still stood. The St. Paul Trust Company still held a mortgage on the property for $100,000 and the college was obligated for $69,000 for real estate in the Macalester addition. Nevertheless the purchase of ten acres of the campus lifted the insistent pressure from the creditors and the specter of bankruptcy for the time being vanished. The college was given a breathing spell. The prestige of Dr. Wallace again rose. However Dr. Ringland seemed unhappy that the trustees had sent the dean rather than the president to confer with Mrs. Thaw.

Unable to raise any considerable amount of money in Minnesota, President Ringland made several trips to the East, but his efforts brought little result. In his report to the Board of Trustees in June 1894, he paid high tribute to the loyalty of the faculty in the difficult situation:

The year has been one of great financial trial to the professors. To them belongs the credit of keeping the college open for the year just ended. The hardships to these professors have been very great and in some cases involve all the accumulations of past years. The church owes a lasting debt of gratitude to the men and women who have held the ship in the storm and have brought that ship to you unharmed at the end of a trip so critical.

President Ringland had determined to resign and return to the ministry. When he received a call from a church in Toledo, Ohio, he accepted and left at once.

XII

President and Tramp

How can ye chant, ye little birds,
And I sae weary, fu' o' care.

ROBERT BURNS

WHEN the Board of Trustees met before commencement. Dean Wallace once more made the annual report. He recommended to them an aggressive financial campaign and again the finding of a president. Thereupon he found himself urged to accept the position; he was indispensable to the college, they said. A secret ballot was taken, and the vote for him was unanimous. They offered him fifteen hundred dollars a year and promised to increase this to two thousand dollars by appeal to private sources. He was hesitant, said that unless the financial condition of the college was righted within five or six weeks, he could not in justice to his family carry on. He would not be president, only acting president, and so he was to list himself in the college catalogue.

On commencement day, to an audience that packed the church, his election was announced. There was vigorous applause and calls for a speech. Dr. Wallace responded briefly, telling the story of the backwoods steward who wrote the bishop to send them a minister. The steward said that they preferred a "sliding elder," and if he could not send them a sliding elder to send a "circus rider," and if he could not send a circus rider, to send them an "exhauster." Dr. Wallace declared that the Board would have to be content with an "exhauster."

145

From this time on, for a period of years, however, James Wallace, though possibly sometimes an exhorter, was more often a circuit rider. For now began for him that seemingly everlasting trek from town to town, church to church, person to person, as he sought money and students for Macalester. This weekend he might be off to Duluth or Rochester, Owatonna, Austin, or Worthington; then he would hurry back for interviews in the Twin Cities and to the routine duties of his office at the college. Next week might find him in Chicago, in Pittsburgh or Columbus, Philadelphia, Washington, or Baltimore, or possibly settling in for a period in New York, wherever he might ferret out wealthy Presbyterians to interest in the college.

Evidently rumors of his success, so far, in getting money had got around, for in June there came a letter from President Scovel of Wooster. Would he come to help in a campaign there for endowment? The hope was held out that after the endowment was raised, he could resume the teaching of Greek and eventually succeed to the headship of the department. It was an attractive offer. It meant that he would be assured a steady salary, would live smong friends and relatives, and return to the life of a scholar. He was torn between the old loyalty to Wooster and the new loyalty to Macalester. If he left Macalester, Dr. Davis and Professor Anderson also would probably leave, and this would mean that the college would close. It was God's will, he decided, that he remain to save the institution for the church, if possible. After commencement, accordingly, he started out, this time for students, with Professors Davis and Downing to assist.

In August Mrs. Wallace gave birth to twins. They were named Janet and Miriam for their mother and aunt, who, James remarked, had been like twins all their lives. From the ordeal Janet had become pale and thin and listless. Her appetite, never strong, was almost gone. The relatives in Wooster were concerned. What would happen to her in that cold house alone with the children through a severe Minnesota winter? James was planning to go East for a month or two before and again after the holidays. Ben and Rob were already in Wooster with their grandmother Wallace. Why should not James bring Janet and the other four with him to Wooster as he went East? She could rest there and have help with the children. James shrank from shunting the care of his large family on his relatives. But he looked again at Janet and saw the wisdom of his mother's and his sister's insistence. In November when he left they were along.

This was James Wallace's first experience of begging in the East. He found it hard. Even the traveling was hard. It would always be. He must stint himself to save a penny here, a quarter there. As head of a Christian college, the railroads in the West gave him clergy rates. In the East they refused; he was not an active pastor. So he sat up all night in a day coach, arriving in the morning, heavy-eyed, and sometimes heavyhearted. He thought, this first time, to find himself a room at a second-class hotel, and did. But Thomas Cochran, a trustee, who had preceded him to New York, moved him promptly to an inexpensive room at the Brevoort, at a dollar a night. The president of a college on such an errand, Cochran felt, must have a good address. James Wallace made up the difference by eating at restaurants. Twenty cents was usual for breakfast, twenty-five to thirty cents for dinner and supper. Once on such a trip he wrote that he was living chiefly on cereals and fruit, "with an occasional order of oysters."

Yet to James Wallace material discomforts had already become almost routine. He was to suffer rather from the humiliations and frustrations of begging. Deep down, too, he was rebellious, for he "had not planned the colossal blunders" that had got the college into debt; they were someone else's doing. "Am I to spend my best years," he wrote, "repairing the damage McCurdy did here? God forbid . . ." He often asked himself why such a task had fallen to his lot.

> What I was sent here for is an inscrutable mystery. I am too diffident to wrestle with men about money and with financial problems so vast.

And again he wrote of the job of a college president:

> If he can read or write, so much the better, but he *must* be able to raise money. I am not a success at raising money.

He loathed begging.

Nevertheless he got from Presbyterian headquarters in New

York the names of wealthy individuals he might well approach and of pastors who might grant him a hearing in their churches. And so he set the pattern of his annual trips to New York. He worked in the city, traipsed to the suburbs and out to New Jersey. Some men he saw in their offices; others he sought out in their homes at night. On Sundays he preached. Collection plates, though sometimes noisy, netted no great sums. Gifts from individuals were usually small, $25 to $100. He went East hoping to find money there for the current expenses of the college, for taxes, interest on the debt, possibly to pay off or reduce the debt itself, sometimes also to try to sell land of the Macalester Addition. Persuading men and women to subscribe to the debts of an obscure and starving little college in the West proved a thankless job. To Janet and the relatives he kept writing: "I have raised $75 today." . . . "I have raised but $325 this week." . . . "Received subscription of $300 this morning, so I am not a dead failure . . . I think I have $500 more virtually pledged."

Yet all the while he was making friends for the college, and now and then through the years he was to find in the East some kind souls who responded as they were able. One day he made a trip to Tarrytown to see a Mrs. Albert G. Monroe, and of this he told:

> Walked 2 miles into the country to her country seat on the Hudson . . . all the way through the rain. She refused before I began but before I left—so much was she pleased—that she gave me a check for $500 and asked me to stay all night!!! She gave me a delicious lunch and treated me most delightfully. There are some fine people in this world.

He had a conference, too, once, with a Mrs. Martin, who furnished him with several leads; and this meeting was the beginning of a friendship with the Martin family that lasted through many years. On another visit a Mrs. Moir gave a timely $500, which brought relief to faculty whose salaries were far behind. Once Dr. Wallace's own salary was $3695 in arrears.

On these visits to the East, Thomas Cochran often gave Dr. Wallace help and encouragement. Sometimes he or his son in New York took him out to a substantial dinner. Sometimes he accompanied him in calling on wealthy prospects. Together they tried several times to interest Helen Gould, but could not. Hetty Green, they thought, might just as well as not give them five hundred dollars for the college, but she did not. They hoped for larger checks from James T. Kennedy, friend of J. J. Hill, from Ralph Vorhees and John P. Blair of Blairstown, New Jersey. But they were disappointed. Once from New York they went to Philadelphia where in Joseph Cochran's church they hoped to find a thousand dollars. They got six hundred. Baltimore and Washington yielded nothing.

In Pittsburgh on his first trip there, there was bitter medicine for Dr. Wallace. A pastor upon whom he called would not even recommend Macalester to his people for their gifts. The Board of Trustees, the pastor felt, should make an assignment and then attempt to buy the plant back when it was put up for sale. But Dr. Wallace took this not too seriously to heart. Dr. Breed, when he had been a pastor in St. Paul, had never been friendly to the college. Yet, except for Mrs. Thaw, Pittsburgh was not happy hunting territory for Dr. Wallace. In 1895 he wrote his wife:

> My visits here made me chafe under the dim prospects of having a good, well-furnished home where we can live as Christians should. Oh, this long torturing poverty, when will it cease? I have had but little success here. The Pittsburghers are dreadfully close. I have delivered circulars, etc. where I have failed to see people and hence must call again.

In Columbus he got no money from the churches and he began seriously to wonder about the future:

> Macalester will probably pull through in time but I am unwilling to have the family go back there and starve and be humiliated as we have been. So in case I fail in this work the home place [in Wooster] will be our refuge. I do not despair of Mac but it is hard to tell how long its profs must live on promises and I cannot do this beyond this year.

In Chicago, at another time, Dr. Wallace was to have an interview with a Mr. Pearsons who had pledged three hundred thousand dollars to western colleges. Mr. Pearsons was a strong advocate of economy. He questioned Dr. Wallace on the number of profes-

sors, students, and so forth at Macalester. He seemed to be trying
to dig up evidence of extravagance, but when Dr. Wallace finished
giving him the details of operational expenses he remarked with
approval, "Yours is the most cheaply managed college I know
of." Pressed to make a gift for the endowment and thus to act as
a lever to pry open the purses of others, he replied, "I have been
that so often. You get some one else to be the lever and I will
jump on it afterwards." Thus was hope deferred again and again.

Of course Macalester was really the responsibility of the Presbyterians within the state of Minnesota. A few years before, while
fiscal secretary, Mr. David Platter had written:

> The east will give money to dot the waste places of Minnesota
> with home missionaries, but not build a college for Minneapolis
> and St. Paul. They say Minneapolis and St. Paul can do that
> themselves, and they are altogether right. Our local pride and
> independence ought to stir the Presbyterians of this state, and
> especially of those two cities, to avoid the reproach of letting
> Macalester College languish and possibly die for lack of loyal
> support.

Eight of the strong Presbyterian congregations had, however, in
those lush days before the panic, gone into debt to build themselves
churches, and they were trying to free themselves first. Besides, in
trying to support both Macalester and Albert Lea the Presbyterians
of Minnesota had long since come to realize that they had taken
on more than they could manage. Dr. Wallace would have been
glad to merge the two; he saw economies in such a union. Yet
whenever the suggestion was made, it met with such opposition
from Albert Lea that the idea after some years was given up. Early
in his administration also, North Dakota's Presbyterian college at
Jamestown had suspended operations because of financial difficulties. Dr. Wallace suggested to them at once that they sell their
property and with the proceeds erect on Macalester's campus a hall
to house their students. These students would then have the use of
the rooms without charge. Board and incidentals would cost each
student about two dollars a week, he estimated. By this plan North
Dakota Presbyterians would be relieved of paying for other buildings and for professors; they would have all the advantages of the

institution with no expense save that of erecting a dormitory. It was perhaps a happy suggestion for the still sparsely settled Northwest, but nothing came of it.

Macalester had at this time buildings which had cost $125,000, a 30-acre campus worth $135,000, and 300 lots in the Macalester Addition valued at $45,000. Much of this, of course, was unproductive real estate on which they had to pay taxes and city levies for improvements. The St. Paul Trust Company still held a mortgage of $100,000 on the property, and there was a considerable floating debt.

Though times were very hard, there was wealth in the state, particularly in the Twin Cities, and Dr. Wallace was determined to pry some of it loose for the college. He already knew Ex-Governor Alexander Ramsey, who had long been entangled in Macalester's history. Out in Worthington he had come to know George Draper Dayton, merchant and banker, later to be head of Minneapolis' leading department store. Mr. Dayton was friendly to Dr. Wallace and to Macalester. He was indeed, since 1894, a member of its Board of Trustees. There was Frederick Weyerhaeuser, lumber magnate, and James J. Hill, "the Empire Builder." He had already contributed, just before Dr. Wallace had taken the reins, $10,000 toward the college emergency. Then there was Rufus Jefferson. Toward these men and others, in the seven long years ahead, he was to direct his efforts. Surely one of them, or all of them working together, could save the college for the church and the state of Minnesota.

It was on R. C. Jefferson, member of St. Paul's House of Hope Church, that in particular he was coming to pin his hopes in these first years of his administration. Mr. Cochran in late 1895 had reported confidentially that Mr. Jefferson had set aside in his will $200,000 for benevolences. He was showing a growing interest in Macalester and Dr. Wallace decided to ask him to be key man in a drive for endowment. He pointed out that Macalester was surrounded by the state university and other denominational colleges and that if it was to carry out its mission of training Presbyterian leaders in the state, it must rank with the best. For this it must have adequate endowment. The only way to start this, he felt, was to have someone make a conditional offer. He had canvassed the field often and thoroughly to find the person to lead off. He had considered the McCormicks of Chicago, and Mr. Pearsons, Mrs. Thaw of Pittsburgh, Ex-Governor Ramsey, Frederick Weyerhaeuser, and J. J. Hill. In each instance there was some reason why the individual would not be able to act as leader. "I always reach the conclusion," he wrote, "that you, Mr. Jefferson, are the only man to whom the college can look hopefully for leadership in this great work." He then suggested that he give $100,000, $150,000, or $200,000 on condition that the college secure from others double that amount. Through such a gift Mr. Jefferson not only would give invincible enthusiasm to the drive for endowment and set an example to other wealthy men, but would establish Macalester as the Princeton of the Northwest and enable it to do a great work for the church. Moreover, it would link Jefferson's name with Macalester for all time and give him the pleasure of seeing the fruits of his benefactions. A few months later Dr. Wallace was to learn that Jefferson had suffered a loss of over $100,000. Still later word came from interested friends that Jefferson and Weyerhaeuser might each give $5000 toward the debt. Nothing happened. In March 1897, in response to an appeal for Macalester in the House of Hope Church, Mr. Jefferson sent a check for one hundred dollars. He might send one hundred dollars more, he said, if it were absolutely necessary." Yet Mr. Jefferson had by no means lost interest.

Dr. Wallace's early experience with James J. Hill was less heartbreaking. Though not a Presbyterian, and indeed critical of Presbyterians for not adequately supporting their college, he was always friendly. To him, also, near the beginning of his administration, Dr. Wallace addressed a letter, and took it in person to the door of his home. He told him of Macalester's possibilities for usefulness, of its financial predicament and of the inability of the churches with debts of their own to come to its aid. Early in 1896 a letter from Mr. John Pringle, financial secretary, to Dr. Wallace, now in New York, told of a call he had made on Mr. Hill. He had been graciously received and given half an hour of time.

He [Mr. Hill] said he knew it was necessity and not impatience which had brought me . . . he said, "I will let you know what

I will do before I leave for New York . . . Tell Dr. Wallace I
shall be in New York the end of the week and to call me about
the college and to arrange for seeing Mr. Kennedy."

Apparently Mr. Pringle had been appealing to him to take over
the salary of a professor. Later, when times improved, Mr. Hill was
to help substantially with the debt.

Through all these lean years Dr. Wallace was writing letters
and preparing circulars to Presbyterians everywhere. He never
let his imagination sleep. Macalester had been sending a large pro-
portion of its ministerial students to Auburn Seminary in New
York State. He therefore wrote to Auburn's president asking him
to bring the needs of Macalester to the attention of his wealthy
friends. When the Presbyterian General Assembly met in Minneapolis and included Macalester in its tour of the Twin Cities, he,
with Mr. Covert and Mr. Thomas Dickson of the executive committee of the trustees, followed up the visit with a letter to all
commissioners reminding them of the crisis facing Macalester and
urging them to a benevolent offering, "great or small," from
churches and from individuals. Again he appealed to the ministers
of the state:

> If the Methodists can raise seventeen cents a member for Ham-
> line, cannot Presbyterian churches raise an average of ten cents
> for Macalester? Such a contribution would enable the college to
> meet its ordinary current expenses without embarrassment.

He broadcast a leaflet giving reasons why the denominational college should live. It had set the standard, he said, of American higher
education; it is the mother of college presidents and America's
most prominent educators; its educational work has been done for
less money than that of any other agency; it's the greatest tax-
saving institution in the state. All these reasons and more he gave
the Presbyterian ministers to use in their pleas for Macalester,
almost every one a focal point for an address on Christian education.

At the worst of the crisis, when the St. Paul Trust Company
seemed about to foreclose their mortgage on the college prop-

erty, he appealed again to the Presbyterians of the state in a letter
entitled "Men of Israel, Help":

> We are at the mercy of our creditors, who can and may force
> an assignment. We are trying to tide over these times till we can
> sell property and get out of debt. To this end we need to raise
> $14,000 this year for current expenses, interest and taxes. We
> desire to borrow also several thousand dollars at a low rate of
> interest to meet pressing creditors.

But James Wallace was not just sitting at his desk turning out
letters and circulars; he was active in the campaign, preaching in
towns and cities, expending all his strength in what often seemed
a hopeless effort. Though in pleading his cause in public he could
assume a hopeful and confident tone, in private and among friends
he was often very close to tears. "This college," he wrote Janet,
"is a burden enough to kill a dozen men." Though in general
his health was good, there were moments when he feared that he
would not hold up under the strain. One fall Saturday afternoon,
he took the train to Austin where he was to preach the next morning. The minister met him at the station. He looked at the haggard
face of Dr. Wallace. "Are you not well?" he said. "I am well," said
Dr. Wallace, "but I am worried. We have no coal to start the
furnace." "No coal?" exclaimed the minister and led him down
Main Street to a dealer whom he knew, and there arranged to have
two carloads shipped to the college. "I never saw a man more
surprised and happy," the pastor later wrote of the incident, and
commented, "He had many such emergencies, but his determination would brook no defeat." Occasionally, however, Dr. Wallace
was too blue to preach, too blue to do anything. On one occasion,
early in his experience of begging, he wrote Janet:

> Yesterday I was booked to preach at Bethlehem (in Minne-
> apolis) again but felt too blue and sent Sharpe in the morn-
> ing and Davis in the evening. So I am out ten dollars. Blues are
> expensive and have been the bane of my life.

And again on the last Sunday of the same year (1895) he was
writing:

. . . I felt too blue even to go to church and stayed in my room all day with the curtains drawn and did not even go to dinner . . . It was dark last year at this time, though I think not so dark as now. Money is very hard to get, harder than last year. If these times continue long, everybody will be broken up I guess. I shall work away, however, I can do nothing else.

Every year he offered his resignation and every year it was laid on the table. Every little while he would tell his family that he could stand it very little longer, maybe a month, maybe till commencement; then he would stop if the money were not raised. "I find myself cooling to this work," he would say, or

I do not think you realize the burden that is on my soul all the time. If I contract a bill for the college however small I am conscious that *I* must raise the money for it and from people too who are not deeply interested. I have never been more firmly resolved to resign or more willing to do it than I am now . . . If I were only martyring myself that would not matter much but I am sacrificing the entire family—putting in money and labor for the college that should go to the benefit of the children.

In early August 1895, while canvassing for funds and students in southern Minnesota, Dr. Wallace received four telegrams. They told him of the death in Wooster of Janet, the chubby, more affectionate one of the twins. He had not known the baby was ill, and did not know the cause of her death until he arrived in Rochester and found letters waiting. Unable to go to his family, he continued to meet his appointments, with an aching heart. On Sunday morning he spoke to a crowded house at the Rochester Presbyterian Church, but that night, August 11, he wrote to his wife:

Janet was too pale to show great physical vigor . . . Her death is indeed sad and I think hearts of stone would weep at seeing such sweetness and innocency pass away . . . Well we are helpless and at the mercy of the world's trials and sorrows. But they are too much for me and a very few more years of life such as we have lived in the last ten years will suffice to end this transient dream. One may well be glad that life is not long and that it is not to be repeated.

Soon other letters came from Wooster, telling of the illness of little Miriam and of her mother. For the next few days Dr. Wallace moved from town to town, often awaiting trains in the night at lonely stations, always in dread of another telegram.

Many times, it was said, he tossed and groaned all night. Sometimes he was bitter:

> I am sick of Mac and wish I had never seen it on earth. The Curse of God seems on the whole work. God has confounded the Presbyterians of Minnesota.

And sometimes he was merely overwhelmed. In early 1896 he wrote:

> The times are growing worse and worse—Two banks suspended in Mpls—one last week and one this. The hardest thing on earth is to preserve faith at all or believe in the beneficence of the divine being. How can a righteous being find any pleasure in such a world in constant rebellion and suffering? Right forever on the scaffold, wrong forever on the throne!

The next morning he added the following sentences:

> Had a good sleep last night . . . A little brighter this morning but my philosophy as much perplexing as ever. If the sheriff would take those silver senators in the U.S. Senate out to the outskirts of the city and shoot them he would do his country a great service.
>
> They are about as great a curse as ever fell over the U.S. and are likely to land the whole country in general bankruptcy . . .
>
> It looks as if the bottom was falling out of the world, and here we are with debts to pay and children to feed and clothe.

Or again he would say, "I cannot endure to have my life measured by the amount of money I can raise." But there were always some brighter moments:

> I have had more encouragement in the canvas than ever before, and the outlook for students is better than I have ever seen it.

The crop in the North West is one of the best in the history of the country.

It was very hard for James Wallace to see others suffering on Macalester's account. He felt a personal responsibility. In Duluth he went to see Mrs. Rice, widow of the Reverend Daniel Rice, who had left a fifty-thousand-dollar property legacy to the college and also scholarship money. He found her feeble and cramped for funds. She was knitting a pair of socks to sell so that she could pay her subscription to the church paper. He wrote Janet:

> . . . No wonder one's spirits flag. If the college can't pay her anything of the 2000 interest they owe her, I will have to give her a part of what I get. She must not be left to such cold-blooded treatment.

In New York he found another widow to whom the college owed a thousand dollars of accumulated interest, and he was humiliated. The Episcopal Diocese had purchased from the St. Paul Trust Company some of the Macalester bonds, and when Dr. Wallace discovered that some of the retired Episcopal ministers were enduring privations because the bonds had defaulted on interest, he was again distressed, though the Episcopal bishop with whom he talked was sympathetic and willing to give the college time to work out its problems.

The hardships suffered by his own faculty, however, were ever present. He had had to employ D. N. Kingery in the department of mathematics at a salary of $400. Later he noticed that young Kingery was not coming to church; he had not the clothes, Dr. Wallace assumed. Professor Downing had owned property in Chicago valued at $2000. With his salary in arrears, he was unable to pay the accumulated taxes and lost it. Downing was being sued also by his landlord for $90 owing on his rent. As an example to other creditors and as a counsel of desperation to friends, in 1897 President Wallace was urging his faculty to cancel part of their claims to back salary. If the college were to go into bankruptcy those claims would not be worth five cents on the dollar; if creditors would all along the line reduce their claims, the college might yet pull through, and the faculty might be better off. Dr. Wallace agreed himself to remit two years of back salary. Two others agreed to remit one year of salary and still others made smaller reductions. During the academic year of 1899–1900 the faculty were receiving only a pittance: Dr. Wallace, $805; Professor Downing, $614; Professor Anderson, $614; Professor Funk, $214; the college engineer, $450.

It was amazing with what good grace and with what loyalty the faculty met the crises of these years. The faculty houses all needed painting. Often they could not be sure till late in the summer whether the college would be opening in the fall at all. They all did everything they could. Professor Davis went about preaching for the college. Professor Boyd surveyed the campus and with the help of students improved the athletic fields and put in a circular driveway. Others helped with the recruiting of students in the summers. They all looked to their leader and held their shoulders high on his account. Only once was there any sign of mutiny —on the part of one instructor.

The students held most of the faculty in high esteem. This one, however, they thought unqualified and they petitioned the administration to remove him. The instructor, in consequence, and his wife, who was also teaching in the college, resigned. Unfortunately their salaries were in arrears and they demanded immediate payment. Dr. Wallace promised that the money would be raised, but there was some delay. The instructor went to court and got judgment for $250. While Dr. Wallace was out of town the ousted man appeared at the men's dormitory with the sheriff and two secondhand dealers prepared to seize and sell off enough college furniture to pay the judgment. The story goes that the complainant had appeared during chapel time, and that Professor Davis, conducting chapel, told the students of the situation and dismissed them. Anyhow, they hurried to their rooms. Quietly they lifted the windows of the second- and third-floor rooms and as the instructor entered, a deluge of water from pitchers and slop jars fell upon him. With wounded pride and drenched clothing he attempted a dignified retreat, but then the college band appeared around the corner, struck up a dirge and escorted him toward the entrance of the campus. A jeering, laughing crowd of students followed. "Rock him! Egg him!" they shouted, and someone hurried over to a grocery to get the eggs. The frightened instructor broke into a run and fled down Grand Avenue to a streetcar. Members of the trustees who had been notified persuaded the sheriff to call off the sale, and a compromise was worked out. When Dr. Wallace returned to the campus he was humiliated to the core by the whole proceeding. He could visualize the lurid headlines in next morning's city papers. In deep gloom he retired supperless to his bedroom. The next morning, to be sure, the papers carried long accounts of the event. But the Macalester community laughed it off.

Among the students also, the optimism and loyalty were heartening and strengthened the desire to preserve the college for them and future generations. The students were well aware of their president's struggles. Once in 1899, when he returned from an extended trip in the East and subscriptions for the debt were beginning to roll in, they showed their appreciation by giving him a "Welcome Home," in chapel. The college orchestra played, the college quartet sang, one of the students gave a welcoming address. Dr. Wallace responded with wit, and then with a serious portrayal of Macalester's need and future hopes. President and students understood each other.

During most of these years Dr. Wallace had not been entirely unaided. Thomas Cochran of the trustees was tireless in his efforts. Thomas Shaw of the Minnesota School of Agriculture came also to the rescue. He was a dynamic Canadian Presbyterian and a firm believer in the church-related college, and, through articles and speeches over the state during weekends, he worked valiantly to rouse Presbyterians to their responsibility for Macalester. During the next few years, it was estimated, he gave to the college toward the liquidation of its debt the equivalent of nine months of free service. A committee, too, made up of some trustees and other influential businessmen, including William B. Dean, Rufus Jefferson and R. A. Kirk, had in early 1897 been set up to help. In late 1896 one of the Board, Mr. R. P. Lewis, had come up with a plan for liquidating the debt. Following his suggestion, a stupendous effort had been made in the winter of 1897 but it had failed. The plan, however, had called for a certain voluntary discounting of the claims of creditors. When the new committee met in the spring they were agreed that not only should subscriptions toward the debt be sought but that some way should be devised to get creditors to reduce their claims, if possible by 30 per cent. The committee members set themselves the task of calling on important creditors. In many instances they met with a generous response. A fuel company with a claim of $2500 agreed to settle for $500. The Episcopal Diocese took a drastic reduction. Even the St. Paul Trust Company pared down its demands. Yet, of course, some creditors balked or demanded a smaller discount than that suggested. As the crisis continued into summer, certain friends of the college guaranteed to provide running expenses for the current year. There was encouragement, too, in the fact that a decision of the Supreme Court had at last made the college campus exempt from taxes.

But there were other troubles. The St. Paul Trust Company, feeling obligated to protect those who had bought Macalester bonds in the refinancing of 1890, had asked the court for permission to sue the original subscribers to the debt, whose notes they held. The threat of this court action hung over Dr. Wallace and his trustees for months, until a compromise was arranged on the basis of discounts. By June of 1898 the debt still was not liquidated, college creditors were growing restive, and the fate of the college still trembled in the balance. This uncertainty constantly weighed on the mind of Dr. Wallace, and he reproached himself for not having secured the money to put the college on a solvent footing. That summer again he felt the college might close forever.

A new administration, however, had come to Washington in 1897, and there was an upsurge in business. Optimism succeeded pessimism. New gold fields and new methods of refining gold built up the nation's gold reserve, and industry was stimulated. By the end of 1898 the prospect of liquidating Macalester's debt was growing brighter. James Wallace wrote:

We shall pull through some way, I think . . . The interest in the college is growing and I doubt if there is a college in the West that has more friends among its constituency.

Presently some subscriptions toward the debt began to come in. Among these was one from J. J. Hill for $10,000, soon to be increased to $18,000 and then to $20,000. R. A. Kirk, W. B. Dean, and Rufus Jefferson had already given $2000 each. A Miss Willard of Auburn, New York, offered to give the last thousand needed to wipe out the debt. Dr. Wallace hoped that by March 1, 1899, all the money might be subscribed. But March first came and went, and still there was the debt. Dr. Wallace had gone East meanwhile and was in Philadelphia where he received a letter from Thomas H. Dickson, president of the Board of Trustees. Mr. Dickson said:

> Your success in Northminster Church astonished us all. It was far ahead of our expectations. I believe there is more money to be had in Philadelphia but you need cooperation and therefore Covert has dropped everything and gone to be with you.

Mr. Dickson reported also that the effort to settle with the creditors of the college for 30 per cent of their claims was moving slowly. But now more subscriptions were coming in. Word came that John Converse of Philadelphia had given $2500. Cyrus McCormick of Chicago gave $1000. W. H. Dunwoody of Minneapolis subscribed $2000, Frederick Weyerhaeuser of St. Paul, George Dayton of Worthington, and T. R. Janney of Minneapolis promised $1000 each. The situation began to take on a hopeful glow. On May 2, Dr. Wallace was able to write his father-in-law:

> The day of deliverance is not far off, and what a deliverance it will be!

By the end of May there was still $7000 to raise, and Dr. Wallace wrote:

> We have reached a crisis in which failing of 7000 our entire work is liable to be of no avail, and the further existence of the college imperilled.

Again commencement passed and the goal receded into the future. In a mood of despondency he penned a letter to his relatives in Wooster:

> Janet, who has been quite ill for several days, waited on by the doctor daily, is now going round. Her illness was due to want of sufficient good food, and soft water, also to anxiety about the college. She is now on her feet again but greatly needs some change.

All our trouble comes from the condition of the college. I have never felt so much like leaving it even if it goes to ruin. It has robbed me of salary, ruined my education, greatly injured Janet's health, seriously affected my own and done no little injury to my reputation. We are so near the end and yet so far that I hang like Sisyphus between success and failure, professional life and death all the time. No wonder we are worn out and wish for death to end our misery. My life here, and Janet's too, has been little short of tragedy. I resigned at the annual meeting or renewed my resignation. The Board urged me to stay by a unanimous and rising vote. This indicates not so much their confidence in me as their desperation. I agreed to remain until July to see if an end could be reached of this dreadful agony.

At about this time another calamity fell. The court ruled that the heirs of a subscriber, who had promised $3500 toward the debt, did not have to pay the money from the estate because of a technical provision in the wording of the original subscription. The decision wiped out almost as much as Dr. Wallace and Mr. Cochran had been able to collect in a year of effort in the East. During the summer and fall the effort to wipe out the debt lost instead of gaining ground. By December $15,000 was still needed. The Board determined to make an earnest plea to the Presbyterian Board for Aid to Colleges for a special grant of $15,000. The Board of Aid refused. They felt it would not be wise for a church organization to commit itself to the plan as worked out by the committee. They felt that plan involved too much that was questionable on grounds of policy and propriety (the asking of creditors to discount their claims), since such a transaction might, though voluntary, involve distress and loss to many parties.

The special committee and the Macalester Board of Trustees, however, all Christian gentlemen, saw nothing unethical in bringing pressure to bear on creditors to scale down their claims, and they asked for a reconsideration. As the year of 1900 advanced, optimism once again pervaded the campus. The Board of Aid for Colleges decided to co-operate and give the college a new start.

They made the appropriation of $15,000 on condition that the debt be fully liquidated.

Near the end of the long struggle there came one note of discord. In December 1900 Dr. Wallace found it necessary to present to the trustees a set of grievances against the field secretary. He, Dr. Wallace complained, was interfering with the administrative affairs of the college: he was trying to hire and fire faculty members and determine the amount of their salaries; he was trying to control the rental of rooms in the dormitories and wished to assume the office of treasurer of the college; several college engineers had resigned because of his interference. These complaints led to serious tension between the president of the Board and Dr. Wallace; he felt that the time had come for Dr. Wallace to step aside and he gave the trustees his ultimatum: Either they would accept Dr. Wallace's resignation, which was permanently on the table, or accept his. The trustees reluctantly accepted the resignation of their chairman and urged Dr. Wallace to continue his leadership of the college.

Another summer came and another fall. At the October Synod meeting, Dr. Wallace made the annual report on the college. He presented a striking appearance, with his straight rugged frame of six feet, his bald head, fringed with flowing locks, his piercing eyes, and bushy sideburns. He was unable to report that the debt was actually paid off. They were still working. They hoped it would be cleared "in a very short time." He expressed the desire to make way for the election of a new president. "The next great work," he said, "is to raise endowment for the college, and to this work a new man would bring new enthusiasm and inspire greater enthusiasm." It was not, however, until May 1, 1901, that at long last the day so devoutly prayed for arrived. The last of the old claims had been settled. The seven-year struggle had ended in victory.

On May 2, Thomas Shaw, now president of the Macalester Board of Trustees, announced the liquidation of the debt in an article for *The North and West*. After commenting on this and what it meant, he went on to say of Dr. Wallace and his faculty:

JAMES WALLACE OF MACALESTER

The story of Macalester College has been a most pathetic one in the past. One almost feels like trying to bury it, dust to dust, ashes to ashes. But some bright lessons . . . shine out from the darkness. The years of self sacrifice on the part of the President and staff to save Macalester ought to be forever kept in imperishable remembrance by the Presbyterians in the Northwest. There ought to be a tablet in the college recording their devotion to an institution which our church can't do without if it is to fulfill its high mission in this great country.

On June 4 at the meeting of the Board the financial report indicated still a deficit of $2300 on the current year. Then and there the trustees subscribed $1000 toward this. By the end of the month Dr. Wallace had found the rest. Macalester was at long last freed from its financial encumbrances.

XIII

On the Campus

His eyen twynkled in his heed aryght
As doon the sterres in the frosty nyght.
GEOFFREY CHAUCER

THROUGH all this weary period of panic and distress James
Wallace held on with a bulldog's pertinacity and courage, and its
blind devotion, sometimes against his instinct and his better judgment. His background, his training, his pride were involved in this
course of action. He resigned repeatedly. When he did so, the
trustees always made him feel that the saving of Macalester was
his duty to the church, and he did not deliberately walk away
from duty. Several times he had chances to go elsewhere. In 1896
a position as head of an academy on Staten Island was offered to
him. It promised a good future and a dependable salary. He did
not like the idea of stepping down from the presidency of a liberal-
arts college to the headship of an academy. However, the offer did
give him the feeling that if the trustees of Macalester would not
make it possible for him to live respectably with his family in St.
Paul, he could go elsewhere. Janet felt more strongly. She wrote:

You certainly ought to use your Staten Island offer as leverage,
and as powerful leverage too: and not only with the Board,
especially the ex-Governor, but with Mr. Jefferson and perhaps
Mr. Hill. Let Mr. Pringle know too, that *you* as well as your
family will no longer submit to this kind of living. Do take a
firm stand . . . After putting your hand to the plow I am not

165

in favor of abandoning it. But we cannot make a good clean furrow in Macalester without plenty of help in removing rocks. Your cry to come to the help of the Lord, to the help of the Lord against the mighty certainly does not meet with the response it should, and I think it is high time to let people know that the time is almost ripe for you to shake off the dust of the Synod of Minnesota if your message does not command more attention.

Emporia College in Kansas approached him, too, with the suggestion that he join their faculty. Again in 1897, when reports were circulating that Macalester would have to close its door, Carleton College made overtures to both Dr. Wallace and to Dr. George W. Davis to come there and bring Macalester students with them. Dr. Wallace gave them to understand that Macalester was a lively corpse and did not intend to let a funeral take place.

It was evident that Dr. Wallace's personality, his wide knowledge and versatility, and his teaching ability had been widely recognized. With his money-raising activities often far afield, on the Macalester campus he continued to be administrative head, leader of faculty and students, friend and counselor, and professor. He was burdened with the choice of faculty, with the curriculum to see that it was meeting needs and current trends, with the welfare of the students, the anxieties of parents, with the manifold demands of what is called college life, and with some actual teaching. In this small college he stood at bat, was pitcher, outfielder, and umpire all in one.

Even as dean in those interims when Macalester had no president, he had been called upon to choose faculty, and he had leaned heavily on the recommendations of friends. Consequently in those early days several came from Wooster, Edward Downing and A. W. Anderson. Lester Brown, instructor for a short time, was son of his old friend, Horatio Brown, in Wooster. D. N. Kingery from Wabash College he knew about from Hugh Kingery, whom he had taught in Wooster. But as his circle widened he drew from other sources. George W. Davis, so long a mainstay of the college, was English born, and a graduate of Auburn Theological Seminary. Mrs. Julia M. Johnson, widow of General Richard M. Johnson, was a graduate of Mt. Holyoke, with college-teaching experience when she came to Macalester's department of English. She also taught French, and was really a dean of women long before Macalester recognized such an office. Miss Grace Whitridge he found teaching elocution in the Twin Cities, and she became a well-loved fixture on the faculty. John Porter Hall was a graduate of Princeton, who had taken his first year at Macalester. Hugh Alexander was a graduate of the college.

Dr. Wallace had high standards for his faculty, in personality, in character, and in teaching ability. If they had graduate training, so much the better, but the college was not yet in a position to demand this of its faculty; they were too poor; the college was too poor. Besides, he came to feel that professors were the gainers and their horizons were broadened if sometimes they had to teach outside their fields. Such experience made them read and study widely, kept them out of ruts. In Macalester this was not privilege, however, but necessity. He wished, in the members of his staff, an innate love of learning, and devotion to the Christian Church. Later he was to warn the trustees of this:

> Making and keeping a college Christian in these days means eternal vigilance. And what above all needs the closest scrutiny is the character and real beliefs of candidates for admission to the faculty. We must keep out men and women who oppose the Christian view of the world or with whom its profession means nothing whatsoever.

On a later occasion in writing of the anniversary celebration of the old Log College at Princeton he went so far as to say:

> The educational road from the old log college to the present has been long and arduous, with ascents at times almost precipitous, and many have been the heroic men that have fallen in that weary way. They counted not their lives dear unto themselves that the Gospel of Christ might find fit expression . . . The grounds for the call of young men and women to devote their lives unselfishly to Christian education are exactly the same as the grounds for entering the Christian ministry or for going to the home or foreign field . . . It is not a question of what is

the maximum salary a professor can command but rather what is the maximum sacrifice he can afford to make.

In 1911 at a meeting of the Educational Association in St. Paul he stressed "Faculty Responsibility for Student Morals." Great educational leaders down through the ages had held, he maintained, that the final end of the educational process is the development of character. He said in part:

> Every student should know and be made to feel that his professors are deeply solicitous about his moral progress. Make each professor a monitor for a limited number of students. When a professor is employed it should be made clear that this monitorship is not an extra duty imposed upon him but an essential function of his professorship.

As he went East on money-raising trips he sometimes visited other institutions: Union Seminary, Columbia University and Teachers College, New York University and Yale. Gradually he enlarged the curriculum. Minnesota had drawn a large population from the Scandinavian countries, and so he put in a teacher of Scandinavian languages. He early saw the need of courses in art for the women. He admonished the instructor of his duties. "I have given him plainly," he wrote Janet, "our view on nude drawings and all those things and he takes a correct view of it." He added instruction in music and in some commercial studies. He saw clearly that if the college was to grow, it would have to expand its offerings in science, and the faculty were in accord. One of the faculty spent the summer remodeling the basement of the east wing, and there a biological laboratory was set up. In their catalogue they announced a scientific course leading to a Bachelor of Science degree. He looked forward to getting a special endowment for the department of the sciences and to the building of a science hall.

In 1905 the curriculum was reorganized to give prevocational training in several fields. A premedical course was set up. At the end of his sophomore year a student could go on to medical school, and then after two years of satisfactory work transfer his credits back to receive a Bachelor's degree from Macalester.

Though James Wallace had always thoroughly enjoyed a good game of baseball, either as participant or spectator, from time to time he flayed the abuses of intercollegiate athletics, and in this he carried his faculty with him. In the spring of 1897 they forbade the use of paid athletes in baseball, and in consequence, that season, had no team. In a few years, however, Macalester was to regain its high standing in the baseball conference. Football, a little later, they joined other colleges in outlawing altogether. In a letter to the college *Bulletin* Dr. Wallace expressed his attitude in briny sarcasm:

The 1905 football season practically closed Saturday with two dead on the field of battle. The day's fatalities bring the total of slain to nineteen, and the injured (record being made of accidents out of the ordinary) to 137 . . . Of course it is a little sad to think of those poor fellows that were killed in football. One can hardly help but sympathize with the bereaved parents and friends. But dear reader, don't stop to think of their broken-hearted parents or the numerous maimed and sprained members. Don't be a ball-baby. Feelings have nothing to do with this. No! No! Think of the wonderful physical development the great football players have gotten. Think of the cheering thousands in the grandstand. Think of the gate receipts. Think of the bovine muscle developed. Think of the thousands of dollars won (or lost) in betting on the game. Think of the splendid drunks that celebrated the victories . . . The authorities of the State Fair should by all means arrange to exhibit a lot of these wonderful football giants next September in one of the barns along with the prize bulls.

We used to be taught that knowledge was power and that old fogy Solomon says over and over again that *Wisdom* is the principal thing. But we now know better. *Muscle* is the principal thing. Brute force is power. Down with brains and up with Sandow and Sullivan.

The article quoted was featured by the St. Paul *Pioneer Press*.

An alumnus recently described Dr. Wallace as having had one stern eye, the other with a twinkle. With his humor, there was combined a kind of inward zeal. Before students and faculty in college chapel he could single out a student for some misconduct and lash him with words till the boy's face glowed with redness and his jaw jerked as if in pain. He did not hesitate to expel boys from the dormitory for a water fight. When a group of students, on the occasion of an initiation into one of the college societies, beat a boy severely, Dr. Wallace denounced the action:

> This spirit of tyranny and the whole . . . initiation business by which Freshmen are compelled to make freaks, fools, and asses of themselves before their professors and fellow students is a species of hazing, a revival or survival of the brutal flagging system that so long disgraced the English schools and universities. Being essentially wrong it easily degenerates into scandalous maltreatment and has not infrequently resulted in death or permanent injury—One purpose of a college is to train young men and women for citizenship and a fine regard for the rights of others.—I wish it well understood that I for one regard it as a serious breach of the first principles of human freedom, as dangerous training in lawlessness, and a plain violation of the Golden Rule.

Yet the boys recognized his essential youthfulness. He could on occasion have his tongue in his cheek. "Why this unseemly levity?" he would say on entering a classroom late, just as they were preparing to take a cut. It was his half-teasing way. And they could respond in kind. An alumnus recalls this incident: "It was the late spring of 1898 and chapel was in session in the large room across the north end of the first floor of the old east wing. The hymns had been sung and the Scripture read and Dr. Wallace, who was leading the devotions, had just said, 'Let us unite in prayer,' when an itinerant bagpipe trio began to play just below the open window back of the pulpit. There was a moment's hesitation, but the good doctor was not the man to yield the hour of prayer to a bagpipe serenade. When the music crescendoed his voice rose to meet it with Christian vigor, and when the bagpipes played more softly, he modulated his tone accordingly. He prayed with accustomed devoutness and at usual length; and simultaneously with his 'amen' the music ceased. For a few seconds there was one of the deadest silences I ever experienced. As the bowed heads came up, every eye turned toward the leader, who was wiping the perspiration from his brow. A pleasant grin spread from ear to ear as he gravely remarked, 'Only Providence could have timed that music so accurately. Chapel dismissed.' "

Another story, often told, is that one day Dr. Wallace castigated a student for his profanity, and he had answered, "Well, if I had your vocabulary I wouldn't have to swear." Once, it is related, some students had taken a cow by night up three flights of stairs into the college chapel. Two days later when all was once more clear, Dr. Wallace ended his vitriolic comments on the incident with a characteristic Scottish anticlimax: "It is consoling to know that we have a contented cow."

The students knew the warmth of his heart. Many and many a one had experienced it, had felt his "unfeigned interest" in the problems and discouragement of a boy or girl and got from this "new strength of heart." To many he was more like an elder brother than a professor. He could be one of them. After commencement in 1899, with two others of the faculty he went off with forty students on a boat trip down the Mississippi, returning that night at eleven. "His intellectual attainments," one alumnus wrote, "were so tempered by his kindness and humbleness of spirit that they [the students] were not only at ease but happy in his presence . . ." With all his burdens he yet found time to know his students, even those of the preparatory department, and to single out those of promise for attention. One of them later wrote him as follows:

> I was possessed with a feeling of deep and sincere gratitude toward you because at a critical period in my life three letters from you, unexpected and unsolicited, came to my father. Like a miracle I returned to Macalester two weeks later to begin my Freshman year . . . I shall always feel grateful to you for your interest, help, and faith in me . . .

Nobody had to be compelled to attend college chapel when Dr. Wallace spoke. He enjoyed speaking now, and often he let himself go and said what was in his heart. Those chapel speeches were remembered sometimes for their invective, and sometimes, too, for their inspiration and charm. Frequently he talked on national and international issues. One day, it is told, a speaker in the Twin Cities had made an address that today might be considered treasonable. James Wallace could not let it pass. At chapel the next day he lashed out at him in words approximately these: "There is not enough sulphur in the state of Minnesota to properly fumigate any hall or public building where —— was permitted to speak." At a later date he once began a chapel talk by saying "I see by the papers that Senator Henry Cabot Lodge is dead. I cannot say that I am one of the mourners." From that he went on to speak to startled students of how Senator Lodge and others like him had hamstrung the League of Nations.

Once in a while in an address to a graduating class one could detect a kind of wistful note, as if he were not sure how much weight Macalester's diploma might carry in the great world; the college, he knew, might have to close its doors forever. In 1895 he said:

What your estimate of this document is I cannot say. It is true indeed that it hails not from an institution so famous and venerable as some in our land. It is true it bears not the signatures of Professors so illustrious as many in the world's great universities. Yet we do believe that it does mean as much to you as those of older institutions mean to their graduates—as much diligence, as much faithfulness, as much interest in the search after truth, as keen discipline of mental powers, as high, as fine cultivation of the moral nature, in short as thorough preparation for the work of life.

He did not question for a moment that the small Christian college *could* give and *did* give something often not to be surpassed, sometimes not even to be equaled by that of larger institutions. In 1897 his farewell words to the seniors expressed this:

. . . The best things of a true education are those of which the class book can take no very accurate note. The exaltation of virtue in the soul, the love of excellence and of culture, heaven-born enthusiasm, a God-given purpose—these are the really great things of education. It is the testimony of Booker T. Washington that his success has been due not so much to the

knowledge and discipline obtained in the classroom . . . as to
the inspiration . . . from the noble and self-sacrificing life of
the president . . . And I am sure it is the hope of all your professors that their lives have exerted in some degree at least a
similar influence upon you; that they may find a lasting place
in your memories, not so much for what they have done as your
instructors, as for what they are as Christian men . . .

Ponder well that composite of the virtues so wonderfully
pictured in the life of your great Teacher, Jesus. There was
great knowledge there, and great wisdom, too, but far above
these was His quenchless love, His infinite sympathy and His
boundless hope. Imitate Him and you shall not err as regards
the virtues of most value in the building of human character.

At another commencement he closed with these words of exhortation:

Love your country and do your utmost, by active participation
in its affairs, to promote its welfare. Beware of rabid socialism
that would destroy the rights of private property, and more the
liberty of the individual in the liberty, or license, of the masses.
Stand for the liberty of a man to work for whomsoever, when-
soever, for whatsoever he may choose. Have this for your guide,
"Nothing is stable except it be just." Cherish the memory of
your Alma Mater. Breathe a prayer for her.

To the academy graduates he said:

. . . It is probably true that England owes her greatness quite
as much to preparatory schools as to her universities. It is no
uncommon thing in reading the biographies of her great men
to find that they attribute their success in life largely to the
influence of their earlier instructors: that in fact Eton and Har-
row had done more for them . . . than Cambridge or Oxford.
Do not forget that the Academy is in some respects a severer
test of the students than the colleges.

Busy and discouraged as Dr. Wallace was, he took time to express himself as a citizen, sometimes in the Macalester *Echo*, sometimes in a Twin Cities paper. During the hot Bryan-McKinley

campaign, when arguments rolled back and forth: free coinage of silver or the gold standard; preservation of the civil service or its abolition; the enforcement or nonenforcement of federal laws in all the states; the safeguarding of the independence or the weakening of the courts; James Wallace analyzed the issues in the *Echo* in as neutral terms as he could muster. However when McKinley won, the students came out with their brass bands and serenaded him and other professors, knowing full well where he really stood. Everyone, including the students, hoped that a new administration would bring in better times for business and for the college.

Again when the Greek-Turkish conflict arose in the spring of 1897 he wrote the St. Paul *Pioneer Press,* commending an editorial and saying:

> It is the same old conflict of centuries ago—occidentalism against orientalism, liberty and progress against despotism and retrogression, education against ignorance, the cross against the crescent. There should be a well organized national movement to aid Greece with all the sinews of warfare, arms and men . . . All honor to the Greeks whose love of kindred and of justice has made it impossible for them to sit still while the so-called concert of nations, with phenomenal incapacity and heartlessness higgle for advantage and barter with the liberties and rights of men . . . The example of America contributing liberally of men and money would prove a mighty inspiration to the Greeks, and would be a potent influence in arousing the patriots of Europe to fly to the aid of Greece.

Of course Dr. Wallace would have liked to be writing and studying and teaching all the time and full time instead of racing about the country pursuing the shadow of one hundred thousand dollars. He was an excellent teacher, direct and clear; and he had "a glow about him," an enthusiasm that made everything he taught, prosaic facts or literature, a fresh and interesting experience. When lecturing on the Gospel he would often have tears in his eyes and show great emotion. Teaching the New Testament was no mere academic exercise; it was a ministry—and in the end his students

were to say: "*He* was the message, far more than what he said."
He gave an impression of "unbounded knowledge," of the Bible,
the classics, of philosophy, economics, and international affairs.
The boys who went on to theological studies found that his training in Greek was invaluable. In the classroom his humor was a delight. He had a mannerism, too, that amused them. In lecturing he
would take off his glasses, rub the lenses between his fingers, and
put the glasses on again to read. They always wondered how he
could see at all. He would have loved to teach in those middle years
far more than he had any chance to do.

For a college president there is no escaping social life. He must
entertain students and he must entertain faculty, formally and in-
formally. This Dr. and Mrs. Wallace did as they could, very simply. In the early days of June, in the commencement season, Mrs.
Wallace could transform the plain old house with daisies from
the field or flowers from the neighbors. Or for the freshmen in
the fall she might stage a Halloween party. Dr. Wallace, tall and
spare, was always a striking figure on these occasions. Though he
did not believe in evening dress for men or women, indeed could
not afford it, he donned a cutaway for church and formal parties.

On one occasion, after Dr. Wallace's retirement, he and Mrs.
Wallace were invited to a reception at President Acheson's for the
faculties of Macalester and Hamline. The invitation suggested formal attire. Dr. Wallace wrote the chairman of the committee suggesting that he stay away since the rooms anyhow would be over-
crowded. He then said:

> Besides, it being a "full dress" affair some of us old fogies, like
> Anderson, Kingery, and myself, can't qualify as we have no
> "full dress" suit and think it a waste of good money to rent or
> buy one. Mrs. Wallace has some good clothes but none that
> reveals as much of the body as common decency will allow.
> Would it not be more interesting if Despot Fashion would re-
> quire the women to come in bathing suits with pink slippers,
> blue garters and a skin colored ribbon around their necks, with
> gold letters stamped thereon, reading: "Modesty be damned"?

On being assured that "full dress" was not required, he replied:

I hope that hastily written note will not be interpreted as a reflection on the women of our faculty. It was not so intended. But to the whole movement of high-brow society to enslave men with a straight-laced, cast iron ritual of conventionality, I am utterly opposed. To be told indirectly or by implication that if you can't come in "full dress" stay away, is a type of devotion to social ritual that I detest.

Ordinarily James Wallace was not fastidious about his clothes, not much concerned if his fringe of gray hair grew a little long or his trousers bagged. He had much too much else to think about. Even if his trousers were patched as they sometimes were, he carried on, as if unmindful, with dignity.

XIV

With His Family

I will arise and go now, for always night and day
I hear lake water lapping with low sounds by the shore;
While I stand on the roadway, or on the pavements grey,
I hear it in the deep heart's core.

WILLIAM BUTLER YEATS

W H E N Janet left Macalester with the family in November 1894, no one realized that she was to stay away almost two years. Her husband, absent much of the time, never saw the moment when it seemed wise to bring his family back, much as he yearned to do so. He was never sure how long he would continue the struggle. Possibly in a month or two he would be going elsewhere. Altogether he thought it easier and cheaper for the family to remain in Wooster among relatives. In Macalester, meanwhile, he lived in his old house, and boarded at "The Elms," the old president's house, which now housed college girls. He and Janet were making the best of a bad situation.

Janet was not strong. Weariness and anxiety had dimmed the one-time sparkle of her eyes so that even her rollicking, wrestling, teasing boys felt it might one day just flicker and go out. James at long distance urged her not to overwork, to go riding often, and to go out and buy some new clothes. "It is sad," he wrote, "that I never have money to dress you as you deserve. It helps a woman wonderfully to dress pretty well." Whenever he could, as he went back and forth, he made pop-in visits to Wooster.

As the first summer came on, she, at least, became sure that she should go back where she belonged, by his side. The children, too, were restless. Robin exclaimed one day, "I do wish I were at home where I could own something. I do want a wagon," and DeWitt chimed in with vehemence: "I want to live in a house that my papa owns and *nobody else* so I can dig a hole in the yard." The relatives were good to them. Grandmother Wallace paid them for working in her garden, for planting beets, setting out cabbages and onions. When they came in there was always "a piece" for them, usually a slice of bread with slabs of butter and a quarter inch of apple butter on the top, sometimes a glass of milk. They loved her and her Scottish burr, particularly her way of saying "gaddles" (girls). Yet they knew that Wooster was not really home. They were crowded in and their father was not here. Yet he still was undecided, thought they should not come.

In October, after baby Janet's death in the summer and the mother's own illness, the family packed Janet off to Battle Creek for rest and treatments in the sanitarium. There James visited her and was relieved to find her looking better, with some of her old cheerfulness. But as her second year away from Macalester stretched out, she grew more rebellious, and wrote:

> I am willing to live on bread (graham bread) and water (filtered water) for Macalester, but it is my right to eat it in my own house with my own dear husband and children around me . . . For more than a year the children and I have been homesick but we have held our peace.

In late spring she wrote again:

> I wish I could settle you as easily as the baby . . . I am in favor of returning before Commencement unless you are *sure* of resigning. And you know *no* Board would accept your resignation. I do not "urge you to stay in that position." I have not done so for a long time. I have only encouraged you in the work you have undertaken but if you are determined to go elsewhere . . .
>
> No, you will probably keep right on at Macalester, rebuked by the Lord for your lack of faith and trust, and your work crowned with success and honor. But I hope you will not be

President, unless the good Lord sends endowment like manna. And, Oh! that He would grant you a new and deeper supply of hope and courage.

At times James felt that she was less than realistic. She had received at Christmas a ten-dollar bill. This she proposed to give to the Macalester missionary society. It worried her that she had given nothing for home and foreign missions for so long and that, on their present twelve hundred dollars a year, they had not been tithing regularly. To this proposal James responded with some heat:

You would be foolish to send one dollar to the Miss. Soc. here. The problem with us is how to get our daily bread and pay our debts. I doubt if any missionaries in our church are as hard pressed as I am . . . I despair of ever living a decent life in this bankrupt world. It is grind, grind, grind till no life, no spirits are left in one . . . If life is to continue long this way I hope my days may soon be numbered. In fact death is to be preferred for all of us.

In the winter Grandmother Wallace died. James, in New York at the time, hurried back for his mother's funeral and returned East again. Another chapter closed for him. His mother had been very dear to him. Her piercing eyes looked right through things, and her sympathy for him and for his work was always warm. For some time she had been paying for clothing for the boys. She had saved money here and there and from time to time would forward him a check to help him with his family in these straitened times. Once, for instance, when in the West, she had planned a trip through Yellowstone Park. Instead, however, she had forwarded to James the money this would have cost.

Not having yet had any encouragement to return to Macalester, in early June of 1896 Janet wrote that she and the children had moved into Belvidere, the old Wallace homestead in the country. She wrote:

I never knew this country place was so charming. Everything is as green as Eden, and now that the shower is over the birds are singing. The house is very comfortably furnished and de-

lightfully roomy after our being packed like sardines for eight-
een months . . . Each of the boys is perceptibly taller since
having a room of his own.

Six weeks later she wrote again:

You know how keenly desirous of returning home we have
been. But now I doubt if any of us will want to leave this home
—it seems so already! In less than six weeks . . .

Somewhat to her husband's alarm, Janet had kept up a correspondence with Mrs. Thaw through all this time. She had urged
James not to be diffident in asking Mrs. Thaw for money for the
college. She was not in the least diffident herself and had dropped
a hint that some of the faculty houses needed repair. Now she was
to receive from Mrs. Thaw a liberal check she had not hinted for,
a gift to the family which she needed. Most of it had at once to
go for debts she had incurred. Nevertheless, even among the children, it caused great rejoicing. Times were hard in the Wallace
family, but somehow they always managed at least to eat, if not
always much, at least regularly. One day Mrs. Wallace spent her
last dollar. The grocery order, amounting to $4.00, she had charged
for the time being to her father. Then Robin came running in
with $4.50 he had earned. "Here is my money," he said, "keep it
for me." Another emergency was past.

Sometimes she felt that her husband was allowing himself to be
imposed upon:

It seems to me that the moment Mr. Lewis [a trustee] says "College will close!" you forget everything else, as Anthony did
when Cleopatra turned sail. Better let the college close than *you*
to close your earthly career. And *that* would not be much worse
than for you to lose your youth and freshness and elasticity. If
you can *clinch* all your talking to those men, and insure the
perpetuity of a college that can pay *living salaries*, well and
good. But have you before God a right to utterly wear out your
family for any cause? I don't mean that we are worn out *now*,
we are not. But how long are we to live on hopes? Thanks to
God and his handmaid, Mrs. Thaw, *we* are perfectly comforta-

ble and this new home is all that heart could wish except for your absence. But *how are you*—physically and mentally?

Janet was actually not only feeling the pinch of poverty but she felt humiliated and almost disgraced that they could not be with James and live as "Christian people should." She spent much time in tears and in prayer. The Wooster relatives thought the situation serious and they warned him, urging him to give up the college. "Why should you," his sister wrote, "forsake your own five bairns, good ones, too, for the sake of even a hundred others?" He came for his vacation with them in August and at the end moved them once more back to their neglected house in Macalester. With deep satisfaction Janet Wallace re-established their home and entered into the college and community life.

Life was normal once again. And they were still poor. As in most families, clothes were handed down from parents to children and from child to child. Janet was skillful at ripping up old garments and making them fit a smaller child. Food was very plain. Each child had assigned tasks around the house, sifting ashes for unburned coal, cleaning lamps, washing dishes, dusting. Outside the home the boys found jobs as they could, to earn a little money, and continued to do so all the time they were growing up.

One thing that helped Dr. Wallace, an old alumnus has written, was his ability to take himself now and then "out of the magnetic field of stress." He remembers being on the campus one day in the dark of the college's depression. "Some of the faculty and students, Dr. Wallace among them, were playing ball. Dr. Wallace was doing his share with all the abandon and enthusiasm of a teenager. In his shirt-sleeves he knocked out a good base-hit, and I can still see him take off for first base, grinning happily."

Back in 1894 he had invested in Wisconsin land the small sum he had from the settling of his father's estate in Ohio. He wanted land so "it would not get away" from him. In his not infrequent visits to St. Croix Falls seeking students and financial support he had often stayed with Major J. S. Baker, a real-estate man, and from him he had made inquiries about unimproved land in Polk County, a district just beginning to develop into a prosperous dairying region. The result was the Baker-Wallace Pool, which acquired four thousand acres, at $1.80 an acre, on the east and west shores of Sucker Lake. In 1901, with the debt finally lifted from the college, Dr. Wallace felt that he could give some attention to the development of a part of this as a vacation retreat for himself and his family. There was a high peninsula along one side, called Pine Island, because loggers in spring had often flooded the neck between it and the mainland. The large trees had been removed from it, leaving only small trees and underbrush. This Pine Island Dr. Wallace now arranged with Mr. Baker to take over for his own use. It had great possibilities if reforested, and would make an admirable place of escape.

From this time on, almost as soon as commencement was over the Wallace family packed their trunks and took off for Pine Island. At first they camped. Cooking was done over a wood fire in the open and served on a table built under a tree. Food consisted largely of oatmeal, corn meal, bread, fish, milk, butter, and vegetables secured from a farmer nearby. After two or three years James purchased one hundred dollars' worth of lumber at a sawmill and Rob and Ben built a cabin, to which later a large screened porch was added. For supplies and mail they rowed down and across the lake a mile and three quarters. Soon Dr. Wallace, with the help of his sons, who could now dig holes to their hearts' content, was beautifying his land. He set out young trees by the thousands; jack, white, red, and Scotch pines; blue, white, and Norway spruce; tamarack, white fir, Douglas fir, and balsam. Pine Island, later to be called Wallace Island, became a paradise of trees.

He set out fruit trees, too, apples especially, and plums, also some small fruits; raspberries, and ever-bearing strawberries. There was a rhubarb bed as well. Then he cleared a sunny spot for a garden, where he grew everything from lettuce, peas, and beans, to watermelon and cantaloupe. In a diary which Aunt Maude kept of the days at "Wappy," there was usually listed the day on which they picked the first sweet corn of the season, the number of tomatoes and cucumbers brought in on a given day. On this day, during a blazing drought, they had all got out and carried water to the garden; on another, "Prof" had planted potatoes or harvested two bushels of plums, or some one of them had gathered a pail of blueberries or blackberries in the woods. Sometimes they went as far as Amery and came back with a crate or two of peaches or some cherries for a pie.

Gradually, too, other facilities were added to the camp. A second cabin was built for overflow, an icehouse, filled during the winter from the lake, and finally a combination garage and barn. After his retirement James and Maude (his second wife) stayed later and later in the season, when nights were frosty and days none too warm. They loved to watch the autumn sun through yellow leaves and the whitecaps on the lake. Even in November they would go out, for a few days at a time to gather in the last of the root crops for their cellar in town, or the jams and jellies made during the summer, and to put the place in order for the winter snows. In the fireplace they had put a heating device to keep them comfortable.

Except in these late-fall visits, they were rarely alone at "Wappy." There was a procession of invited guests, their friends and their children's friends, and "their sisters and their cousins and their aunts." They made them all welcome. The children themselves, after they had scattered, loved to come back for a few days or a week or two, bringing their children. All the grandchildren learned to swim there; and their first experiences paddling in the lake were duly recorded. People would drive out from St. Paul and Minneapolis for lunch or supper and would often spend the night; sometimes they would stay several days; once in a while they would bring a tent along, set it up on the place, and spend a week or two.

For the children, "Wappy" was perhaps the home they loved best; it was a place where they had chores to do, yes, but mostly they had fun. They did things there with their father and mother, with each other. They learned to dive, to manage a boat in a storm; when the waves were too high they walked around the lake for the milk, through the woods. They took long moonlit trips in the canoe, had sings before a roaring fire, supper or marshmallow roasts on the beach, but perhaps most of all they enjoyed those icy dips at dawn. They adopted at "Wappy" a family custom of "summer birthdays." Each child chose his (or her) own summer date—a kind of extra dividend.

They would decorate the table with greenery for the occasion, make an arch of ferns over the table; there were simple presents, some real, some merely jokes. There would be a special dinner, always chicken bought from some neighboring farmer, and always ice cream made from real country cream. Those were happy family times, into which their father entered with gay abandon.

It was a shame, he thought, that so beautiful a sheet of water should be known as Sucker Lake. The Indians, he ascertained, had called it Wahpuggaisee. He took the matter up with authorities in Washington and had the name officially changed to Wapogasset. "Wappy" it was called in the family for short. He helped also to organize the Lake Wapogasset Improvement Association, which, among other things, stocked the lake with fish and built a dam at the outlet to hold the lake the year round at about the same level. Later he was to help also in establishing a public park for the community. Often in his later days at the camp he would be asked to go on Sunday to preach at some village. Once, it is recorded, on such an occasion he chose as his subject the old prophets and crop failures. He spoke with feeling; his own garden was burning up.

Though he could not stay at "Wappy" all through the summers, Dr. Wallace could go and come, and there fish and row, chop wood, clear underbrush, and plant. He drew new vigor from his contacts with the soil; his life outdoors helped to keep him young in body and in spirit; there he went back to his boyhood on the farm. He could get away from official duties, too, and relax in old clothes. He could even on occasion shave off his sideburns, and did, greatly to Janet's consternation one morning when she thought she saw a stranger working round the woodpile. It is said she refused to let him leave the camp until he had grown them back.

During the years of his presidency the children were rapidly growing up. He had from their early years shown great satisfaction in them, noting their several traits and tendencies, teasing them, instructing them, and loving them. In 1901 Helen and Ben both read papers at the junior entertainment and "did themselves much credit . . . I was surprised especially at Benny's paper." A year later they were both graduated from Macalester College with honors. He was proud to see his daughter's commencement oration spoken of in the Minneapolis *Journal* as notable for its diction and for the means it suggested for the idealization of life. He was still prouder two years later when Ben, at the age of twenty-two, was chosen first Rhodes scholar from the state of Minnesota and was sent to Oxford University, England, for three years.

James Wallace had himself been receiving recognition of various sorts. In June of 1899 Wooster College had conferred on him, *in absentia*, the degree of Doctor of Laws. Dr. Wallace was at that time in no mood for degrees and tried his best to refuse. He wrote the secretary of the college trustees in Wooster a characteristic note:

> Yours of the 17th informing me that the Board of Trustees on the recommendation of the Faculty has conferred on me the degree of LL.D. is received. Appreciating very heartily this high opinion and good intent of these honorable bodies I must decline emphatically to accept the title. God knows I have had trouble enough wearing the degree I already have and to add another literary degree to a man whose mind, soul and strength have been occupied in wrestling with a college debt as high as the Colossus of Rhodes is worse—much worse than cruelty to animals . . . Please, therefore, assure the brethren that their "favor" is strongly and emphatically declined. In fact they ought to apologize.

In 1903 McCormick Theological Seminary in Chicago notified him of his election to its Board of Trustees, a recognition of his spiritual attainments and practical judgment. This quiet, unassuming man was coming to be known all through the Middle West. A letter from Mrs. Thaw enclosed one from Daniel S. Gregory, former president of Lake Forest University, who said of him: "I know of no man on the continent who has been doing a nobler or more self-sacrificing work than he has been doing, and I know, also, that he has had the opportunity of making changes that would have been greatly to his pecuniary advantage."

In the spring of 1904 one of these offers came from Lane
Theological Seminary in Cincinnati. It wished him to be president. Dr. Wallace wavered in his decision. His father-in-law and
others urged him to accept. He was the man for the place. The
seminary was well located to appeal to students north and south,
theologically neither too liberal nor too conservative. The milder
climate would benefit Janet's health, which had been declining.
He would have adequate salary, and have a chance to teach
Greek exegesis, a field for which he was well equipped. Once
again he was torn between two loves—the love for Macalester
for which he had toiled and suffered, and the love of teaching
Greek to eager students in a quiet retreat. Macalester, however,
was just launching its endowment drive, and he feared for what
his resignation might do to this. Finally he sent a night letter
to Cincinnati, declining the offer. The trustees, thinking it use-
less to urge him further after these few weeks of waiting, elected
that same afternoon their own chairman to the presidency. On
further thought and prayer, however, Dr. Wallace decided to
accept after all and dispatched another telegram, this time to
the chairman at his home. The telegram was slipped under the
door after the chairman had left for the Board meeting. Instead
of going home after the meeting, the chairman went off to his
summer cottage and did not find the telegram until sometime
during the next day. In the meantime the papers had announced
Dr. McKibbin's election and it was too late. The final decision
was made for Dr. Wallace and he stayed to push Macalester's
endowment drive.

XV

The End of a Chapter

The world is too much with us; late and soon,
Getting and spending, we lay waste our powers.
WILLIAM WORDSWORTH

IN the fall of 1901 Macalester opened without debt or deficit.
Through all that year there was a general good feeling and a
spirit of hopefulness among faculty and students. Of course,
there was yet no backlog of endowment and so no regular income upon which to draw for the month-to-month operating
expenses. The temptation was strong for the friends of Macalester
to sit back now and rejoice and enjoy a breathing spell, but for
a harried president there could be no peace. By Christmas, salaries
were again somewhat in arrears, and President Wallace found
himself digging into his own resources (the Baker-Wallace Pool)
for a hundred and fifty dollars so that one of his professors could
go home over the holidays to see his parents. Nevertheless by
June of 1902 they were once more in the clear, and again in
1903 he could announce no deficit. Generous friends of the
college had come to the rescue in time.

In his report to the Synod in the fall of 1902 President Wallace
had appealed to them to awake to their obligations in raising
an endowment. At his suggestion they did pass a resolution commending such an effort to the Presbyterians of the state. "It is
the deliberate judgment of the Synod," they said, "that the hour
for this undertaking has struck." The occasion was the conditional

offer of Mr. George D. Dayton. He would give toward the endowment $100,000 if $400,000 more were raised, or $250,000 toward a million. Unfortunately no date was set for the end of the campaign. Though Synod pledged their support, yet apparently they expected the Macalester Board of Trustees and the president to do the work. They did not take hold. Nor did the businessmen of the Twin Cities. Some of them indeed thought Mr. Dayton's offer fantastic.

Both Dr. Wallace and his faculty were annoyed at the prevalent attitude. They felt no easing of their personal financial obligations. In early 1904 Dr. Wallace was saying: "I do not think that we have ever found it so impossible to live within our income as this year," and he went on to tell of a cloak Mrs. Wallace had bought, reduced to thirty-five dollars. "It is," he said, "a handsome garment, and one she very much needed. I am very glad she bought it, though it will be hard to pay for it." The upswing in business had not yet reached the academic level.

That winter of 1904 the Board finally chose to launch its drive for endowment. In the old Aberdeen Hotel in St. Paul they gave a banquet honoring James Wallace to a selected group of forty men. Mr. Dayton renewed his offer and in his speech challenged both their patriotism and their loyalty to Christian education. He was "consecrating his business life to this end." He told them:

> . . . it is patriotism for us to establish on a certain and substantial foundation just such an institution as I have outlined and make it a power for good citizenship after we are dead and forgotten.
> . . . You who are conservative business men can here find an investment that will pay you dividends of increasing satisfaction as the years go by—an investment more enduring and more valuable than stocks and bonds, because here human lives will be ennobled, strengthened, Christianized, and sent out to bless the world.

The newspapers the next morning announced that $250,000 toward the half million had been conditionally subscribed. Dr. Wallace had received many personal tributes at this meeting.

He was greatly moved, but knew that these have little value in themselves. He called for prompt and vigorous action. He and his faculty needed meat, not celery with salt alone.

This time the ministers of the Twin Cities organized for the drive. The president of the Board, the fiscal secretary, one or two others, and, of course, Dr. Wallace threw themselves into the effort. But summer is a lean time; one finds people with money more easily when trees are bare and summer hotels are closed. The tempo of the drive slowed down. President Wallace longed to give it all up in favor of a younger man. Perhaps he should accept the offer to become a field secretary for the Presbyterian Temperance Committee. He believed after all in the movement, had often spoken in the Twin Cities for temperance. Yet again he held tight to the old plow handle; somehow he could not let go.

In the fall he made his usual report to Synod. He was able to say that at last Macalester had enrolled, during the preceding year, better than two hundred students. Its three most pressing needs now were endowment, a science building, and a women's dormitory. The experiment in coeducation had been a success. Synod's response was disappointing. They seemed to feel still that the trustees should raise endowment from the wealthy few. President Wallace and his Board held that Macalester was the responsibility of the whole church membership.

In the summer the Board had authorized the publication of a Macalester College *Bulletin* for the promotion of the campaign and had made President Wallace editor. This was to take the place of the *Echo,* edited and published by the students. It was to contain news of the college and the alumni as well as promotional material. In this, gifts were announced from time to time: five thousand dollars from this person, one thousand dollars from that, and many smaller sacrificial gifts. The alumni had been urged to do what they could, and many had given beyond their means. Some gifts seemed "more like the currency of heaven than of earth." The *Bulletin,* even though it added to his duties, gave Dr. Wallace an opportunity to speak his mind on college policies and college problems, and he made good use of it, particularly in denouncing the abuses of college athletics.

In the spring of 1905, once more, word came from Mrs. Thaw. All through these hapless years she had indeed kept a watchful eye on Macalester. Once she had inquired as to the chance of selling any of her land out there. Again she had asked for details of the college budget, and, reading them, had protested the drastic cut Dr. Wallace had taken in his own salary. In 1895 she had sent the manager of the Thaw estate out to look over the Macalester Addition. He had seemed well pleased and, leaving, had remarked that the Thaw children would have some money to invest before long. Actually one son, Edward, had later bought a block of this Addition for $7800, and Mrs. Thaw herself had taken $8000 more of it. On all of this they had been paying taxes and the various assessments for improvements. Now they deeded this, with the ten acres of her original purchase, back to the college, free of encumbrances. It was the heart-warming gesture of a gracious Christian lady. With this the total benefactions of the Thaw family to Macalester had amounted to $45,800, $5000 of which was a cash gift and the remainder the value of the property given back.

That same spring Dr. Wallace made up his mind to ask Andrew Carnegie for a science building, fireproofed and fully equipped. To this end he went East to present his plea in person. On the way he made several stops. In Philadelphia John Converse gave him $5000 for endowment. In Princeton he visited John Hall, former member of the Macalester faculty, who had accepted an instructorship at Princeton, and who was now wishing he could return to Macalester. There "surveying its [Princeton's] glory and then thinking of little humble Macalester," Dr. Wallace found the tears welling often in his eyes. In New York he made his headquarters at the Biblical Seminary on Lexington Avenue. Of this, a friend of college days, Dr. W. W. White, was president. Unfortunately Dr. Wallace was unable to gain an interview with Mr. Carnegie, although he was greeted cordially by his representative, who promised to bring the material prepared to the attention of his chief. Deeply disappointed at his failure, Dr. Wallace went back to the seminary and confided in all frankness his discouragement over the Macalester situation to his old friend.

To his surprise Dr. White suggested that he take a position in the Biblical Seminary. This new-type seminary, its founder thought, had a great future; he was planning to enlarge its faculty and expand its reach, by summer schools, to Winona Lake, Indiana, and other regions. Dr. Wallace was interested; he was weary of constant travel, of soliciting money from apathetic people, and he longed for a quiet study where he could read and think and do some writing. The indifference of the churches, the slow progress toward the goal of endowment, the constant irritation over the college's inability to pay salaries promptly, made him willing to explore this possibility. He went back to Macalester to ponder it, telling only his family of the suggestion.

He had already made it clear that he wished the trustees to hunt a successor. Even the St. Paul *Pioneer Press* had quoted him as saying:

> I have carried the college through its economic stress and it seems wise to me that the institution should find some strong man to carry on the work.

But no one yet had acted on his suggestion. Through the spring and the summer on the home front, therefore, he continued to seek endowment, current funds, and students. As he had opportunity he studied plans, costs, specifications of recently built women's dormitories at other colleges. The one that seemed most nearly to be what he wished for Macalester was that of the Western College for Women at Oxford, Ohio. He hoped that within the next year the money would be in hand and excavation be begun.

In September a telegram from Dr. White notified him that the Biblical Seminary earnestly desired his services, at once, if possible. They were offering him three thousand dollars for the first year, with every prospect of an increase and permanent appointment later. There he would teach Greek, both elementary and advanced, one or two classes in English Bible, be dean of the summer school at Winona Lake, and have certain other duties. It was rumored that Miss Helen Gould was back of the institution and would be giving it one million dollars. It was time now to tell the trustees of the offer. They passed a resolution urging him to remain, advancing his salary to two thousand dollars a year, assuring him that his and other faculty salaries would be met from month to month. One of them wrote him that it would be a disaster for him to leave now. Dr. Wallace remained, but held the other offer in abeyance. He would not leave at least until after Christmas.

All fall of 1905 he and Mrs. Wallace debated the issues. They feared the unfamiliar, were unsure how well they would transplant at their age. Besides, since Mr. Hall had gone to Princeton, Dr. Wallace had once more been teaching Greek and finding the work enjoyable. At the office, too, he now finally had the help of a stenographer for two hours a week. Their children, especially Helen and DeWitt, urged them to go. A leave of absence would be a boon to both Dr. and Mrs. Wallace; both needed change and relief from constant suspense. To be sure, he had served notice on the Synod some time ago that to avoid a breakdown he was forced to give up carrying the active financial burden of the college. Two members of the Board had presented Macalester's case to Rockefeller's General Education Board and Dr. Wallace was hopeful that Macalester would be put on the list for a grant. They had called also on Carnegie. He felt, however, that it would still take a year or two to put Macalester on its financial feet. He was aggrieved that the wealth of the Twin Cities had not yet risen to Mr. Dayton's offer. Yet the St. Paul Y.M.C.A. had raised $250,000 in a month. He said:

> . . . If Macalester College was fairly well endowed it would do more for the moral and spiritual betterment of this world than any half dozen Young Men's Christian Associations in America.

Dr. Wallace was firmly convinced that the growth of the college depended on the expansion of its scientific department. Exasperated over the failure of men of means to respond to the challenge of Mr. Dayton, he evolved a substitute plan. He wrote to Mr. Dayton pointing out that the great scientific schools at Princeton, Yale, Harvard, Lafayette and other colleges had each been started by some individual making a large gift. He suggested that he give $150,000 or $200,000 for a school of science at

Macalester on the condition that others subscribe to the fund. He proposed that the school be named The George D. Dayton School of Science and that Mr. Dayton take charge of the investment of the endowment and add to it as he was able from time to time. After much heart searching, Mr. Dayton replied, "It is not wise for one man at this stage to do too much." He added:

> There must be a combination of interest and money in order to make the institution a certain success and I am inclined to believe that it is wiser to wait a little longer in the hope that some of the men who can and ought, will do handsomely by it.

So this dream, too, faded. But before many months, word came that the Carnegie Foundation had granted to Macalester College $30,000 for a science hall, provided an additional $150,000 be raised. Dr. Wallace at once wrote thanking them and requesting that they increase the gift to $50,000, provided that the trustees raise additional funds. This they later did.

Once more at commencement, 1906, Dr. Wallace reported to his Board a deficit, greater than usual. They listened with grave faces, and then, as he wrote in the *Bulletin:*

> When the exact amount needed was ascertained, R. A. Kirk put his shoulder to one wheel and R. C. Jefferson to another and Thomas R. Janney to a third and George D. Dayton to a fourth: and in about ten minutes the chariot of Macalester College was out of the financial ditch and upon solid ground.

This over, Dr. Wallace asked for leave of absence for a year. Reluctantly the Board granted his request. The committee on a new president must now begin a diligent search. Dr. Wallace hoped that he could start his leave at once, but with no new president in sight he felt it his duty to stay through the summer to lead the canvass for students. He had given Dr. White his word, however, that he would be on hand at the opening of the seminary in October.

It was high time that Dr. and Mrs. Wallace had a change of clime, both weather-wise and spirit-wise. Mrs. Wallace, never strong, had long needed freedom from overwork and care. She had borne seven children, had reared five of them, though of these Miriam was still a young girl. The daughter Helen was right when she remarked: There had been "too much cold house and irregular salary," for both of them. Even when, the year before, the trustees had promised faithfully regular payments, it had been December before they had received even the first half of the September salary. No, it was good that they were going. James Wallace himself felt nearly at his tether's end.

XVI

On Leave

Sweet are the thoughts that savour of content
The quiet mind is richer than a crown.

ROBERT GREENE

AT the end of September 1906 Dr. and Mrs. Wallace went East, he to his new work in New York, and she with Miriam to East Northfield, Massachusetts. Dr. Wallace thought that her health would improve more rapidly in the quiet of a New England town than in noisy New York. They had chosen East Northfield because there she would also be near DeWitt, who had entered Mt. Hermon School.

Dr. Wallace was soon happily at work in the Biblical Seminary. "I have great studies before me," he wrote. He was teaching interpretation or hermeneutics, education, history of religions, etc., and Greek Testament. His classes were largely of women between twenty-five and forty, training as lay workers of various sorts, some to go as missionaries, some to assist in churches in this country. They were eager, purposeful students. He found himself spending many hours studying the various interpretations of parts of the Scriptures and rejoicing in the experience. He would like, he felt, to write a book on Isaiah, for school use, another on Jesus as a teacher. A teacher himself, he was quick to discern methods and aims in the work of another of an earlier day. He was full of ideas.

Here in New York he had once more time to think and a

chance to listen. In the brisk atmosphere of this cosmopolitan city
he could feel his soul expanding. One Sunday he could go to hear
Hugh Black, whose books he had read, on another, perhaps Dr.
Aked of Liverpool. "Great preaching," he wrote, "is the most
uplifting power on earth," and he was happy to come under its
influence. In the spring of his first year there, the National Ar-
bitration and Peace Congress was held in Carnegie Hall. He was
asked to represent Macalester. This movement, he felt, was at
the heart of things. To be a part of it moved him deeply. Soon
afterward, it was told, he was speaking on peace in a church in
Pennsylvania, at Montrose, with such vigor and enthusiasm that
as he finished, a lawyer listener could hardly restrain himself
from shouting, "Go on!" He lectured on the subject in various
churches and reports came back of people much impressed with
his learning, his wide-ranging illustrations, with his actual eloquence. On such occasions he had a firm outline, but his language was often largely impromptu. He knew he had one qualifi-
cation for speaking—"The hearty response in my own heart to
the truth I utter." Of a Washington's Birthday address he gave
to the students at the Biblical Seminary he wrote to his wife, because he knew the account would please her. He had received
much applause, many congratulations. "A great speech.—We
must use you more in public," said his old friend Dr. White of
the seminary.

Here, too, in New York, he saw old friends as they passed
through, met others, with no thought of seeking money. He followed up his friendship with the Martin family, made years before, and he and John C. Martin became warm friends. To his
surprise and pleasure, one day Martin offered him ten thousand
dollars for the founding of a department of Bible at Macalester,
provided he, James Wallace, would be its head, and provided
that fifteen thousand dollars additional could be found for the
purpose. One Sunday at Fifth Avenue Baptist Church he met
John D. Rockefeller, Sr., and they greeted each other pleasantly. One day Dr. Wallace went down to the New York Tombs
to visit Harry Thaw, a former student at Wooster Academy, now
confined there awaiting trial for the shooting of Stanford White,
the architect. White had allegedly been intimate with Thaw's

young wife, the actress, Evelyn Nesbit. He had a pleasant talk with him about old times, his mother, life in prison. Then Mrs. Thaw, Sr., appeared, and with her he had a pleasant visit, too, and she had asked him to call at her hotel. He had found sitting outside the cell "the amiable, rather sweet, confiding young wife," and he "pitied her exceedingly . . . No doubt she had been a giddy, indiscreet, and foolish girl, but perhaps more sinned against than sinning." Dr. Wallace was open-minded and generous in his estimates. Later when he was subpoenaed by the prosecution, he told the bearer of the subpoena that it had been a mistake to call him, for "he would have to testify that the boy was abnormal."

When they were on the eastern seaboard, Europe seemed nearer. The salt air quickened their imaginations. In the spring of 1907 Janet decided to accompany her sister Miriam Maude to England. Ben was in Oxford and the time was right. They went over on a freighter carrying cattle. James had written them not to worry about anything at home but to "Enjoy life, be happy, be thankful. Be well. Be careless. Stay long enough." He had hoped the trip would rest and refresh Janet. It did. She thoroughly enjoyed every moment. She was the best walker aboard ship, and was never sick a moment. England she loved, particularly seeing Ben, his quarters, and his friends at Oxford. But before the end of May the sisters were landing again, in Philadelphia.

In New York they were surprised to find that James, now, was scheduled to sail on June 2, on the *Irene*, for Naples. On the morning of his sailing he became engrossed in a conversation with a friend uptown and forgot to look at his watch. When finally he remembered, he was almost too late. Baggage in hand, he fled to the wharf, only to find that the *Irene* had already pulled out into the river. He chartered a launch, was taken out, and climbed up over the side. Thus began a trip that was in every way a success. The sea was smooth, and to his great satisfaction he found aboard an old friend, a former Macalester student of the class of 1899. From Naples he went on to Athens, where he brushed up his Greek, renewed old friendships, and revisited spots he had explored as a young man. On the way back, he, too, went to Oxford. Then on August 6 he and Ben, his period as

Rhodes scholar completed, sailed for home together. It was a
happy summer. On this side, he went first to Oak Bluffs, Massachusetts, where Mrs. Wallace had been staying since her return.

Dr. Wallace was surprised to find that Janet, with her usual
temerity, had in his absence done what he had feared to do; she
had written R. A. Kirk, vice-president of the Macalester Board,
telling him how much good the year of leave had done her husband, and had raised the question of extending this another year.
The request had been granted. Dr. Wallace went back with
pleasure to the Biblical Seminary. Janet, whose health had been
only temporarily improved by her trip, went to Battle Creek
again. Dr. Wallace worried about her: "I fear that Janet's health
is critical . . . Her vitality is low—diabetic tendency." Later
she went to Clifton Springs to the sanitarium.

Of course both of them avidly devoured every bit of news
from Macalester. In early January of 1907 the Board of Trustees
had found the successor to Dr. Wallace as president. He was T.
Morey Hodgman, a Presbyterian elder and a professor at the
University of Nebraska, who had had considerable administrative experience. Before electing him, they had finally to act on
Dr. Wallace's often tabled resignation, and in doing so they
found occasion to express to him a little of what was in their
hearts. B. H. Schriber, secretary of the Board, wrote:

> While taking this action which you have requested, the Di-
> rectors, both as a Board and as individuals, desire to express
> their appreciation of the great services you have rendered the
> college during the years you have been its chief executive.
> By an unfaltering devotion to the interests of the institution;
> by continuous effort in its behalf, many times at the cost to
> yourself of personal sacrifice; by perseverance and patience in
> your labors in times of great discouragement; by admirable
> work in the class room, and by a sympathetic communication
> with its constituents throughout the whole state, you have
> been the chief instrument in making the college what it has
> become, an institution with not only a good history but a
> good outlook as well.

You were made President of the college when it was greatly

embarrassed financially; it is now without debt. Your first classes were small; the college now has a large enrollment of students. You found it difficult during most of the years of your administration to secure funds in large amounts for the institution; now friends have appeared, many of them made by your faith and faithfulness, whose purpose it is to provide for the college a substantial endowment.

. . . you have set a high moral standard for the college and by your doctrine and example you have made an atmosphere in which it is easy for the young to embrace and to conform their lives to the best standards. Our institution has no better testimonial than the men and women of worth whose characters are made strong while in Macalester under your superintending care.

At the end they had expressed the desire that Dr. Wallace, after the leave of absence, continue with the college in the professorship he had filled so long, and they requested him also to act as dean. In the fall of 1907 the new President Hodgman announced to the Synod that Dr. Wallace had been made vice-president in special charge of the religious work of the institution. His salary was fixed at $2000, with the free use of his former residence. At the same time President Hodgman had announced that "for reasons satisfactory to himself Mr. George Dayton had withdrawn his offer of $100,000 provided $400,000 more be raised."

In December of 1907 the new dormitory for women was dedicated. Wallace Hall had been named in honor of him who had dreamed and planned for the building for years. It had been finished free of debt. Dr. and Mrs. Wallace, unable to be present, were represented by their son Robert, who in their name presented the dormitory with a picture of Dante and Beatrice and a set of Shakespeare's works. James Wallace's picture hung on one of its walls, his books lay on a table in the living room.

At the end of their second year Dr. and Mrs. Wallace headed for Macalester. They stopped in Wooster to visit relatives. Janet's mother had died in the spring and they wished especially to be with Dr. Davis, who now that his wife had gone, leaned much on the daughters. Dr. Wallace was scheduled to give the baccalaureate address at Macalester for the class of 1908, to which his son Robert belonged. Commencement for him was a home-coming. He addressed the students at the last chapel service of the year. Then on Sunday he delivered his sermon, "The Gospel of God,—the Power of God, the Wisdom of God." It was strong and effective, the product of much thinking. At the graduation exercises President Hodgman spoke of the struggle of Dr. Wallace which he had won against great odds. Macalester, he said, had entered a new era. He gave the Wallace administration credit for initiating the action which led to the building of Wallace Hall, the securing of $50,000 from Andrew Carnegie for a science hall, a $75,000 pledge from the General Education Board (Rockefeller) and a $50,000 pledge from James J. Hill for endowment. The Hodgman administration was pushing to secure a total of $450,000. There still remained $95,000 to be raised.

From various remarks and incidents Dr. Wallace gathered that President Hodgman did not wish him to return to Macalester. Accordingly he requested the trustees for a third year of leave. Then, commencement over, he and his family went off to their camp at Lake Wapogasset and there spent a large part of the summer outdoors.

It appeared presently that President Hodgman bitterly resented the strings attached to the Martin offer of $10,000. He wrote Dr. Wallace, accusing him of pushing himself upon the college. "I was simply brought here," he said, "to bring this institution out of a hole and get it in shape for you to enjoy the rest of your life. Were you and your friends willing to do your share towards making your return possible, I should not feel so strongly upon the matter, but you are all simply waiting for me to do the work."

Cut to the quick, Dr. Wallace sent an extract of the letter to several of the trustees. Mr. R. A. Kirk wrote back:

> It goes without saying that none of us approves the letter . . . Dr. Hodgman was very much worked up about the condition of the endowment fund, and especially at the failure to increase the Biblical Department Fund and permitted himself to write in a way that I do not doubt he has already regretted,

though, as yet, the matter has not been taken up with him. Dr. Hodgman wrote that letter without conferring with any member of the Board and no one knew of its having been sent until after it had gone.

Mr. Thomas A. Dickson, former president of the Board, with whom Dr. Wallace had once crossed swords, but who was now again on terms of happy friendship, called the letter brutal, said he had read it "with mingled pain and indignation." Professor Shaw, too, was incensed, but felt things should be hushed up until the endowment was completed. He passed on to Dr. Wallace in confidence the news that Frederick Weyerhaeuser was planning to give $50,000 to the endowment fund. He hoped that the goal would be reached by the commencement of 1909. Professor Anderson also wrote Dr. Wallace in the winter: "Prexy may not want you back, but I feel sure that everyone else does." Late in May of that year another letter from Mr. Shaw urged Dr. Wallace to make it clear to the trustees that he was ready to come back if the Board still desired him.

The decision as to what to do was not easy. Dr. White had invited him to continue at Biblical Seminary. Dr. Wallace enjoyed his teaching there and his outside speaking engagements. He liked the theory of the seminary curriculum, with the Bible placed at the center and all other studies circling about it to clarify its message and make it significant in all the various areas of thought and action. But the seminary, like Macalester, was bedeviled with financial problems; even there the salaries fell into arrears. Besides, where would they live if they were to stay permanently at the seminary? Janet could not endure the noise of New York. James was not happy to think of daily commuting from the suburbs. The Presbyterian Board of Temperance had again indicated that it would like to have him as a field secretary. And the president of James Millikin University, of Illinois, had written inviting him to apply for the position of professor of Bible there.

When the final moment for decision came, Dr. and Mrs. Wallace followed the leanings of their hearts. Old friends urged their return. Dean Anderson wrote that both church and col-

lege had suffered religiously since their departure and it would
be a calamity if they failed to come back. The one real obstacle
was the attitude of the president. Dr. Wallace hoped that by
keeping himself in the background and doing a good job in the
department of Bible he could in time overcome the president's
opposition. He wrote the Board that he was ready to return if
it so desired. A telegram soon came back from Professor Downing following commencement in 1910. It read:

> Trustees announced your return. Financial help provided.
> Zeus and victory.

It was rumored that George D. Dayton had underwritten part
of Dr. Wallace's salary. To the joy of everyone, early in the
summer the $450,000 goal was reached. In this was the $10,000
gift of Mr. Martin. Dr. Wallace had tried to persuade Mr. Martin to raise this to $20,000 or even $25,000, but Mr. Martin felt
he could not. This failure had probably been back of Dr. Hodgman's initial antagonism to Dr. Wallace.

His return to Macalester settled, Dr. Wallace could now devote himself to the preparation of a series of lectures he had
promised to give during the summer, at Montreat, North Caro-
lina. There Dr. White was conducting one of the extension
summer schools of his seminary. These lectures were to be on
the teachings of the Bible as related to free institutions, political
economy, international law, socialism, etc. Here Dr. Wallace
was in his element. From the middle of July to the middle of
August he lectured every other day. It was a satisfying experience for him and for his listeners. Here, too, he could lift his
eyes to the hills and there find peace, grateful rest for a tired
body and quiet for his soul that needed to gather strength for
the year ahead. Wherever he looked, there were green meadows,
and valleys and woodland, and in the distance the mist-covered
mountains.

He knew, however happy he would be to be teaching again
at Macalester, that there would be strains. As an ex-president,
with a host of friends in the faculty and the community, he must
watch his step. He had made up his mind to stay strictly out of
all administrative matters, to devote himself entirely to his own

department. After all, the setting up of this new department would be a real job. Frederick Weyerhaeuser had endowed the Bible department with $50,000. In addition there was the $10,000 of John C. Martin for the Bible-training department. He was in charge of both and would have three other professors helping him, Dr. Davis, Professors Anderson and McRae. He planned to offer twelve wide-ranging courses, covering not only several aspects of the Bible but related fields in language, history, and philosophy. He conceived the aim as twofold: to provide a well-graded instruction in the Bible for all Macalester students; and to offer special courses for those preparing for some form of Christian activity as lay workers. The church was entering, he felt, an era of the laity; the field was ripe for lay workers of every kind. Yet the theological seminaries were not open to them.

His work the last three years had been itself a preparation for this program. He was full of eagerness, was taking back many books, maps, relief maps, charts of various sorts to make his teaching realistic. He regretted only that he was not to teach the Greek New Testament. When Professor Hall had returned from Princeton to Macalester to teach, he had taken that course over and he would not give it up. There was much to think about, these days at Montreat.

Janet had gone ahead with Miriam to Macalester. She had hoped to have the old home ready for his coming in mid-August. She was vexed no little to discover that the administration was planning to use the house as a duplex, and they were expected to share it with another faculty family. She wrote to James and he advised her to go to "Wappy" and await his arrival. Once there, his first chore was to rent a house. This he found at 1628 Laurel Avenue, and they moved in at once. Miriam was now the only child at home. But at the end of August all the family, including Helen and her baby Janet, came back for a reunion, to make the new house a home.

College opened in September. What joy it was to be again with old friends, to greet them and to be welcomed by them, to go to church again in the old spot, to teach what he liked to teach, in the place he loved the best! Dr. Hodgman treated him

with a strained courtesy. That was to be expected. Dr. Wallace
kept himself in the background, devoted himself wholly to his
work. There were controversies in the faculty, in which old and
dear friends were involved, but he took no part in them. Envy
and jealousy were not characteristic of Dr. Wallace, and he sin-
cerely delighted in every advance made under the leadership of
his dynamic successor. He rejoiced to see the new science hall
go up, to know of a growing endowment, to watch the curriculum being expanded. He was disturbed when in the spring the
seniors, who had been freshmen when he had left Macalester,
asked him to deliver their baccalaureate address. He thanked
them but declined. They insisted, and finally he did yield, apparently without arousing Dr. Hodgman's ill will. Little by little,
by his sincere humility and his co-operation he was winning
the respect and confidence of the president.

As spring opened up and the ground thawed out, he was glad
from time to time to spend a day at Lake Wapogasset, improving
his land there. He put in a young orchard of apple, cherry, plum,
and walnut trees, and a row of willows along one shore.

Of course, too, he supplied pulpits here and there, and made
addresses before various organizations, on national and international subjects and on prohibition, too. In May of 1911 he was
asked to be first president of the Macalester College Peace Society, branch of the Minnesota Peace Society. Its purpose was
"to promote international peace, and the settlement of all controversies according to the principles of arbitral justice." Dr.
Wallace saw the teachings of the Bible as the key to a peace that
in time would conquer the world. In the Macalester *Bulletin*
he wrote:

> And when the Bible shall have done its work there shall be
> universal peace; right shall be supreme over wrong; society
> shall be like the garden of the Lord; the human mind shall be
> wondrously illumined; and all the powers of the world shall
> acknowledge the dominion of Jesus Christ, the Son of God.

The Bible was the center of all his thinking. He opposed La
Follette of Wisconsin when he was seeking the nomination
against Taft, because he was an "egotist and unbeliever."

At the end of his first year back at Macalester he was asked to be a "ruling elder" in the church there. It must have been with some pride that he accepted the office and was ordained to it in September 1910, thinking of his patriarchal father, in whose footsteps he was following. For nearly thirty years he, too, was yet to serve his church in this capacity. Like his forebears, he did not hesitate to speak out and if a pastor was neglectful in the preparation of his sermons, he was known to go to him in utter frankness and tell him of his failings. There was no pride of superiority in the admonitions; they were the well-thought-out advice of a friend, a man humble before his God, who craved a stronger leadership for the church.

On another occasion, years later, there was growing dissatisfaction with a minister of the Macalester church and efforts were being made to have him resign. Dr. Wallace thought the complaints quite unjust and addressed to the officers of the church a letter of protest, in which he said:

> If our pastor and myself were called before the bar of God to give an account of our stewardship toward our church, he as pastor and I as elder and member, I have not any doubt the verdict would be more to his credit than to mine . . .
>
> There are some facts connected with the history of our church since —— came that convince me that it would be well if the men of our church would judiciously raise in their minds this same question: How do I stand as a member (and maybe an officer) of this church before the bar of God in comparison with ——? Viewed as pastor and preacher, have I performed my duties as faithfully as he has performed his?

He praised the minister's preaching and pointed out that, proportionately, the membership had increased more than that of any other church in the presbytery during this pastor's incumbency.

Through all his life so far, he had hoped someday to make investments which he and Janet could lean upon when they reached retirement age. So far, beside his island home at "Wappy," he had 800 acres of wild Wisconsin land worth about $8.00 an acre. He had bought also a 160-acre farm in Cass County,

Minnesota, had shares in a lead mine in Colorado. In 1910, also, he invested in a Minneapolis company holding coal lands in British Columbia. He bought the stock at fifty cents the share, believing it was bound soon to double its value. With two other men he was sent out to look over the company's property and was impressed. He added 500 more shares to the 4500 he already had. Unfortunately, however good the vein of coal may have been, the management was dishonest and the company was plunged into bankruptcy. He had some stock in iron mines north of Duluth and wrote of wishing that he could, with a brother, invest in fruit lands in Mexico. The lead mine in Colorado paid some dividends but eventually it was closed down. It had always been more of a worry than an investment.

Like many another academic, Dr. Wallace could be easily taken in; he was too confident of the essential integrity of man, and sharps sometimes traded on that confidence. When he had moved to New York, for instance, he had gone to a cheap store in St. Paul to buy a suitcase. The new bag stood the trip to New York with him, but when he expressed it across town from the station it gave way. On close examination he then discovered that it was not leather at all, but paper cunningly devised to look like leather. The salesman had deceived him, saying it was leather. He was incensed, was going to write to the owner of the store, was provoked also at himself for being taken in. But he didn't really learn to distrust sales talk.

One other time a solicitor for a proposed book, *Past and Present of St. Paul*, talked him into letting them put his picture and a brief biography into it. He had agreed on condition that the book should adequately present the story of higher education in St. Paul and the part that Macalester had had in this. This solicitor gave him assurance that this would be done. But the promises were not carried out. He wrote in consequence a blistering letter to the publishers:

I need not tell you that all this is of the very essence of fraud . . . Doubtless you will make a good deal of money out of this work . . . But I want to say for my part, I would no more buy a book published by your house or edited by Mr. Hennessy than I would lend money to a man who had robbed me in the dead of night . . . Rather, however, than have any trouble with your agent I paid $5.00 for the book. I have seriously questioned whether to put the book into the college library or to put it into my furnace . . . You have doubtless made money out of the book but I want to say to you and Mr. Hennessy, you and your money be damned.

James Wallace woke up too often after the thief had fled; he was essentially a guileless man.

In June of 1911 he was shocked and grieved at the sudden death of his brother Robert in Colorado. The brother had been at the head of the Monte Vista bank and was a revered and outstanding member of the community. But greater griefs were to come before long. In 1913 Janet grew weaker. She had little faith in doctors or their medicines, particularly those of the allopathic school. She might take a dose of a prescription and then refuse to take the rest. She preferred to trust her instinct and her diet. Dr. T. K. Davis had planned to go with his daughter Bess to Florida for the winter, and James arranged that Janet should go along and enjoy the sunshine there. Instead she had to take to her bed at home for six weeks. In January 1914 she lapsed into unconsciousness and was taken to a sanitarium. There she responded to the feeding and to the drugs administered, and Dr. Wallace hoped that she might before long be able to go South to recuperate.

In the meantime he learned, however, of Florida's extreme laws on race segregation and he was outraged; he would send Janet somewhere else, but not to Florida; all Christian people should boycott Florida. He wrote to his father-in-law:

Florida has a law forbidding white teachers to teach colored people. It is a law that was inspired by the devil and conceived in the bottomless pit. Curses of heaven on the demons that enacted such a law. I shall try to find some decent state to which to send Janet if she gets able to go. Every Northern man in the South should denounce the law by letters to the papers, to the Governor and then get up and leave the state till it emerges from barbarism and heathenism.

But Janet's improvement was temporary. She never was able even to return home. On March 27, 1914, she died. She was fifty-six years old. For thirty-six years she and her devoted husband had struggled through life together. Though ready and indeed eager to assist anyone at any time, she had made her husband and her family her world in a peculiar sense; she was "a genius" in social matters, and yet those who knew her well felt that even in her entertaining she was acting really for them. Bearing every trial uncomplainingly and bravely, a spiritual stalwart, she was nevertheless practical in just those spots where her husband was often impractical. She complemented him. Where he was out-spoken, she was gentle; where he was excited, she was serene; where he was inclined to be a rebel, she was rather a martyr. And yet in many ways she was completely impractical where he was practical. He was bowed down with grief as he took her body to Wooster to be interred.

He accused himself for the tragic suffering of her life, yet another wrote of him, to him:

> If ever I met the true *gentleman*—whose acts stand out in sunshine and shadow—it is you, and especially in your treatment of your wife.

As the next few months wore on, he meditated much on her and on their life together. Of this he wrote her father:

> I miss dear Janet almost every hour and I cannot review the past without bitter regrets and the feeling that her life was a sad and tragic one—too hard, too sacrificial for one of her delicate nature . . . While I was fighting with beasts at Ephesus she was pinched and starved and troubled at home. The only consolation in it there is, is that she took it all so patiently and uncomplainingly, and, despite the crucifixion she underwent, she fulfilled a great mission . . .
>
> Perhaps the hard conditions are necessary to make virtues shine. At any rate they did shine in her and I think gentleness

and unselfishness rarely has found finer embodiment than in her.

Not long after Janet's death Dr. Wallace bought a house at 68 South Snelling Avenue, across from the campus. Here his daughter Miriam, now a student at Macalester, assumed the duties of homemaker. Aunt Miriam came over from Minneapolis and spent weekends with them.

and most frespectfully that he resigned their confidence that in

According to ... Dr. Walker ... into a range of ... Sailing ... waters ... from the camp at ... Here he ... begins a ... situation in ... ... after ... passed ... over him. His ... and ... ... works with them.

XVII

War Years

Lay the proud usurpers low!
Tyrants fall in every foe!
Liberty's in every blow!
Let us do, or die!

ROBERT BURNS

A T sixty-five James Wallace could already look back on a full life. He had been in his way both pioneer and crusader, pioneer in charting the way for a young and not well-established college, crusader in battling the cause of Christian education. He had grown up in the tradition. As a boy he had listened to his father debating the North-South issues, and had heard him called a "black abolitionist." He had tried his own hand at crusading as a young man, in local politics and against the liquor traffic. His whole life at Macalester had been a struggle for what he felt to be the right, against all hazards. Like many a pioneer, he had lost, too soon, the delicate and gentle wife who had gone along with him and shared his hardships. He was alone now, but his convictions showed no weakening. He still had much to do. The issues during the next twenty-five years would be different, but they would still call for all the best in him.

In June of 1914 two shots in Sarajevo set the world on fire. James Wallace was dumfounded at the war, had thought that peace among the great nations was about to be finally established. He wrote his father-in-law:

It is a judgment day for the nations that have trusted in standing armies and military force and have repudiated the Gospel
of Peace, good will, brotherhood and sweet reasonableness.
They have worshiped Mars, now Mars demands rivers of
blood.

It is the colossal disgrace of Christendom and will put back
the Kingdom of Christ for generations. Think of the hates
and bitterness engendered!! Our missionaries will be unable
to look the heathen in the face. The blame rests wholly with
Austria and Germany.

Dr. Wallace sought to understand the background, and read ex-
tensively on the subject, tracing the philosophical, psychological,
and political aspects of the struggle to their roots far back in
history. His soul was stirred to its depths. Along with many other
Americans, he regarded the Wilson-Bryan policy of neutrality as
weak and cowardly. Christian nations, he felt, had an obligation
to protest vigorously against oppression and brutality and to act
in defense of the weak and the wronged. He regarded this as a
struggle beween despotism and freedom, between paganism and
Christianity, and wrong against right. He could not be neutral
nor remain silent. Again in writing to his father-in-law he said:

Germany's leadership has my deepest execration. Her treatment of Belgium is an iniquity so unspeakable . . . it couldn't
be atoned for if Germany were destroyed. Her use of asphyx-
iating gases, fire bombs on men, women, and children—civil-
ians, her submarine warfare on merchant ships, her acquiesc-
ing in the Turkish Holy War under which the butchery of
Armenians goes on and which she hoped would result in the
slaughter of all Christians in Africa, Egypt, and India, marks
Germany as the outlaw of all nations. The simple reason is
that while she has advanced in science and learning she has
utterly deteriorated in morals owing to her infidelity, militar-
ism, atheistic evolution.

Now I am on the Roosevelt-Taft Hibben platform—Peace
and Preparedness. Nothing but force counts with Germany,
just as nothing but force counted with ancient Sparta and
Nineveh—great military powers . . . Should Germany win—

a thing unthinkable—then it is only a question of time till we shall have to fight these modern, worse-than-Huns. Let us do it while we have company, as Admiral Mahan wisely advised England.

In 1916 Elihu Root spoke out against the position of the Wilson administration in words which Dr. Wallace warmly seconded:

A single expression by the Government of the United States, a single sentence denying assent and recording disapproval of what Germany did in Belgium, would have given to the people of America that leadership to which they were entitled in their earnest groping for the light . . . The American Government failed to rise to the demands of the great occasion. Gone were the old love of justice, the old passion for liberty, the old sympathy with the oppressed, the old ideals of an America helping the world toward a better future, and there remained in the eyes of mankind only solicitude for trade and profit and prosperity and wealth . . . Every note of remonstrance against interference with trade, or even against the destruction of life, has been projected against the background of an abandonment of the principles for which America once stood, and has been weakened by the popular feeling among the peoples of Europe, whose hearts are lifted up by the impulses of patriotism and sacrifice, that America has become weak and sordid.

This expressed exactly Dr. Wallace's own view. He had advanced far beyond protest; he was willing to bring victory to the Allied cause. Later in the year when Hughes and Wilson were contending for the Presidency, James Wallace favored Hughes.

When Wilson finally severed diplomatic relations with Germany in February of 1917, the Macalester campus divided into two groups. Eighty-seven students sent a statement to all Minnesota congressmen and senators, commending those who were resisting the pressures to force the country into war. A congressman in Duluth rushed into print and denounced them as cowards and un-American. There was much unfavorable publicity in the St. Paul papers. To counteract this, members of the faculty, with three exceptions, under the leadership of James Wallace sent this telegram to President Wilson:

> Believing that permanent world peace is impossible until the bloody despotism of the Turkish Empire and the arrogant absolutism of the Hohenzollerns are destroyed, we urge that the United States owes it to the cause of democracy, to the rights of humanity and to its own good name to engage actively in the war and help overthrow these tyrannous and lawless survivors of a barbaric age.

President Hodgman in turn told reporters that he disclaimed responsibility for the telegram, had not been shown it before it was sent. He made a long statement to the press in which at the end he said:

> Any man, or group of men, who, on insufficient knowledge of the intimate facts, urges war at this stage are a hindrance rather than a help to President Wilson. He and Congress can be safely left to do the right thing.

It appeared that President Hodgman, who had come from Nebraska, was a friend of William Jennings Bryan and supported his views on world peace.

Finally, however, Woodrow Wilson became convinced, and on April 6 Congress declared war. The day before, James Wallace had gone to Bemidji, Minnesota, to be the main speaker in a patriotic gathering in the town hall. His bold stand, his dynamic personality, his knowledge of history had brought him many requests for speeches before all sorts of audiences. After a parade in which he rode with the mayor and other dignitaries, he addressed a packed audience. He praised the German people for their fine contribution to the cultural and scientific progress of mankind, but he condemned their government. He lauded the Russians for their revolution in which the people overthrew the czars and set up a democracy. He declared it America's duty to join the Allies and save the world from the tyranny of dictators. He went on to say:

I have been teaching the Bible all my life and I believe in peace, but only when in justice. God is a pacifist only when right prevails. If we followed the course outlined by Mr. Bryan, when the Prussian pirates ordered us off the Atlantic Ocean, we would shift our boats over to the Pacific, and if they attacked us there, why then we could pull them up on the beach and build a shed over them to keep them from getting wet. I cannot interpret the Bible in a manner that will stultify manhood and demoralize common sense . . . Many have asked if the matter could not be arbitrated, but despots will never arbitrate . . . If Germany should be successful in her submarine warfare and should starve England to submission, the first demand would be for the British and French navies, and then where would the United States be? I invited in several friends and had a jollification when Baghdad fell and I expect to have another in two or three weeks when Constantinople falls; and I will dance before the Lord with joy, as the Bible says, when Constantinople falls.

He was interrupted frequently by applause.

When the U-boats began to sink American merchantmen he said, "It will stir the American war blood all the more." The "Four-Minute Men" had been mobilized over the country to address theaters, clubs, churches, about the war. There was everywhere an urgent demand for speakers who were prepared and intelligent on the subject. Dr. Wallace could qualify and he was happy to help marshal public opinion, to voice his convictions of the duty of every Christian American man or woman to support the war. The enemy must be beaten to his knees in complete surrender, the war lords brought to justice. In the spring of 1918 Dr. Wallace was asked to preach at the morning service of the Presbyterian church at Dawson, Minnesota. The headlines that morning stated that the Germans were ready to make their great bid for victory, their push on Paris. When Dr. Wallace stood up to preach he remarked that in the light of the news he would not use the sermon he had prepared. Instead he would speak on "Christianity Up Against It." He launched into a sketch of the crises the church had faced since the days of Christ and the apostles to the present time. The congregation sat spellbound as he showed how the church had come through other crises victoriously. Then he expressed his confidence that evil would not in the long run prevail.

He wrote letters to papers and magazines. In one to the *Outlook* in the summer of 1918, he said in part:

> To ask us as disciples of Christ to forgive a man or men who have committed a great crime under sudden anger or great provocation, and who later give evidence of repentance—that is practicable and consonant with reason and sound morals. But to ask us to forgive men or nations that make criminality a profession or who deliberately adopt murder, piracy, and brigandage as lawful means of achieving victory and world dominion, without any evidence of repentance—at such teaching the human soul revolts and reason stands aghast.

He addressed the Synod in Worthington, bringing to them at the end a series of eleven resolutions. In these he urged that the church, if it were to fulfill its mission, "must enter more deeply into the international mind and purpose of Jesus Christ!"; that this war be recognized as a "holy crusade in behalf of righteousness, freedom, and the inalienable rights of all peoples and nations"; that the Synod urge the administration in Washington "to make no possible compromise with the enemy"; that prior to any discussion of peace, "the Kaiser and his associated criminals, whether in Germany or in Turkey, who are justly held responsible for the revolting crimes in Belgium, France, Serbia, Poland, Armenia, and on the high seas, be delivered up, to be fairly tried and to suffer the due reward of their crimes." He concluded with the words:

> To all of which let every minister and every Christian believer, yea, let all the people say, "Amen."

The assembly rose to its feet and passed his resolutions with enthusiastic applause.

Meantime early in 1917 his son, DeWitt, had enlisted, trained a while at Camp Dodge, and then asked to be sent overseas.

When he was wounded by shrapnel in the stomach and the neck and from the hospital wrote his father of it in a light vein, his father cabled back:

> Letter received. Contents delight us. Brave Cheers for your courage. We are proud of you. War to the hilt on the Hun. Play the man and may heaven protect you and bless you.

When the armistice came and then when Wilson went to Paris with his Fourteen Points, Dr. Wallace followed every detail in the newspapers with the profoundest hope, and with the prayer, that the world might really now become safe for democracy, that the small nations of the world might take their rightful place with the great, that righteousness might at last prevail, and that peace might come, safeguarded by an active and powerful League of Nations and World Court. He was doomed to watch his hopes fade, to see Wilson come back with the mangled remains of his Fourteen Points embodied in the League of Nations Covenant, to witness the repudiation of the League by members of Congress he had thought were men. He listened to their long debates, heard their many reservations, saw their stalling practices, with deep indignation. Their behavior was treasonable, he felt, and in the end his heart was very nearly broken. So long as there was any hope he made himself heard in favor of the League to every audience he could command. He introduced a resolution before the Presbyterian Ministers' Association of St. Paul, congratulating President Wilson on what he had accomplished at Versailles, and urging the two Minnesota senators to give the Covenant of the League their sympathetic and favorable consideration. The resolution said in part:

> While we do not consider ourselves qualified to pronounce on its exact merits [the Covenant of the League], we are persuaded that its objects and aims, as stated in the preamble, are so great, so just and honorable, and the provisions for securing these objects as stated so judicious, reasonable and complete, that this constitution will take its place in history as one of the greatest, if not the greatest, landmarks of the progress of our race.

Then he went to the Presbyterian Synod of Minnesota with another resolution: the League, even though it was "clearly imperfect at some points . . . embodied and applied Christian principles to so large a degree that the United States should heartily and speedily endorse it." Dr. Wallace felt that the United States held a moral responsibility to the world to step out of its isolationism and take its part in helping to establish a peaceful and democratic government wherever that need is evident. He took issue with the editor of the Minneapolis *Tribune* who had criticized Wilson for compromising in his effort to have the League accepted. The framers of our Constitution, he pointed out, had had in several instances to compromise in order to get it ratified. Little Rhode Island, for instance, had been granted the same number of senators as New York. He went on to say:

> Does the editor have to be told that all governments are made up of compromises and that an absolutely just constitution for states has never yet been drawn? . . . Even a superficial knowledge of European history and politics makes it perfectly clear that not even divine Omniscience, even if ably assisted by Henry Cabot Lodge from Hubdom, could have drawn a perfect league and treaty that would have had the slightest chance of adoption.
>
> The League of Nations is a great enterprise. As in all great enterprises there are risks. How do men determine whether in any case the risks should be run? By dwelling only on the real or possible defects of the enterprise? Or also by considering its basic facts and principles? The Constitution triumphed exactly because a majority refused to allow the defects of parts to hide the merits of the whole.

Dr. Wallace favored the approval of the League of Nations with as few reservations as possible, though he did suggest six he would be willing to accept. When on November 26, 1919, it appeared that the enemies of the League had scored a victory, Dr. Wallace addressed Macalester students in the chapel. There he gave way to his bitterness over what he called "peanut statesmanship" and "catering to hyphenated voters":

If I had my way I would put the United States Senators in cages and send them around the country with Ringling Brothers circus as the greatest exhibition of political incompetence the world has ever seen. I am a Republican but I do not speak from a party viewpoint, but merely from the standpoint of the universal good. The lesson from such pecuniary, microscopic statesmanship is that the country needs training in political leadership.

There had been other causes, too, in these times, that stimulated his public utterance. He had always a strong attachment to the British Empire, and the Catholic independence movement in southern Ireland evoked his hostility. When De Valera was booked for an address in St. Paul, Dr. Wallace in an article for the *Pioneer Press* challenged him to comment on various points:

Explain why you were not shot as a traitor . . . when you joined in a plot to make Ireland a German base of military operations against Great Britain.

Comment freely on the asinine mind of any man who supposes that Great Britain will ever consent to driving the Ulsterites out of the British Empire against their will after the sacrifices they have made and the loyalty they have exhibited in the last war.

If the British government is as tyrannical as you say it is, explain why the Scotch Irish are contented and prosperous and resolved to remain under that government, cost what it will.

Dr. Wallace had hailed also the enactment of the Eighteenth Amendment as a great milestone in the progress toward a Christianized social order. In this he had a sense of personal triumph, for all through the years he had thrown his influence against the manufacture and sale of intoxicating beverages. He had thought "local option" a great advance, and had confidently looked forward to the day of national prohibition. It was with deep disappointment that, later, he saw the Volstead Act revoked.

In the meantime, at the college there had been a change. In 1917, after ten years of devoted service, Dr. Hodgman resigned

to become manager of a teachers' agency. Some months later he
had been succeeded by the Reverend Elmer A. Bess, Presbyterian
minister and student pastor at the University of Iowa. Dr. Hodgman had contributed much to the advancement of the college,
in building, endowment, and in the development of the curriculum. Dr. Bess, however, was a warm supporter of the Allied
cause. James Wallace welcomed him. The two became warm
friends.

In Dr. Wallace's own life, too, there had been changes. He had
continued to spend most of his summers at "Wappy," and there
friends and relatives had come to see him. He enjoyed the open-
air life, enjoyed also improving his land. He set out more seed-
lings. Sometimes, however, lonely as he was in his personal life,
and distressed at the world scene, he felt tired and worn and
so wrote Maude:

> This hard work over there tuckers me out and when night
> comes and I turn my weary feet homeward with the sad re-
> flections on the dear one who will walk these shores no more
> and on the children scattered far and wide, then I feel like a
> pilgrim indeed and there easily occurs to me the words my
> father often used in his prayers in his later years, "The places
> that know us now will soon know us no more forever."

Four years had passed since he had written that, and much had
happened. Helen, his daughter, was a minister's wife now in Indiana. Ben was an expert with the Tariff Commission in Washington. Rob had taken a forestry course at Yale University and
was now in Oregon. DeWitt had recently returned from the
war with the idea of a magazine he wished to start. Miriam, who
had been his housekeeper through these years, had been graduated in 1918 from Macalester, and now in July of 1920 had married a childhood playmate, Michael Scanlon, and gone off.

The July wedding of Miriam was soon followed by that of
Dr. Wallace himself to Miriam Maude Davis, Janet's beloved
sister. Janet had hoped that, when she was gone, James would
marry her; and so had told him. When he first approached Maude
on the subject, she put him off. She felt it much too soon; she
could not take Janet's place yet. She kept him waiting six years.

Meantime she continued as reference librarian in the Minneapolis Public Library, and came over weekends to assist young Miriam in the direction of the house. This was a happy occasion for everyone, this morning of August fourteenth, when on a bluff overlooking Lake Wapogasset they were quietly married by the Reverend Elmer Bess, President of Macalester College.

It was a wedding in the woods, simple, homely, and rather touchingly beautiful. Miriam Maude's best friend from the Minneapolis library came to be an attendant, bearing flowers from her associates. She arrived early to help with the preparations. Everyone helped, even Maude herself until it was time for her to dress for the event. She was all in white—a dainty voile blouse for which she had shopped with greatest care, a matching skirt she had made herself, a wide white satin belt, dressmaker-fashioned, and on her feet white oxfords for the procession over rough ground to the bluff. The porch of the cabin had been made a bower of greenery for the luncheon, and on the long camp table, covered with new white oilcloth, ferns had been arranged and a bowl of white flowers, city-bought. There were at the end not enough dishes to go round, so they used the new tin plates. Several of the children and grandchildren were present. Next to their own mother the children loved Aunt Maude. She had come in and out of the Wallace home since in 1888 she had accompanied them from Wooster; she had shared their vicissitudes, and many a time in a pinch she had come to their financial assistance. Now they welcomed her warmly as "Mother Maude." James Wallace was now seventy-one, Miriam Maude, sixty-four. They were to live happily together for nearly twenty years.

XVIII

Retirement

Nae falsehood to dread, and nae malice to fear,
But truth to delight me, and friendship to cheer;
Of a' roads to happiness ever were tried,
There's nane half so sure as ane's ain fireside.
ELIZABETH HAMILTON

THE years ahead were to be a time of increased recognition. Often in the old days he had feared that he was wasting his efforts; now he knew that he had been but laying a foundation, that upon which Hodgman and Bess had been able to build. In the spring of 1923 Bess had tangled with labor organizations, had resigned and gone West. The trustees had decided to make this a James Wallace commencement and to ask him to make the main address. His character and standing in the community were such as to offset to some extent the unfavorable publicity of the spring. Besides, they would like to indicate to him and others a little of the sincere appreciation they felt for his life and services. James Wallace was now seventy-four. He had served the cause of Christian education at Wooster and Macalester for forty-nine years.

The exercises were held in the Central Presbyterian Church with the mayor of St. Paul and other dignitaries on the platform. In an address entitled "Days Should Speak and Years Should Teach Wisdom," he interpreted for his audience the function, as he saw it, of a professor in a small Christian college:

In recent years the conception of a college or university professor has undergone a great change. Especially is this true in our great universities in which a professor is expected to be a good specialist in some one branch of learning; to have a classroom schedule of six, eight, or at most ten hours a week; to devote much or most of his time to original research; to make original contributions in books or magazines to the sum of knowledge; it is not by his work in classrooms or by his devotion to his students that his success is judged so much as by his literary productiveness.

Now judged by this standard my college life has been in a great degree a failure. . . . That it [my literary productiveness] is painfully insignificant I am well aware and have felt deeply the humiliation of it.

My apology is the old view of a college professorship: That his first allegiance is to his students, and his second allegiance is wholehearted devotion to the interests of the college, serving it in any way, in any capacity that its needs, best interests, and highest welfare demand—and then sacrificing to its needs all his personal ambition respecting authorship and highly technical scholarship.

This sacrifice I made—reluctantly, yet willingly, and it is the joy of my life today that I did so. The interests of the college were worth infinitely more than the realization of my personal ambitions.

Besides teaching Greek and, later, the Biblical studies, I have at one time or another taught some Old English, some rhetoric, some history, for a time sociology, political economy, constitutional history, and international law because the poverty of the college demanded it, because we were fighting off the sheriff until the dawn of a better day. It was a terrible thing to have to do it but it had great compensations. It gave me a broader, if not a deeper, scholarship; it made me a better citizen, a better Christian, a better all-round college man. Best of all, it was a great service to the college at the time. This is what all our older professors at Macalester have had to do. This is what the professors and presidents that have laid the foundations of nearly all the older Christian colleges have had to do. And so doing, I believe they were bigger, broader men, rendering a nobler service to the cause of higher education than they could possibly have done by exclusive devotion to some highly specialized form of scholarship. I am of the old school . . . I would vastly prefer to have an excellent general knowledge of Latin language and literature than to know everything conceivable about the dative case. I am afraid of the dative case men. They are mighty apt to be fools or indifferent about the great matters of citizenship and religion. I believe every professor should be required to teach some branch or branches outside his own specialty. It would save him from insufferable narrowness. It is for this reason that I believe all students should be required to take psychology, political economy, sociology, and a good course in history. These studies are essential to breadth and to the preparation for good citizenship—an aim every college should keep in mind.

I wish to say further, that if I have rendered any considerable service to Macalester College it has been due largely to the breadth of my interests in learning.

At the end George D. Dayton, an old friend, now president of the Board of Trustees, announced that the Board had made James Wallace president emeritus, while continuing him as head of the Bible-training department. In addition, they conferred on him, a layman, the honorary degree of Doctor of Divinity. No other event, Mr. Dayton said, in the history of Macalester during his twenty-nine years as trustee, had given him such real pleasure and satisfaction as to confer this degree. In the citation he said:

The purity of your diction, the clarity of your thought, the free flow of your sentiment, all result from the thorough study of, and intimate acquaintance with, the Book of Books, the Bible. All those of us who have sat at your feet and . . . been elevated by your conceptions of deity have felt that the Great Teacher was using you, a human being, as the vehicle of the divine thoughts and divine ideals.

Here is where you have given your greatest contribution

of religious influence and religious instruction, illustrating in your own daily life and intercourse, the precepts, principles, and results of the religious atmosphere and of the thoughts inspired by intimacy with the Master, who is King of Kings and Lord of Lords. Your knowledge of theology and your scholarship in religious education rank so high, both in fact and in the opinion of the public, that you are entitled to recognition. . . .

Though Dr. Wallace decried the fact that he had had time to publish so little scholarly work, he had made his published work count, nevertheless, in influencing public opinion, and he was still doing so. After the Great War a wave of pacifism swept the country. War settled nothing, it was fashionable to say. James Wallace rebelled. He wrote an article on the "Great Gains of the Great War," which received wide circulation in the papers. After enumerating the gains of each small nation, and of the world in the elimination of the Hohenzollern, Hapsburg, and Romanov dynasties, he continued:

Never in any war, perhaps not in any five wars, has justice had so many triumphs. There are some sore spots in Europe, of course . . . but Europe today rests on a foundation of justice, vastly broader and deeper than she has ever known before. Now, there is real ground to hope that a great beginning has been made for a United States of Europe. Before the Great War such an idea was unthinkable, chimerical.

Count the emancipated peoples in Denmark, Finland, Poland, Czecho-Slovakia, Italy, Jugo-Slavia, Rumania, Estonia, Latvia, Lithuania, Greece, France (Alsace-Loraine), Palestine, Syria, China, not to speak of Arabia and Mesopotamia, and tell me, when in any war, in any century, freedom and justice have had so many great triumphs?

The holding of these peoples in duress by governments which they hated constituted a body of problems before which pacifism was and would have been as helpless as a flea bite on the back of a turtle. . . .

The trouble with pacifism as a sole reliance for peace is that it cannot be preached and applied where it is most needed.

Try it on the military men of Prussia, who are lying in wait for an opportune time to overthrow the German Republic. Try it on the Bolsheviki, who, with a million of men in arms, await an opportunity to help set up communism in Germany. . . . Exercise a little historical imagination and consider how pacifism worked on old Xerxes when planning the invasion of Greece and what would have become of that country and Europe if the heroes of Marathon, Salamis, and Plataea had blindly put their trust in such teaching. The pious and the good may accept pacifism, but what about the Alexanders, the Napoleons, the Frederics the Great, the Abdul Hamids, who regard pacifism as cowardly and an invitation to conquest?

. . . How does Isaiah read? And the word of "pacifism" shall be peace and the effect of pacifism—? Not by a thousand miles. "The work of righteousness shall be peace and the effect of righteousness quietness and confidence forever."

The advent of a world ruled by righteousness is certain to come . . . but it has made progress not alone by preaching peace, but also because many valiant men have preferred liberty even at the cost of death on the battlefield rather than life under the heel of the tyrant. The lesson of history is that wars will cease when tyrants and tyranny are no more, and that time and that event were mightily hastened by the Great War.

At the memorial service held in the college for Woodrow Wilson in early February 1924 Dr. Wallace spoke with deep emotion of the great architect of the League of Nations:

. . . The final illness and death of Woodrow Wilson has stirred my soul to a conflict of emotions—profound grief, a sore bereavement, and a keen admiration for the great martyr, coupled with seething execration of the Lilliputian minds that, with hellish craft and whispered slanders, have, for four long years and more, wrought for the utter destruction of Woodrow Wilson's reputation and influence and the complete undoing of all his work. . . . History will write down Woodrow Wilson as the world's greatest and most eloquent

expositor of universal democracy. . . . In Pericles' great funeral oration he declared the whole world the tomb of heroes.
So with Woodrow Wilson. It matters nothing where his body
lies. History will make the whole world his tomb.

In May of that year James Wallace was sent as a commis-
sioner to the Presbyterian General Assembly at Grand Rapids,
Michigan. As a member of the Bills and Overtures Committee,
he helped, along with William Jennings Bryan and others, to
draft a strong resolution on international peace, though it is
doubtful whether he really endorsed all its provisions as it was
finally written and passed.

In the meantime a new president had again come to Macalester; Dr. John C. Acheson, formerly president of Pennsylvania
College for Women and recently president of Kentucky College
for Women. With his coming, and a change in economic condi-
tions, Macalester was able to build the long-awaited gymnasium,
suitable also for convocations, and to add to its faculty. Dr.
Wallace took solid satisfaction in all of this.

When in March of 1926 he reached his seventy-seventh birthday he asked the Board of Trustees to be allowed to retire. He
was still physically vigorous and mentally keen but he was finding it difficult always to hear his students in the classroom. The
administration was loath to see him go and asked him to continue until they could find additional personnel for the department. He remained therefore for another college year. Perhaps
it was somewhat ironic that only a month after he had asked for
retirement he was elected to Phi Beta Kappa at Wooster. In being
granted its charter, the Wooster chapter had been allowed to
elect those alumni whose college standing and subsequent record
through the years seemed to merit this honor. Late as it came
in his career, he wore the key with satisfaction.

With the end of teaching in June of 1927 there now began
for James Wallace a period of leisure and travel. The first summer he spent as usual at Wallace Island. When fall came he and
Mrs. Wallace took off to the southwestern states. Before Christmas, when the snow was already lying deep in Minnesota, they
sailed on a slow freighter for Egypt. Mr. Dayton, Thomas Cochran, Jr., and others had made this trip possible. From Gibraltar

to Alexandria the voyage was full of thrills, in spite of winds
and rough waves. Persons and places from the classics and from
the Bible appeared before the eyes of their imagination as they
passed well-known islands or put into ports: at Carthage, Hanni-
bal and his mighty army; Augustine with his *Confessions* and
City of God at Hippo; St. Paul shipwrecked on the shores of
Malta; Simon, who bore the cross for Jesus, at Cyrenaica.

In Egypt Dr. Wallace had relatives and old friends connected
with the United Presbyterian missionary and educational work.
His niece, Janet Wallace, had married Robert W. McClenahan,
now dean of oriental studies at the American University of Cairo.
The Reverend John Alexander, at Asyut, was an old patriarch
from Wooster whom he had known when both were boys. The
Wallaces indeed had expert guidance to the museums, the
Sphinx, the pyramids and tombs of the pharaohs, trained inter-
preters of the modern cultural, economic, and political developments of this ancient land. A five-hundred-mile trip up the Nile
brought them to Luxor and the ruins of ancient temples of Kar-
nak. From Egypt they took a train to Palestine. There they
stayed for a while at the American Colony in Jerusalem, a group
of sixty persons practicing Christian communism. Abraham and
Jacob, Joshua and the Judges, Samuel, Saul, David and their
contemporaries came to life for them as they visited the scenes
of their exploits. In imagination they followed Jesus from Jericho
up over the Mount of Olives to Bethany, and thought of Him
riding into the Holy City on the colt of an ass while the throng
shouted their hosannas. They followed Him through Gethsemane
to Pilate's judgment hall, and out the Via Dolorosa to Calvary and
the tomb in the garden. Bethlehem, Nazareth, Mount Carmel,
Capernaum, the Sea of Galilee, they tripped to them all, with the
enthusiasm of those far younger. Dr. Wallace wrote back:

> . . . It is some fun to see Maude riding a donkey. Especially
> going up a hillside at an angle of 60°, and then down
> again . . . I need a dictaphone to treasure up her exclama-
> tions.

It was a memorable trip in every way, and the Wallaces returned refreshed in body and in spirit. Now James could settle

down to study, writing, and possibly to some lecturing. He had brought back with him a collection of lantern slides.

One book he had long had in mind, a history of his forebears, the Wallaces and the Bruces and their descendants. He was proud of his Scottish ancestry. The years were taking their toll and unless he soon prepared this book, many of those from whom he could still get information would be gone. All his own brothers were gone, even now his brothers-in-law. He started searching out relatives, writing letters for birth dates and places, asking for reminiscences and as accurate facts as could be found in old records. He went to libraries, too, for research. He had indeed a fond hope that he might establish descent from Sir William Wallace, Scottish patriot, who led an unsuccessful revolt against Edward I of England and who had been executed therefor. At length he had his facts together and in 1930 the book was published, *The Wallace-Bruce and Closely Related Families*. It was full of genealogies, and dates, but it was also full of stories of the kith and kin and brief characterizations, of old David Liddell, for instance, whose house down Millbrook way was open, it seemed, to all who could not pay for lodging. One Saturday night he housed a traveling Irishman. But when the next morning the man said he would be going, David Liddell replied, "Na, na, you'll na be breaking the Sabbath by traveling aboot on the Lord's day." The man sat down, but before long once more opened the conversation. "That's a good stove there. About how much did that stove cost?" "We'll na," said David, "be talking aboot the price o' stoves on the Sabbath day." And there was Christina Bruce whose Scottish gift of understatement was reputed very strong. One day she praised her grandson and his schoolmate, but what she said was, "I daur say that there are waur (worse) boys than the twa." James Wallace had been disappointed to find that Sir William Wallace had left no male descendant. But he added,

. . . this effort to trace lineal descent . . . is putting the emphasis in the wrong place. The far more important question is, Are we worthy heirs of his character and spirit, of his love of liberty, of his heroism, and ardent patriotism? Character is the real aristocracy.

Not only in his ancestors but in his children Dr. Wallace could take a reasonable pride. In 1928 Ben had been chosen as a member of the Kemmerer Commission to go to Shanghai to help China put her finances on a sounder basis. He and his wife, Katharine Seelye Wallace, were gone for several years. By this time, too, DeWitt's little magazine, *Reader's Digest*, was being well received.

On Dr. Wallace's eightieth birthday, March 12, 1929, a special convocation was held in the college chapel, at which his portrait, painted by the well-known portrait artist, Nicholas R. Brewer, was presented to the college. Dr. Wallace himself would not attend; he somehow did not feel it seemly to be present in the flesh. When he saw the portrait later, he declared, "It looks positively sleepy."

XIX

Looking to the Future

> *Happy is the man that findeth wisdom, and the man that getteth understanding. . . . Length of days is in her right hand; and in her left hand riches and honour. Her ways are ways of pleasantness, and all her paths are peace.*
>
> PROVERBS 3: 13, 16, 17

T H E years of retirement were meaning much and were to mean even more to James Wallace. He had time to read widely, to think, to speak what was in his heart. He had time to sit down quietly with friends at home, to keep up a voluminous correspondence with those at a distance. He had time to visit with his sons and daughters, to admonish and tease their sons and daughters, to visit his sisters, and there look again at the scenes of his youth. He had time to travel, to rejoice in the beauty of the world, and to think on its creator. Now he could consult his memories, laugh at life's incongruities and inconsistencies, evaluate his own small part, and wish that it had been better and greater. Time did not lag.

He read much. All those dragging years of his presidency had seemed to him lean and barren. He had longed to get back to his books. Now he could. The daily papers, of course, particularly the New York *Times*, had always been before him, the magazines also, but in later years he could peruse them more thoroughly and more thoughtfully. He followed the march of

events with eager interest and some despondency, though it was
not in his nature to be anything but optimistic for the long run.
With equal zeal he watched the activities of the church at large,
of its missionaries in far places, its ministry at home, its colleges, and its assemblies.

He had had little time for fiction, though occasionally he had
been wont to read, or listen while Janet read aloud some good Scottish tale. Tears rose to his eyes as he saw in his mind old Dr. Mac-
Lure of Drumtochty carried by on his last trip, through the deep
snows, and heard in thought the faithful Jess neighing to him from
the stable. He loved to read and quote Burns' poetry. Nearly every
year he was asked by some Scottish society to address them, and
he hastened to refresh himself on *Tam o' Shanter* and other poems.
The Cotter's Saturday Night reminded him of his own childhood
on the farm:

> The cheerfu' supper done, wi' serious face,
> They, round the ingle, form a circle wide;
> The sire turns o'er, with patriarchal grace,
> The big ha'-bible, ance his father's pride:
>
> . . . .
>
> The priest-like father reads the sacred page,
> How Abram was the friend of God on high;
>
> . . . .
>
> How He, who bore in Heaven the second name,
> Had not on earth whereon to lay his head;
>
> . . . .
>
> Then kneeling down to Heaven's Eternal King,
> The saint, the father, and the husband prays:
> Hope "springs exulting on triumphant wing,"
> That thus they all shall meet in future days,
> There, ever bask in uncreated rays,
> No more to sigh, or shed the bitter tear . . .
>
> . . . .

These were the old familar things. *Scots, wha hae wi' Wallace
Bled* he often quoted. Wallace and Bruce and Bannockburn all
were of his heritage. Often in conversation he would recall the
louse of Burns' poem:

"O wad some Power the giftie gie us
To see oursels as ithers see us."

That was usually when he was laughing at himself. And sometimes, in a melancholy state of mind after tramping the streets
and ringing doorbells for Macalester, he had quoted another line
of Burns:

"For man was made to mourn"

though in his deepest heart's core, he didn't really believe it.

But all this reading had been incidental. The classics, of course,
he knew and loved to go back to, Vergil, and Ovid, Homer,
Sophocles, and Aristophanes. He was familiar with Socrates'
teachings as presented in Plato's *Dialogues*, with Plato's *Republic*, with Aristotle's treatises on *Politics* and other themes, with
Cicero's philosophic dissertations. He read in biography, widely
in history; and his whole tendency was to interpret it in terms
of scriptural teaching. The First World War and its aftermath
had stimulated much reading. Besides, when he had returned to
Macalester to teach and to teach only, he had given a course
on Christianity and the State, which led him into studies as
broad as the world itself.

Yet in American history as related to this he had been especially
interested. Lincoln, and Washington, too, he revered. "It was
hardly too much to say," he was to write later, "that it was the
profound impression of righteousness and justice of Almighty
God and its wide and impartial application to the affairs of men,
as revealed in the Bible, that made Abraham Lincoln the statesman he was." He regarded the one-time popular debunking of
American heroes as the "work of small minds—minds with a
ghoulish bent":

Writers who cannot see facts and events in their relative importance are not fit to write biography or history.

Of this, in connection with Washington, he wrote:

Considering the extraordinary achievements, character, and
influence of Washington, of what consequence was it, if under
some provocation, he swore or lost his temper, or that his let-

ters home do not reveal the ardent affection we should have
expected.

He had studied Woodrow Wilson's *State*, his inaugurals, and
other addresses. He greatly admired Wilson. His program for
peace was, he felt, inevitably right, based, as it was, "on the principle of justice to all peoples and nationalities, and their right
to live on equal terms of liberty and safety with one another,
whether they be strong or weak." He felt with Wilson:

> Justice and only justice shall be our motto. The feelings with
> which we face this new age of right and opportunity sweep
> across our heartstrings like some air out of God's own pres-
> ence, where justice and mercy are reconciled, and the Judge
> and the brother are one.

There is, James Wallace believed, and wrote:

> . . . a moral order in the world to which the State must take
> account and to which its legislation must in general conform.
> There has been no deep antagonism between the ethics of
> our religion and the ethics of the State. They have been rec-
> ognized as essentially the same.

The Kellogg-Briand Pact of 1928 had cheered his heart, and he
had taken great satisfaction in the fact that Secretary Kellogg
was from St. Paul. But soon the distant rumblings of war began
to spread through the world. The new aggressions of Japan in
Manchuria and China, of Mussolini in Abyssinia, and now the
blatherings of Hitler stirred him to the depths. To understand
all this he needed to read more and more in history and philosophies that were anathema to him. He familiarized himself with
the doctrines of Nietzsche, of Schopenhauer, of Oswald Speng-
ler, Karl Marx, delved even into Hitler's *Mein Kampf*. Just to
think of man as a beast, of nations taught to prey upon nations!
The hordes of the devil were loose on the earth! He did what
he could. He favored everywhere the embargo on Japanese
products, joined actively in boycotting their merchandise, took
off his silk ties and substituted others. In 1936 he wrote a letter
to the New York *Times* which appeared under the caption

"Hamstringing the League." (This was later included in the *Yearbook of Public Opinion*.) In this he charged:

Only a League made up of nations that really believe in its peaceful and war-averting purposes can have any hope of success. What has Japan's and Italy's membership in the Kellogg-Briand Pact done but brought upon it disgrace if not actual ruin? The United States does believe in the peaceful purposes of the League but her hypercritical, halting, baffling action toward the League has definitely encouraged both Japan and Italy to treat the League as they have done.

Again in 1937 he wrote the *Times* on our policy of neutrality:

Such policy [of neutrality] is following the line of least resistance. It is safety before principle. It is peace at any price. It is the policy of the priest that went by on the other side. It is flat denial of the moral unity of the world. It is aiding the strong nation as against the weak.

The assumption of the defenders of a fixed policy of neutrality that both parties to a war are alike guilty or that it is impossible to tell which is the more guilty is rarely true. . . .

There are several facts that Congress and the government do not seem to have realized: Treaties, pacts, convenants do not enforce themselves. Treaties not lived up to or enforced speedily become dead letters. Standing for world peace means accepting world responsibility. America being one of the most powerful and influential of the nations that honestly believe in world peace has corresponding responsibility and accountability for the maintenance of that peace.

Again in September 1937 he wrote the editor of the St. Paul *Dispatch:*

Japan's well planned campaign to destroy China as a free and independent state is the greatest crisis since 1914. Great China is to be reduced to a puppet state. . . . All China's vast resources are to be completely controlled by Japan. When and if that comes about, and Japan has built a navy two or three times the size of her present one, possibly then it may dawn upon the minds of the isolationists, pacifists and neutralists into what a fool's paradise they have led our country. . . .

The policy of neutrality makes it impossible even to make any effective protest.

Nothing the United States could have done would have pleased Tokio so much as the effective way in which the United States has tied its own hands. Are the isolationists, pacifists and neutralists, statesmen, or are they fools? We have good reason to fear the answer which Japan's war on China will give to that question.

James Wallace was called upon to speak much on world affairs within the state of Minnesota. He raised a vigorous voice. We were seeing, he said, the results of our repudiation of the League.

But he felt that he could do nothing better in his remaining years of life than to gather together in a book the fruits of his studies, and meditations and discussions. To this he applied himself diligently. He called it *Fundamentals of Christian Statesmanship*. In it he traced the teachings of the Old and New Testaments on the character and duties of rulers and the nature of the Kingdom-of-God ideal; the concept of the state, held by political leaders in America, Britain, and Germany; the contributions Christianity has made to the state through the character of Jesus and his teachings on such subjects as the family, education, social welfare, wealth, war, and peace; and the ideas of the state, held by ancient and modern philosophers. He concluded

that the State rests on justice, equity and loving-kindness and is not a law unto itself, that the individual citizen being of inestimable worth, has certain inalienable rights which even the State has no right to ignore; that all men of whatsoever race, color, or condition are of such moral worth and of such capacity to receive truth that they deserve the message and concern of our religion; that as race and color prejudices are potent causes of hatred, strife, and war, the Christian doctrine of the unity of the race, of the common creatorship and fatherhood of God and the consequent brotherhood of man are the best means known to man of reducing or removing that prejudice; that while right . . . justice, and equity are supreme virtues for the State they need to be supplemented by love, sympathy, service, and sacrifice—the supreme virtues as taught by the Church.

In Isaiah and the other prophets, in Proverbs, the Psalms, Job, as well as in the Gospels and Epistles he found the fundamental principles of government and man's relationship with man.

One of the marked characteristics of Isaiah's statesmanship [he wrote] is his keen appreciation of good government . . . one object of his prophecies was to set forth the contrast between government thoroughly bad and government ideally good—the former cursed with greed, discord, anarchy, defeat; the latter just, equitable, peaceful, prosperous, enduring. In his picture of the ideal of Messianic future the outstanding feature is the perfection and beneficence of the State. It is the supreme institution of society.

Dr. Wallace completed the book as he reached his ninetieth birthday. His son Benjamin indexed it for him and prepared it for the press in August of that year. It did not appear until shortly after Dr. Wallace's death.

Realizing, that spring, that he had not long to live, he felt the urge to leave behind him also for his countrymen a short political testament that might continue, when he was gone, to plead the cause of world organization. He wrote consequently a pamphlet, *The Great Betrayal*. In it he reviewed the struggle to set up a League of Nations with a World Court. He pointed the finger of scorn at those he saw as responsible for its failure. He wrote:

It [his conclusion] is: That the policy pursued after the Great War by those that became the leaders of the Republican party was the most treasonable toward the great cause of world peace, justice, cooperation, and the settlement of disputes around the council table,—the most treasonable, I say, and the most disastrous that can be found in modern history. . . .

Betrayal already achieved was continued in and after the election of 1920. The Republicans framed an ambiguous platform and their presidential candidate made ambiguous speeches. Thirty-one of their most respected leaders joined in a solemn appeal to the American people to vote the Republican ticket as the best means of assuring American entry into an association of nations. A more shameless misrepresentation cannot be found in the annals of partisan lies, but millions believed these hitherto respectable leaders. As the strength of their appeal lay in their previous leadership in advocacy of the League of Nations, their treason to the cause of world order is, if possible, more damnable than that of its open opponents—to whom they surrendered complete control of the party as soon as it came into power. I name none of these men. Let their memory rot!

He went on to point out the powerlessness of the League of Nations with the United States on the outside. He held that the Neutrality Act favored the oppressors and lowered the prestige of the United States in the eyes of the world. He went on to say:

My last word to my fellow countrymen is: Realize the responsibility and the power of this colossus among the nations. Desert the leaders who in the words of the prophet Jeremiah, made us in the eyes of the world "an astonishment and a hissing." They have brought our whole civilization to the brink of another catastrophe. Again, as in 1919, it is crystal clear that there can never be tolerable security for any nation—until enough of the nations firmly combine to insist that the peace shall be kept.

During the last ten years of his life Dr. Wallace had been much concerned, too, for the future of the college. He kept a watchful eye over the department of religion lest its professors go off on tangents or attempt to pontificate in realms in which they had no expert knowledge. He was also watchful of the department of political science. In his estimation this chair was next in importance to that of philosophy, and its occupant should be a strong Christian who would not take the secular view of history and politics. He would not have the college drift from its old channel into the open sea of secularism. So long as Dr. Acheson was president he was satisfied and happy, but when he suddenly died Dr. Wallace was filled with apprehension. What now? Even in his address at the funeral he took pains to contrast those countries in which education is "the handmaid of religion and the church" with those in which it does obedience to the state. He wrote the Board of Trustees a long letter in which he set forth Macalester's historic connection with the Presbyterian Synod of Minnesota. "Not in the last 500 years," he asserted, "has the argument for the Christian college and its Christian philosophy of God, man, and the world needed and demanded more vigorous and courageous assertions than now," when "rank paganism and new gods and despotisms and philosophies" are abroad in the world. When Dr. Charles J. Turck, former president of Centre College, was elected president Dr. Wallace was once more at ease. The college he loved would go on in the old way and the old faith.

In many ways the college still depended on Dr. Wallace. Even though long retired, he had spoken for the faculty at Dr. Acheson's funeral. Reviewing Dr. Acheson's indefatigable efforts for the college, he had said, ". . . the cross which Dr. Acheson had to carry all the time was the discrepancy between what the college was and what he knew it should be." It was a cross he himself had carried as president; and in a way it was a continuing experience. He rejoiced at every advance the college made that lessened that discrepancy, warned of the danger of any slipping back, at any point.

In June of 1938 he was asked to give the farewell address to the seniors, and he admonished them:

. . . Be not weary of well-doing for the State. Democracy has often failed and ours has no sure guarantee of success. As it cost much to win it, it is likely to cost even more to save it. We beg you to accept responsibility for its welfare.

. . . Make it your life purpose to be good churchmen. The Church has glaring faults. The numerous sects of Protestantism are a scandal. The infallibility and absolutism of Rome, in the light of history, are preposterous. Yet the Church has the world's greatest message, teaching that this is a moral universe, that back of all material phenomena there is a Being of infinite perfections; that He is so friendly that He is called Father, and mankind are His children; that His character is the ultimate basis of morals; that there is a solidarity of the races, and interdependence of the nations, and ultimate brotherhood of man, a coming kingdom of heaven, an assured hope of immortality. Here is a great philosophy of God, man, and the universe. To be a good churchman is to be in tune with the Infinite.

But he had much more than admonition to give. On the occasion of dedicating a new pipe organ in the gymnasium, to be used at all convocations, he was asked to give the dedicatory prayer. In this those who knew him best felt that the prayer revealed not only his own appreciation of the value of music in worship and other aspects of human experience, but its rich influences in his own life: such as Janet singing to her children and playing the organ, and his venerable father leading in the singing of the Psalms at family prayers in the old farm home.

Particularly [he said] . . . on this occasion do we give Thee thanks and praise for the blessed ministry of music that aids us so wonderfully in expressing the varied moods and experiences of our minds and hearts. We thank Thee that Thou hast made music the charming companion of our lives even from the first lullabies we hear on our mother's knees till the last requiem is said at our demise: that it soothes our sorrows, heightens our joys and is a necessary accompaniment of the festivities of our social life. Still more do we thank Thee, O God, that Thy wisdom has made music so noble, so essential a part of our religion: that in Thy holy sanctuaries Sunday after Sunday millions of Thy children raise their voices in song and praise to Thee.

And for that vast library of psalms, hymns, and spiritual songs by which Thy children make melody in their hearts unto the Lord—for these, too, we must thank Thee as their original source and inspiration.

Early in 1936 Macalester College celebrated its fiftieth year on the present campus in St. Paul. Men of wide reputation were called

Macalester College coeds pinning a home-coming button on Dr. James Wallace in his eighty-ninth year.

in to add color to the occasion. Dr. Wallace made the historical address and wrote an article on the college which was featured by the Twin City papers. His portrait was placed on display in one of the downtown department-store windows.

Founders' Day at Macalester College is an annual tribute to the memory of James Wallace, as it is observed on the Friday nearest to his birthday. It was established under the leadership of Professor Grace B. Whitridge on March 12, 1938, the eighty-ninth birthday of Dr. Wallace. Trustees, faculty, alumni and friends gathered in the college gymnasium, donned Scottish bonnets and plaids and sat down to a banquet. Dr. Wallace made an address on Edward Duffield Neill and a member of the faculty paid a tribute to Dr. Wallace as the one who headed the movement that saved the college from extinction in the dark days of its financial crisis. Over a national radio hookup Dr. Wallace addressed the widely scattered alumni in the following words:

All hail! Dr. Jimmy salutes you. Your Alma Mater sends most hearty greetings and congratulations. She is proud of her off-spring. You are her trained messengers of good to all the world. Heaven's blessing rests upon you. Cherish high hopes for the future of dear old Macalester.

Again on Founders' Day, 1939, his ninetieth birthday, he was made the hero of the occasion and gave the main address and again spoke to the alumni over the radio. Greetings by letter and telegram poured in from everywhere.

The last few years he had had reason to be happy over many things. For one, one of the ablest businessmen of the Twin Cities, after retiring as head of a great concern, had become president of the Board of Trustees and pledged himself to give much of his time to Macalester's material development. Dr. Wallace's son DeWitt, with his wife, Lila Bell Acheson Wallace, too, had established the Reader's Digest Foundation and from this were giving the college one hundred thousand dollars a year for five years. When Dr. Wallace heard this news, all he could say was "Well, I declare!" But he was deeply gratified. The gift was not only helping the college in a significant way but it was carrying on the tradition. His sister Mary wrote concerning it:

I have been thinking of Father and Mother, how their influence and training will be carried on through this gift. . . . [They] were always so deeply interested in education. . . . This also went back to grandfather and grandmother Bruce who left Scotland for the simple reason that they could not educate their children with what they were able to make in Scotland.

In 1938, indeed, $800,000 altogether had been pledged toward an additional million of endowment. There were smaller gifts, too, that made his heart glad. One of the members of the class of 1913 had sent $200 to start a $5000 James Wallace Loan Fund for needy students.

In the winter of 1933 Dr. and Mrs. Wallace had been encouraged to go to the Southwest. While they were in Albuquerque they received a telegram inviting them, before going back, to visit their children in the East, and informing them that DeWitt had bought for them a house in St. Paul, of which they were to take possession on their return. For some time DeWitt had been urging his father to sell the old home at 68 South Snelling and move to a comfortable apartment, where housekeeping would be easier for Mother Maude, but they had consistently ignored this advice. Now it had been done for them. It was a bungalow under the elms and maples at 112 Cambridge Street. With exquisite taste Lila had refurbished the new house from top to bottom, having the old and well-loved furniture done over whenever possible, buying new to supplement this when it seemed best. She personally superintended every detail, even to choosing a housekeeper for them, and then she wrote Mother Maude, to prepare her:

I'll be seeing you before long.—I hope it will be a happy time. . . . I've had some bad hours in the night over it. . . . What bothered me most was going into your house and disturbing any of your things. Perhaps it was a necessary evil, but I was very unhappy about it. Men just can't know how we women feel about our houses.—It was DeWitt's very great desire to make things lovely for you and Daddy Wallace that prompted it all. . . . He is so proud of you both and has such a deep desire for you to have comforts and joys, that it's great fun to help carry out his plans.

When Dr. and Mrs. Wallace came back to St. Paul they were accompanied by Lila and DeWitt. Rob and Nina, who lived but a few blocks away, escorted them to the new home. There they found Dr. Wallace's books on the shelves, Mrs. Wallace's personal things tucked away in the drawers. One day sometime later a friend calling on Mrs. Wallace remarked to her, "This is the prettiest house on this street." "It is," Mrs. Wallace replied, "the prettiest house in St. Paul." There, looked after and comfortable, they were to spend their remaining years. There he was busy with his books and addresses, with letters and friends. Alumni dropped in to see him when they returned to the city. Faculty, trustees, churchmen, neighbors, friends from here and there came in to call. In the summers at "Wappy" some of his family often came for a few days at a time.

Periodically, too, he and Maude made trips East to see the children, to Washington to see Ben and Katharine, to New York and Pleasantville, where DeWitt and Lila had their home, to Philadelphia where Miriam lived, or to Gettysburg to see Helen and John. On these trips they would stop in Wooster, too, to visit his sisters, Margaret and Mary, and to look again upon the old haunts. He wanted to attend services in the old United Presbyterian Church and sit in his father's pew. He loved to be taken on drives around the countryside, out to the old farm particularly. Here was where he and Will had been about to have a great battle with one of the neighbor boys and "Maggie," finding it out, had intervened; here was the creek through the woods where they had waded and tried to catch minnows; there old Jimmy Ball had lived, and here the old Union School. What arguments had gone on there! Here was old "Auntie Frazier's" place—and he would chuckle. He well remembered her. She had been used to taking a little toddy for her stomach's sake. One Sabbath morning when they were all about to start to church she complained of feeling ill. Her children urged her to have a toddy. "Na, na," she said, "ye wouldna' hae me drunk in the kirk." He would want to go to Millbrook to see the granddaughters of old Margaret Bruce Lowe, long since gone, or to Millersburg to see the Taylors, or to Canaan Center where he had gone to the academy. Everywhere he would rejoice in the fields of corn and wheat and potatoes, in the greenness of the fields, and most of all in the views from the hilltops. Here, he would say as he looked off across a valley, he would like to build a house, and here, and here—and here. Indeed he loved the beauty of the earth, and quoted gladly from the 65th Psalm:

> Thou visitest the earth and waterest it, thou greatly enrichest it; the river of God is full of water: thou providest them grain, when thou hast so prepared the earth. Thou waterest its furrows abundantly; thou settlest the ridges thereof: thou makest it soft with showers; thou blessest the springing thereof. Thou crownest the years with thy goodness; and thy paths drop fatness. . . .

And then, sometimes, as memories came flooding back from his long life, he would take to telling stories, occasionally of the heartbreaks and discouragements of the treadmill of his presidency, more often of the amusing encounters he had had. There were the two elderly sisters who came to call on him and Maude one sunny winter afternoon. They had been carrying suitcases, which they left on the porch. They all had a pleasant visit, but the call was prolonged. Maude went out to look after the evening meal and still they stayed. They were asked to eat with them. Dr. Wallace suggested that the suitcases would be safer inside. They agreed. He brought them into the front hall. Eight, nine, ten o'clock came; the sisters showed no inclination to leave. Would they stay the night? They would. Dr. Wallace carried the suitcases to the guest room. That was the beginning of the longest social call on record. The sisters stayed a year. Exasperated, but amused as well, Dr. Wallace never called the sheriff, never lost his temper. Long ago in his administration these two had contributed to the college five hundred dollars. He saw it all clearly now. Evidently—he told the story half shamefacedly—the time had come for them to replenish their coffers at his expense.

Then there was the grandson of old Eliza Douglas, who took offense at what Dr. Wallace had said of his branch of the family in the Wallace-Bruce history. He had indeed told of how old Aunt Eliza Douglas in the early days could be seen sitting in her rocker out at the farm, solacing herself with a corncob pipe; of a son of hers who had imbibed too freely though he had risen to considerable local prominence. The grandson had written that he would sue but for the fact that James Wallace was "obscure, stupid and a man in his dotage." Dr. Wallace hadn't answered at once, but at Christmas time he wrote the grandson:

I am sorry to hear about my dotage, obscurity and general stupidity, but to quote from your uncle Ben Douglas:

"Life has joys for all of those
Who shun its vices as their foes:
And hope will cancel petty woes,
Without it, all were gloom."

and besides

This is the Christmas time of year
And we should seek to bring good cheer
To every sort of human kind,
However dumb, however blind.

James Wallace enjoyed writing jingles, and usually at Christmas time in his later years he sent out some verses of his own as a Christmas greeting.

So, with work at home, summers at "Wappy," visits here and there, he rolled up the years to ninety. His step was firm, his shoulders held erect; there was still a glint in his eye, and his mind was as vigorous as ever. But he was deaf, and so, often, he did not wait for others to do the talking; he talked himself, and his family and friends were glad to listen. In the spring of 1939, however, he knew that he was near his end. Helen came from the East to be with him, the other children came for a few days at a time as they could. He had a cheerful word for each. He awaited death with no fear and no complaint. He enjoyed a laugh as much as ever. His attitude was not that of one going on an adventure, but of one going home. One who visited him during those days wrote back:

How I wish I had talked to him about what he expected to find across the divide. I think he would have said something like this: "Well, of course I don't really know but I'm confident it won't be a place or a life of idleness, ease, or luxury. On the contrary I think it will be a place of growth, opportunity, and infinite possibilities of advancement. If this life is a training school for the next, then the next must be one of highly interesting and spiritually profitable activities. And when I say *spiritually profitable* I mean in the broadest sense. The life to come is not static." That is what I think he might have said, but how I should have liked to hear him say it.

So on August 23, 1939, James Wallace was gathered to his fathers. Everyone who knew him rejoiced that he did not live to see Europe once more in arms. But if in heaven he knew and was following the course of events on earth, one could hear him hurling imprecations at the rulers and politicians who had brought on this world-wide catastrophe when they had been given every chance to establish peace and a new world order. He would be echoing the words of "de Lawd" in *Green Pastures*, which he had once seen in New York:

I tried to make dis a good earth. I've given you ev'y chance. I sent you warriors and prophets. I've given you laws and commandments, and you betrayed my trust. Ev'ything I've given you, you've defiled. Ev'y time I've fo'given you, you've mocked me. . . . Listen, you chillun of darkness, yo' Lawd is tired. I'm tired of de struggle to make you worthy of de breath I gave you. . . . Listen to the words of yo' Lawd God Jehovah . . . I repent of dese people dat I have made and I will deliver dem no more.

Citizens of my beloved land [he had written in *The Great Betrayal*], forget two decades of disastrous defeat. Remember that no part of the world can ever be a decent place in which to trade, and live, and hope while every armed nation retains the power to imperil civilization itself whenever it chooses. Let the greatest of all nations resume again the leadership which none other can supply. O, my Countrymen, advance firmly to the establishment of effective organization for international law and order.

Postscript

For though the daye be never so long,
At last the bell ringeth to evensong.
STEPHEN HAWES (1523)

T H R O U G H all the years James Wallace had been the re-
cipient of many tributes. These he had brushed off lightly,
though his family cherished them, and even he could hardly
forget. There was that morning in chapel long ago when Edward
Downing, versifier of the faculty, had read a poem of which
two verses were devoted to him:

> Behold the man who stands alone,
> Like some tall tree upon the plain,
> Who ever feels the wound and pain
> Of wind and storm, without a moan.
>
> He holds his place. His noble form
> Though tested harder than we know,
> And sometimes bending very low
> Still rises greater than the storm.

At the time of the Wallace commencement in 1923, the faculty
had sent him a letter of appreciation:

We, the members of the Faculty of Macalester College, who
have known you and the life of this college as no others have

been privileged to know them, would not let this occasion pass unnoticed.

We have known you as an intimate friend. We have come to rely on your sympathy and your strength. We have known, much more than others, how helpful you are even to those whose burden is lighter than your own.

We have admired the range of your interests. Nothing human is foreign to you. We have been stimulated by your love of scholarship and learning. We have wondered at your varied store of knowledge and have been charmed with the aptness of your language and the liveliness of your humor.

We have felt your devotion to all the higher interests of men. The righting of injustice and wrong, the relief of the suffering and oppressed, the lifting of men from barrenness and pettiness to breadth and richness of spiritual life, the destruction of selfishness, suspicion and hatred,—in a word, the building of the Kingdom of God in the hearts of men, we have seen as the dominant interest and purpose of your life.

Finally, we have known better than any others how your spirit and personality have shaped the life and ideals of this college; how members of the faculty, as they have come in from time to time, have been consciously and unconsciously molded by them; how young men and women, students of the college, as they have gone out from us, have carried into the world the spirit of self-forgetful worship of God and service to man.

We believe that there is no deeper joy in life than that which comes from comradeship with genuine manhood in the promotion of men's high spiritual interests. We have enjoyed the comradeship with you.

We rejoice in your vigorous, abounding health. We hope and pray that you may yet have many more years to give full strength to the great task.

Then before his ninetieth birthday a letter had gone out from the college, apprising college presidents throughout the country of the approaching celebration. Many had answered. Among these had been Harold Dodds of Princeton, and Hugh P. Baker of Massachusetts State College. The latter had attended Macalester preparatory department years before and remembered Dr. Wallace with awe and respect. Arthur G. Crane of the University of Wyoming wrote gaily:

> A strong man is known by what he can take as well as by what he can give. You must be a tough one.

One of the most gratifying came from the president of the University of Minnesota, Guy Stanton Ford, who said:

> Neither the history of Macalester nor of any other good cause in the Northwest will be complete without a tribute to you. Mine is, however, a personal one, whose background is my sense of good fortune in having known and worked with you for what others call lost causes, but that you and I know will go on until they are solved and solved right. I wish you more years to lead us as you have in the ninety years now behind you. In this I speak for the University of Minnesota as well as Mrs. Ford and myself.

All through the summer before his death, letters kept coming to him from many old students and friends. He was made aware how greatly he was revered and loved.

His funeral he had himself planned. He had wished it to be in the Macalester Presbyterian Church, had wished then to be taken to Wooster. This was done. Instead of flowers, he had, characteristically, requested contributions to the China Relief Fund.

Even the physician who attended him during the last painful weeks had derived much pleasure in talking with him. He had felt real reluctance, he told the family, in giving drugs that beclouded so interesting a mind.

At his death the Twin City papers had carried long sketches of his life, and the St. Paul *Pioneer Press* in an editorial said:

> He did not find his classical interests incompatible with a life of action, for he was even in his later years alive and alert to the world around him, an eager observer and participant. In these activities he displayed those qualities of moderateness,

balance, humanism which are so typical of the classical spirit. The modern world could make use of such qualities. Certainly it would be the richer for more men like President Emeritus Wallace.

Mayor Fallon of St. Paul sent condolences "on the loss of one of our great citizens." And Governor Harold E. Stassen wrote:

It is difficult, if not impossible, to measure the extent of our loss. Dr. Wallace's contribution to the people of Minnesota and the Northwest in his long years as teacher, dean and president of Macalester College, lives primarily in the inspiration, love of knowledge, and vision he was able to give hundreds of young men and young women who came within his influence.

It was always gratifying to me, as it must have been to many others, in this day to see a man so keenly alert and so devoted to study and the contemplation of the riches to be found in books. His was truly a remarkable life.

Some spoke of the "vigor and sparkle" of his speaking, of his "ebullient optimism"; others of "the courage and faith" that "knew no defeat." The Reverend Joseph Cochran of Macalester's first graduating class wrote, "His friendship for me has been one of the most precious experiences of my life," and another member of that class, the Reverend William P. Lee, said:

There was no other like him. He was not only teacher to a host of us but he was God's prophet. He spoke so directly and truly and unconsciously for his Lord . . . he seems to me still to speak as of old as no other man ever did to me—with such a twinkling, sparkling, irresistible wisdom. He was so great in his soul, with the greatness like Elijah.

A little later a memorial service was held at the college for Dr. Wallace. Among the speeches made by trustees and faculty and alumni, that of Mel Hobart, 1908, deserves quotation:

In classroom and out—humor, fun, joy of life—they were the glorious sunshine of a great spirit shed where it was most potent.

There was a passion for righteousness in Dr. Wallace, and a zeal for justice in the affairs of men and nations, that impressed itself upon all that sat before him, and which made it impossible for him to be indifferent or neutral in respect of any issue that bore on human freedom. . . .

There were many occasions in this generation past when his heart was stirred by movements and acts of oppression, bigotry, violence, and terrorism. Many of us have witnessed his reaction to these things, and none of us will ever forget the days when his burning indignation expressed itself in such sweeping torrents of phillipic eloquence as roused within us a deep sense of awfulness of these sins against the human spirit, and exalted before us truth and justice and freedom as the rightful heritage of mankind. These were no longer abstractions, but in that electric presence, in the sound of that ringing voice, became profoundly moving, living, vital principles in which the destinies of mankind were bound up.

Trustees and faculty spread upon their books resolutions in his honor. That of the trustees read:

Dr. Wallace guided Macalester College through the most perilous years of its development. He chose as a young man to give his life-service to this college in the northwest, forsaking the certainty of academic advancement in another institution for the exciting adventure of building a new institution where the need for Christian education was greater. It was his courage and vision that kept Macalester College open when other minds had determined to close it. It was his strong religious convictions that put the stamp of the Christian religion upon the purposes and procedures of the college. It was his sacrificial example that led the faculty to suffer financial deprivation in order that the institution might continue to live. . . .

His life was the life of a Christian citizen taking full part in every civic enterprise which promised to advance the Kingdom of God. There was a dignity in his presence and a reserve of intellectual power and independence that enabled him to meet on terms of mutual respect the greatest leaders of

education, commerce, and finance. He was universally recognized as a man who in character and intellectual ability ranked
with the most illustrious builders of American life. Dr. Wallace's death has left upon us all the sense of departed greatness,

> "As when a kingly cedar green with boughs.
> Goes down with a great shout among the hills,
> And leaves a lonesome place against the sky."

And the faculty resolutions had ended with the words: "We
shall ever rejoice in the wealth of untarnishable memories which
abide with us."

Out at Lake Wapogasset, too, there were many others who
mourned his loss, men and women, many of whom had never
seen Macalester. In the summer of 1941 the citizens of Amery,
Wisconsin, and of the region round about the lake gathered in
the park at the outlet of the lake. Once before, they had gathered to do Dr. Wallace honor on a birthday and had presented
him eighty-eight roses. This time, however, they were dedicating
a bronze tablet to his memory. It was fastened to a huge ten-ton
granite boulder that had been brought to the park for the
purpose. The inscription read:

IN GRATEFUL APPRECIATION OF
THE HIGH CHARACTER AND
INTELLIGENT AND UNSELFISH
SERVICE OF

DR. JAMES WALLACE

IN THE ESTABLISHMENT OF
THIS PARK
AND MANY OTHER PUBLIC SERVICES
THIS TABLET IS DEDICATED
1941

The tributes paid James Wallace in life and death indicate the
measure of his influence on those who came under the spell of

his personality. The wide range of his knowledge, his ability to trace the causative relation between historic ideas and events and contemporary life, and the vigor with which he threw himself into the battle for a better world filled many with amazement and admiration. At times he lashed out against the evils of his day with the eloquent invectives of an Old Testament prophet. But at heart he was a humble man with a keen sense of his own limitations. The teachings of the Scriptures and the chastening experiences of life left him with a kind heart, full of sympathy for the downtrodden and the underprivileged. We can write him down as a man of deep devotion to his creator, to his church, to his country, and to the college for which he had toiled and travailed. To those who knew him well in a social way, he was a genial companion, a charming conversationalist, full of wit and humor, and playful in repartee.

Many of those who sat in his classes as they read this inadequate record of the life of *James Wallace of Macalester* are apt to exclaim with moistened eye, "Grand old Doc Jimmy, he meant a lot to me!" As succeeding generations of students come to the campus, they will find in James Wallace a heroic figure challenging them to the highest and best.